UNDERSTANDING YOUR FAMILY CHEMISTRY

Understanding Your Family Chemistry

How Your Genetic Blueprint and Family History Affect Your Temperament, Relationships, Emotions, and Health

Drs. David and Sharon Sneed

VINE
BOOKS

Servant Publications
Ann Arbor, Michigan

Vine Books is an imprint of Servant Publications especially
designed to serve Evangelical Christians.

The names and characterizations in this book drawn from the
authors's case studies or his personal experience are rendered
pseudonymously and as fictional composites. Any similarity between
the names and characterizations of these individuals and real people
is unintended and purely coincidental.

Unless otherwise noted, all Scripture quotations in this book are
from the Holy Bible, New International Version. Copyright © 1973,
1983, International Bible Society. Used by permission of Zondervan
Bible Publishers.

Published by Servant Publications
P.O. Box 8617
Ann Arbor, Michigan 48107

Cover design by Michael Andaloro
Text design by K. Kelly Nelson

92 93 94 95 96 10 9 8 7 6 5 4 3 2 1

Printed in the United States of America
ISBN 0-89283-738-1

Library of Congress Cataloging-in-Publication Data

Sneed, David, 1953–
    Understanding your family chemistry / David and Sharon Sneed.
      p. c.m.
    ISBN 0-89283-738-1
    1. Family—Mental health. 2. Problem families—Rehabilitation.
3. Intergenerational relations. 4. Diseases—Genetic aspects.
I. Sneed, Sharon. 1953– .
RC488.5S615   1992
155.2'3—dc20   92-10853

Dedicated to our children,

Shannon Michelle Sneed
Lauren Elizabeth Sneed
Jonathan David Sneed
and the richness they add to every day.

CONTENTS

ACKNOWLEDGMENTS

We gratefully thank our own families for bringing us into this world and loving us from the beginning. We also thank our patient and understanding children, Shannon, Lauren, and Jonathan, who "made their own fun" during times when the writing of this manuscript required our full attention.

Special thanks go to Ann Spangler and Beth Feia, editors at Servant Publications, for their intuitive sense about what needs to be written and read. They are insightful, professional, and have a genuine concern about their authors and readers. Their ideas formed much of the framework of this book.

The Twelve Step recovery section at the end of this book was primarily written by James Walter, Th.M., the associate pastor of counseling at Westlake Bible Church in Austin, Texas. We have seen Jim do much more than write books. He is about the business of changing lives, using God's infinite power. Who better to speak of family recovery than a man such as this? We are deeply endebted to Jim for his help in this project.

We also would like to thank Nancy Wood, Kay and Hugh Sparks, Shelley McAfee, and Cindy Powell for their valuable comments on the flow of the manuscript.

INTRODUCTION

WHO HASN'T WONDERED WHY they act the way they do or marveled at the distinct differences in their children who are in so many other ways very similar. Our book, *Understanding Your Family Chemistry*, answers questions about how our genetic potential and the influences of our environment blend together to create unique individuals and families. Written by practicing health professionals, the book offers you practical advice to help you better understand both individual and family predispositions.

By understanding the power of genetic predisposition you can better participate in personalized health care to avoid such health problems as heart disease and cancer as well as emotional problems such as depression and anxiety. We give special attention to addictive problems and the unique health concerns of women.

We also offer new insight into the special pressure that families face at different stages of their lives. This information coupled with effective advice on dealing with emotional conflict within the family makes this book an invaluable help to the family seeking improved physical and emotional well-being.

Our many years in medical practice and counseling as well as the practical experience within our own family of five encouraged us to write not just about the problems of life but also to point to a path of recovery and renewal for the family or individual seeking a better life.

Understanding Your Family Chemistry recognizes the individual and the family as complete beings with physical, emotional, and spiritual feelings and needs. We encourage you to take this opportunity to complete personal inventory in each of these areas of your life as a first step toward maximizing your personal and family potential health and well-being.

To this end the final part of the book presents an entirely new approach to family health leading to physical, emotional, and spiritual recovery via a family-oriented twelve step program. This program offers hope and healing to troubled families and renewal to strong families.

The anecdotes and personal style of the book lead you on an enjoyable journey of improved understanding of yourself and your family. *Understanding Your Family Chemistry* provides easy-to-read, up-to-date medical information, sound emotional support, and pastoral family counseling to give hope and healing to body, mind, and soul.

Drs. David and Sharon Sneed

CHAPTER 1

Family Chemistry: What Is It?

To the rest of the world, Jerry looked like a man who had it all. Just thirty-three years old, he was a rising young manager with an up-and-coming computer firm, an upbeat person, always full of stories and jokes. He had an attractive and accomplished wife named Alice and a three-year-old son named Royce.

For some years Jerry had been a patient at our medical clinic. When he came in for his annual check-up, I noticed that he seemed different and commented on it. To my surprise, that was all it took to unleash a long and agonized monologue. Apparently, Jerry needed to vent some of his deepest feelings and concerns, ones that went to the heart of who he really was and what he might become in future years.

Jerry had grown up in a small, midwestern city. His dad sold cars at a local dealership. Ever since his teen years, his dad drank heavily "with the guys" on weekends. Eventually, he was starting each work day with an "eye-opener" and falling into bed each night after his fourth "nightcap." Jerry had been both physically and emotionally abused by his father. His dad, of course, did not remember these episodes when he was sober—which he seldom was.

Not surprisingly, Jerry's father was also unable to produce a dependable income for the family. His mother was forced to return to work while the boys were still quite young. She used to tell Jerry and his brothers, "Your father isn't a bad man. He just tips the bottle a bit too much now and then. He really doesn't lose his temper at other times. It's the alcohol talking when he's harsh, boys. He really loves you. Always remember that. Your father really does love you."

As the years went by, Jerry's brothers also became alcoholics. His mother developed a dependency on a prescription medication she had initially used for relief from tension headaches. Years later, she is still taking the pills, even though the headaches have long since disappeared.

Having a child of his own was a major undertaking for Jerry, a responsibility he did not consider lightly. Haunted by his past, he was determined not to repeat it. Like an auto-rewind tape that constantly replayed in his head, Jerry kept thinking, "I don't want my son to live like I did. I don't want it to be for him the way it was for me. I want to stop this hurtful sickness that seems to take over in my family."

A year ago, Jerry's father died. Since then, his mother and brothers have pressured him and Alice to move back to his hometown. They assure him that he could find a good job with a salary and benefits package equal to what he already has. But every time the subject comes up, Jerry gives some lame excuse. He does not want to return even for a brief visit, much less for any kind of extended stay.

Why is moving back to the city where his family lives so unthinkable to him? Jerry is afraid of what he has seen happen to his family. He doesn't want it to happen to him, to Alice, to Royce. Even though Jerry loves his mother and brothers deeply, he can figure out no other way to keep himself out of harm's way than to remove himself from his past life altogether. "As I look at my family, sometimes I'm afraid I might still go that same way," he told me tearfully.

As we listened to Jerry's story, it became clear that we needed to do more than simply monitor his vital signs and write prescriptions for him. Our job was to fortify this young man in his effort to break the deadly intergenerational cycle of addiction, to defy his dark legacy of family dysfunction, and to reassure Jerry that it *could* be different for himself and for his family.

We have done the same for men who were afraid they were going to die of a heart attack at age forty-five, just because their fathers had died that way. We have helped women from cancer-prone families take preventive measures to maximize their own chances of avoiding this dread disease.

"Family chemistry" is the amalgamation of factors that makes each of us who we are. It includes our genetic backgrounds, as well as all the behavioral attitudes that we have learned by example. Yes, we are all our parents' children. Yes, we have inherited their genetic legacy and predispositions. Yes, things like alcoholism, cancer, heart disease, mental illness, high blood pressure, depression, and baldness are hereditary, at least to some degree. But that does not mean they are inevitable. Our family chemistry plays a key role in making us who we are—but not the *only* role, and not necessarily the *primary* role.

Our family chemistry plays a key role in
making us who we are—but not the only *role,*
and not necessarily the primary *role.*

In this book, you will begin to understand how you came to be who you are through both genetic and environmental inheritance. You'll learn what genes are and how they make us unique. You'll also learn how family relationships can cause you harm, as well as how they can be healed. Most importantly, you'll learn how to face the negative elements of your family chemistry—like Jerry's predisposition to alcoholism—and live victoriously through faith, knowledge, and simple precautions.

FROM GENERATION TO GENERATION

Consider your parents for a moment. What were they like? What did they look like? How did they act? How did they live their lives? What physical and emotional tendencies governed their lives that might be passed down to you?

When we think about family chemistry, most of us think mainly about the *genetic* inheritance we received from our biological parents. And in fact, our genes do have a lot to do with why we are the way we are. We all know that such traits as hair and eye color are genetically determined. Scientists believe that many aspects of our personality are also the result of our genetic inheritance.

But family chemistry also has to do with what we might call "environmental" factors. For example, the way family members responded to life and to each other while we were growing up shapes the way *we* behave today. Personality, temperament, and tendencies toward depression and anxiety are inheritable traits, to a certain extent. But there are no absolutes, and no lines of demarcation showing where *nature* ends and *nurture* begins.

But is it within our power to overcome the intergenerational factors that play havoc with our family chemistry? Or must we inescapably fall victim to the problems encoded in our genes and reinforced by our upbringing?

By understanding the impact of both aspects of family chemistry—nature and nurture—we can learn a great deal that can help us and our children live happier, healthier lives.

We are not helpless victims. This is the trap of fatalism. In most instances, we are a prisoner neither of our genes nor of a difficult environmental background. Within certain limits, there is a wide variation of outcomes we can achieve, whatever our starting point. By understanding the impact of both aspects of family chemistry—nature *and* nurture—we can learn a great deal that can help us and our children live happier, healthier lives.

Suppose, for example, that both your parents were compulsive overeaters who brought you up with the same destructive habits they had always used. Let's further suppose that your grandparents on both sides of the family were similarly afflicted. With this type of background, we can substantiate a case for your being strongly predisposed—both genetically and environmentally—to obesity. Most likely, you already struggle with your weight. You might even consider yourself a food addict because you are emotionally entangled in a love/hate relationship with food.

Let's consider the options. You could give up and resign yourself to being fifty or more pounds overweight for the rest of your life. *Or you can choose to make changes.* You can institute some environmental controls and learn to live comfortably within twenty pounds of your ideal weight. The choice, in most cases, is yours to make.

Moreover—and here's the kicker—your kids don't have to be overweight at all. Knowing that obesity and compulsive eating are familial traits, you can set out to make things different for the next generation. You can eliminate bad habits in the supermarket, at the supper table, and in restaurants, before your children learn to imitate you. You can help them learn how to cope with life so they aren't driven to eat in order to salve emotional pain.

Are such changes easy? No. They take firm resolve and hard work. But it can be done. And not just for overeating, but for whatever problem "runs in the family"—from depression to substance abuse to cancer. Often we stick our heads in the sand like ostriches, ignoring the impact of our family chemistry, or just give up and give in to the seemingly inevitable repetition of past problems. Instead, we can learn to practice good stewardship over our bodies and our families. We can decide to promote the best possible environment for ourselves and our families.

Whether we feel good or bad about our families at the moment, the fact remains that we are tied to them. We share with them genetic ties, memories, love, tenderness—and probably some difficult times we might choose to forget. Some of these ties are unbreakable, no matter what relational estrangement or isolation may have taken place. There are no perfect people and certainly no perfect families. But learning to accept this fact, and then to live nonjudgmentally toward ourselves and others, will help improve family relations as well as heal our own wounds.

In many respects, the buck *can* stop here. Understanding the emotional, physical, and genetic shortcomings in our makeup can help us deal with them in a healthier manner, sometimes even prevent them from occurring altogether. This knowledge allows us to be good stewards of our bodies and a help instead of a hindrance to our families. Discovering who we are, and why, will help us deal with our lives, our health, and our families—past, present, and future.

Predisposition has to do not with what must *be, but with what* might *be. The health problems we will be discussing are problems that are often preventable with "beforehand" understanding and action.*

The dictionary definition of "predispose" is "to incline beforehand; to give a tendency or bias to; to render susceptible." In this book, we will look at a number of diseases to which you might be predisposed for one reason or another. Does that sound morbid or depressing? It shouldn't. Predisposition has to do not with what *must* be, but with what *might* be. The health problems we will be discussing are problems that are often preventable with "beforehand" understanding and action. That's good news!

Without claiming to have written a comprehensive family recovery book, it is our goal to help you better understand family relationships and communication. Though we have not provided an exhaustive health book resource, we have made suggestions for lifestyle changes which should help you cope with many major illnesses.

This book is about understanding the truly complex person you are: where you came from, where you are now, and what you can do to maximize health and happiness in your own life and that of your family. Our insights are based on a simple belief that we have seen borne out again and again in the lives of our patients: *Family chemistry can be changed.* In this book, we'll show you how.

CHAPTER 2

Diseases that "Run in the Family"

J IM CAME TO OUR office for a routine physical exam — the kind required by some employers at the beginning of each year. He was retired from the army and now employed at a microchip manufacturing company. Jim had just turned fifty and was not aware of any major health problems. In fact, for the most part, he felt fine.

After completing his physical exam and accompanying blood tests, we were all surprised to see that the "slightly elevated" levels of the past few years were suddenly well into the danger zones. We found that Jim now had high blood pressure, high cholesterol, and high blood sugar. He was also noticeably overweight.

You could see on Jim's face that the impetus for change had finally arrived. He spoke ruefully of the sinking feeling we all get when we realize that something has gone wrong that might have been prevented. We took the opportunity to assure Jim that he shouldn't feel guilty for being genetically predisposed to these conditions. But while it makes no sense to feel guilty for something that was not under his control, it *was* important to determine what *was* within his control and to make whatever changes were possible.

We identified several areas that could be changed. First, Jim needed to lose at least thirty pounds—fifty would be even better. He needed to cut back on extremely salty foods and follow a low-fat, low-cholesterol diet. Once those efforts were underway, Jim needed to begin a graduated exercise program. Finally, his wife needed to stop smoking so that Jim would not suffer the effects of passive smoke inhalation and further increase his risk of heart disease.

Sharon helped Jim get started on an aggressive but liveable diet. He also began a program of walking for exercise. The results were immediate and dramatic. Within six months, Jim had lost the fifty pounds. The elevated blood pressure, cholesterol, and blood sugar levels had disappeared. Jim was completely normal and healthy—in a word, cured.

Suzanne, Jim's wife, had become part of the process from the beginning. Though very involved with a home-based business of her own, she wanted to help where she could. Suzanne sat in on Jim's nutrition consultations and learned how to handle food purchasing and meal preparation to his advantage. She even discovered how to make many of her favorite recipes with minimal fat and cholesterol content.

Convincing Suzanne to stop smoking, however, was another matter. She joked that "me and cigs go back a long way." We assured her that cigarettes were no laughing matter—that in fact, smoking is *the* major health risk to Americans. Never having considered the consequences of passive smoking, Suzanne had no idea that her bad habit could profoundly affect those who lived with her. Even though she had unsuccessfully tried to quit on four other occasions, Suzanne agreed to try once again. This time she used a program offered through the American Cancer Society, with the help of some prescription medications we could offer through the clinic.

It wasn't easy, but over the next year, Suzanne succeeded at beating her nicotine addiction. As of this writing, she has not smoked a cigarette for more than three years. Jim has been just as supportive of her efforts as she was of his. He knew that cigarette smoke in the house could only increase his own chances of heart disease. Even so, Jim was patient and did not provoke his wife when not smoking seemed out of her reach.

Jim and Suzanne are a marvelous success story. They functioned as a team, helping and supporting each other, being patient rather than nagging. They did not look for immediate results, but simply tried to take more steps forward than they took backward. They accepted one another's situations, and did what they could to maximize one another's chances of success. And in the end, they triumphed together!

PREDISPOSITION AND DISEASE

"Human disease may be considered as an imbalance between stresses placed on persons by the environment in which they live, and the inborn capacity of each person's body to cope with these stresses."[1] If we look at disease from this angle, we can see that both our environment and our genetic make-up contribute toward nearly all forms of ill health. This even includes such health problems as infections and accidents, whose source may seem to lie entirely outside our genes or our backgrounds.

But in fact, our genetic makeup will determine to a great extent what infectious diseases we are susceptible to and how quickly we are able to recover from them. And our genes may even determine how soon sutures and accidental wounds will heal when compared to the same injuries suffered by another person.

Prior knowledge of predisposition to a particular disease can give you many added years of health if preventive action is taken at an early age.

In this chapter, we'll look at some of the more noteworthy diseases with significant genetic ties—those toward which we "inherit" a predisposition, diseases that can "run in the family." As we have noted, many people resist learning such information. Why talk about something as negative as health problems you can't do anything about? But the fact is, *prior knowledge of predisposition to a particular disease can give you many added years of health if preventive action is taken at an early age.*

Ignoring the fact that your dad died of an early heart attack is not the solution. Don't bury your head in the sand about such issues. Instead, take account of what health problems you may face as a result of your genetic makeup, and then use modern medical knowledge and techniques to forestall or prevent them from occurring in your own life.

Let's look at some of the most significant "inheritable" health problems and review their particular risk factors. Most importantly, let's discuss what you can start to do *right now* to overcome whatever predisposition to them you may have inherited.

CANCER

Joyce first came to our office shortly after she and her husband moved to town. They were looking for a new doctor for themselves and their two boys, ages six and three. We had seen them for several minor illnesses before Joyce came in for an annual exam and pap smear. In the course of taking down her medical history, we learned that Joyce's mother had been diagnosed with breast cancer several years ago and that one of her aunts had also had this type of cancer.

We discussed with Joyce the implications this history had for her own genetic predisposition to cancer. We taught her how to give herself a breast self-examination and how to arrange for regular mammograms in the future. Two years later, during her annual exam, Joyce mentioned that she had shared with her older sister the information we had given her about the family's possible predisposition to breast cancer. Her sister had immediately gone for an exam and a tiny spot had appeared on her mammogram. That spot turned out to be a small breast cancer, which the doctor was able to remove simply and completely. He was very optimistic that Joyce's sister would require no further treatment.

No one likes to think about cancer, and none of us wants to believe that we may be at greater risk of cancer because of our family chemistry. But if there *is* a history of cancer in our background, then there is a good chance that we *are* at increased risk. And wishful thinking won't make that risk go away. A program of careful surveillance and early detection tests is vital.

Joyce's is a family-chemistry story with a happy ending. Because her sister went in for her cancer screening right away, she was able to catch her breast cancer at a very early stage. And because Joyce herself is faithfully pursuing a program of regular examinations and screenings, her own chances of avoiding serious trouble are vastly reduced.

Let's take a closer look at this mystifying, frightening disease called cancer.

Cell growth run amok. The growth and development of the human body is essentially the growth and development of *cells*. The body has an astonishingly complex system for initiating, and then slowing or stopping, the rapid development of various kinds of cells at various points in the development process.

For example, development of a baby's major organs is well underway within a mother's womb during the first trimester of pregnancy. From there, the organs increase in size until they are fully grown, which occurs sometime in young adulthood. Then, for reasons science still does not fully understand, they cease to enlarge.

All the while, however, the tissues of the skin and the intestinal lining continue to renew themselves, sloughing off old cells at the surface and regenerating new cells beneath the surface. If the skin or the intestinal lining is cut—whether by a wound or by a surgeon's scalpel—the process of cell division and multiplication increases until the wound is closed. Similarly, if it is necessary to remove a diseased kidney, the other kidney enlarges to meet the body's demands.[2]

The essence of cancer is cell growth run amok. Occasionally, amid the enormous complexity of these cell-growth dynamics, mutant cells develop and the body becomes unable to control the reproduction of this new and different tissue. The change to such uncontrolled growth is called *neoplasia*, and the resulting growth is called a *neoplasm*. More commonly, we refer to a neoplasm as a *tumor*, which simply means "swelling."

Occasionally, amid the enormous complexity of these cell-growth dynamics, mutant cells develop and the body becomes unable to control the reproduction of this new and different tissue.

Tumors can be either benign or malignant. Benign tumors do not spread into adjacent tissue, although they may cause pressures on otherwise healthy tissues. They can usually be surgically removed without further complications. Malignant tumors, by contrast, spread by growing into nearby tissues. Another kind of cancer, called *metastatic* cancer, occurs from a few cells entering the blood or lymph system and floating to new and previously unaffected parts of the body. Other types of cancer include *carcinomas*, which are tumors of the epithelial tissue (such as the skin), and *sarcomas*, or tumors found in the connective tissue.

The word "cancer" is derived from the Latin word for "crab." Though not all cancers develop with the suggested finger-like extensions, we still refer to all neoplasms as cancer. Two other terms to have in your vocabulary are *carcinogenic* and *oncogenic*, both of which simply refer to things that seem to initiate the development of a tumor. They are frequently used in the media to describe environmental factors that may cause cancer.

Researchers estimate that five percent of patients attending most cancer clinics have a hereditary cancer syndrome,[3] in which a dominant gene has caused cancers of the breast, ovary, brain, gastrointestinal system, and blood. These are referred to as "cancer-prone families." Beyond this small percentage, other cancer victims may have a predisposing cancer gene that can be "turned on" by environmental factors including chemicals, specific viruses, radiation, and sun exposure.

Breast cancer. New statistics say that as many as one in nine women will likely develop breast cancer in their lifetime. Many risk factors have been identified—none more important than a family history of the disease. When considering the genetic aspects, the most important risk factors are whether other family members had breast cancer and the age at which their cancer began.

Environmental risk factors for the development of breast cancer include:

Alcohol consumption. A detailed review of the research linking alcohol consumption with breast cancer leads to the conclusion that there is a strong connection between the two.[4] It also seems that the more alcohol consumed, the greater the risk for breast cancer. Even a few drinks per week could significantly increase the incidence of breast cancer in susceptible individuals. If your family history includes breast cancer, don't drink alcohol at all.

High-calorie, high-fat diet. Studies indicate that the high-calorie diet rich in saturated fats common to many Americans and other Westerners promotes breast cancer to some extent. Low-fat and fiber-rich diets, on the other hand, may help reduce the incidence of breast cancer. Obesity, particularly after menopause, is also associated with increased risk.[5]

Colorectal cancer. Cancer of the lower digestive tract which includes the colon and rectum is the second most common form of cancer in North America. Once again, five percent of all colon cancers are thought to be among cancer-prone families that inherit this trait genetically. Another twenty-five percent have some less direct sort of genetic involvement. The remaining seventy percent of colon cancers are primarily influenced by environmental factors, especially diet.[6]

Though breakfast cereal boxes would lead us to believe that the data unequivocally supports the use of a high-fiber diet to protect against colon cancer, the research is actually not so clear cut. Many of the studies used fresh vegetables as their source of fiber, thus improving the nutritional quality of the diet in other ways as well. Since an increased intake of vitamin C, vitamin A, and calcium may also help to prevent this disease, it is possible that these may play a role equal to or greater than fiber itself.

In any case, the risk of colon cancer increases with low vegetable intake and, perhaps, low fiber. A high-fat intake is yet another factor that can cause colon cancer. This is especially true for saturated fats. Studies have also shown a positive association between meat consumption and colon cancer. The incidence of colorectal cancer may also be increased in persons who consistently drink alcohol, especially beer.

Lung cancer. In industrialized countries, more men die of lung cancer than any other form of cancer—and women are unfortunately starting to catch up. Without question, the major cause of these deaths is cigarette smoking. Occupational exposure to asbestos, nickel, and radiation also serve as risk factors.

The genetic and environmental connection among smokers is clear. People who grow up in households where smokers are present are more likely to become smokers themselves. Moreover, there also seems to be a predisposing genetic factor. If you have a close relative with lung cancer, and you yourself smoke cigarettes, your risk of lung cancer is increased fourteen times over that of the general population[7]—not to mention the increased risk of heart disease.

If you have a close relative with lung cancer,
and you yourself smoke cigarettes,
your risk of lung cancer is increased fourteen times.

Other types of cancers. *Leukemia* has a strong genetic component, especially when there is a chromosomal abnormality such as Down's syndrome. There are still many unanswered questions regarding *prostate cancer*, though the risk appears to be greater for men consuming a high-fat diet and who are overweight.[8]

Stomach cancer is associated with diets containing high amounts of salt-preserved foods and nitrates, as well as low levels of fruits and vegetables. *Esophageal (throat) cancer* is associated with the use of tobacco and alcohol, both when they are used individually and especially when they are used in combination.[9]

CANCER PREVENTION: TAKING IT SERIOUSLY

The idea that we may be genetically predisposed toward cancer is not a pleasant thought. If there is a long history of cancer in your family, you may already have an unnatural fear of the disease. If this dread disease has taken a loved one from your presence, you probably loathe the very word "cancer." Yet understanding the risk factors, especially those forms of the disease to which you may be predisposed, is vitally important. Early cancer detection and prevention methods are constantly making strides, enabling more lives to be saved every year.

An old joke says, "Everything I like is either illegal, immoral, or fattening." Increasingly, it seems that all of us may be predisposed to some form of cancer and that many of the things we like the best are actually harmful to us. Still, there is a certain anti-cancer lifestyle that we should all follow. If your family has had many cases of cancer, then these guidelines become all the more important for you personally. Examine your lifestyle to see what changes should be made.

Primary prevention: avoiding factors that might lead to the development of cancer.

Smoking. Cigarette smoking is responsible for eighty-five percent of lung cancer cases among men and seventy-five percent among women. Smoking accounts for about thirty percent of all cancer deaths. Those who smoke two or more packs of cigarettes a day have lung cancer mortality rates fifteen to twenty-five times greater than nonsmokers. Five years after a person stops smoking, his or her risk of lung cancer becomes similar to that of someone who has never smoked at all.

Sunlight. Almost all of the more than six hundred thousand cases of non-melanoma skin cancer diagnosed each year in the United States are considered sun-related. Recent evidence shows that sun exposure is a major factor in the development of melanoma. The incidence increases for those living nearer the equator and with light skin complexions.

Alcohol. Oral cancer and cancers of the larynx, throat, esophagus, and liver occur more frequently among heavy drinkers of alcohol, especially those who also smoke.

Smokeless tobacco. Use of chewing tobacco or snuff tobacco increases the risk of cancer of the mouth, larynx, throat, and esophagus, and is highly habit-forming.

Radiation. Excessive exposure to ionizing radiation can increase cancer risk. Most medical and dental x-rays are adjusted to deliver the lowest dose possible without sacrificing image quality. Excessive radon exposure in homes may increase risk of lung cancer, especially in cigarette smokers. If levels are found to be too high, remedial actions should be taken.

Occupational hazards. Exposure to several different industrial agents (nickel, chromate, asbestos, vinyl chloride, etc.) increases the risk of various cancers. Risk from asbestos is greatly increased when combined with cigarette smoking.

Nutrition. Risk of colon, breast, and uterine cancers increases in obese people. High-fat diets may contribute to development of cancers of the breast, colon, and prostate. High-fiber foods may help reduce risk of colon cancer. A varied diet containing plenty of vegetables and fruits, rich in vitamins A and C, may reduce risk for a wide range of cancers. Salt-cured, smoked, and nitrite-cured foods have been linked to esophageal and stomach cancer.

Secondary prevention: diagnosing cancer or precursor conditions as early as possible.

Colorectal tests. The American Cancer Society recommends three tests for early detection of colon and rectal cancer in people without symptoms. The *digital rectal examination* and *stool blood test,* performed by a physician during an office visit, should be done every year after the age of forty. The *proctosigmoidoscopy* examination should be carried out every three to five years after age fifty, based on the advice of a physician.

Pap test for cervical cancer. Women who are or have been sexually active, or have reached the age of eighteen, should have an annual pap test and pelvic examination. After a woman has had three or more consecutive satisfactory annual examinations, the pap test may be performed less frequently at the discretion of the physician.

Breast cancer. The American Cancer Society recommends the monthly practice of breast self-examination (BSE) by women twenty years and older as a routine good health habit. Physical examination of the breast should be done every three years from ages twenty to forty, and then every year. The ACS recommends a mammogram every year for asymptomatic women age fifty and over, and a baseline mammogram between ages thirty-five and thirty-nine. Women aged forty to forty-nine should have mammography every one to two years, depending on physical and mammographic findings, and upon genetic risk factors.

HEART DISEASE

Having just turned forty-six, Oscar was depressed about being on the downhill side of life. On top of that, his annual exam had revealed that his blood-sugar levels had gone through the roof and that his cholesterol levels weren't far behind. Years before, his father had died suddenly of his first heart attack when he was only forty-eight years old. Oscar still remembered the overwhelming shock that came over his family when they got the news. Only that morning they had seen their father off to work, never dreaming that it was the last time they would see him alive.

Oscar remembered trying to be strong for his mother and younger brothers and sisters. He even went into his parents' bathroom to clear away some of his father's things which had been used only a few short hours before. With glazed eyes, he stared in disbelief at his dad's razor which he now held in his trembling hands. Oscar wondered: what would the fate of his family now be? For that matter, what would *his* fate be?

In a family like this, everyone should ideally have some medical screening done for cholesterol and other blood chemistry abnormalities. Unfortunately, this has been a routine part of medical exams for only the last ten years or so. When Oscar came to us, he already had some significant health problems from the genetic legacy he inherited from his father's side of the family. But he was not a defeatist. Oscar was not ready to give up and anticipate dropping dead of a heart attack, just because that had been his father's fate. Instead, he was prepared to make lifestyle changes to enhance his chances for good health and a long life.

Oscar had already quit smoking years before. His blood pressure was normal. The only remaining risk factor he could change was to decrease his levels of serum cholesterol and triglycerides by weight loss, exercise, and an improved diet. When he reached the lowest levels possible through a self-help regimen, he was placed on a prescription medication that helped further lower his blood lipids to normal levels.

At fifty-one, Oscar is now in perfect health for his age and hopes to enjoy life for years to come. His is a textbook example of someone with a hereditary predisposition to a life-threatening disease who decided to make the most of opportunities for prevention.

Heart attack. Ischemic heart disease, or what we more commonly call coronary heart disease or "heart attack," is the most common cause of death in the United States, claiming some five hundred and fifty thousand lives per year. The role of genetic factors in the occurrence of this disease is not in doubt. However, environmental and behavioral factors like smoking, high-fat and high-cholesterol diets, and inactivity, also play major roles.

Many a patient has told us of a friend or relative who managed to smoke two packs of cigarettes a day, drink a lot of alcohol, eat poorly, abuse themselves in many other ways, and still live to age eighty. Impressive? Perhaps. But what might that person's longevity have been had they made the right health choices? Sooner or later, lifestyle catches up with us all, even those who for a time seem to be "exceptions to the rule."

Let's delve further into some of the factors that can contribute toward heart disease—and learn what we can do about them.

---

*Sooner or later, lifestyle catches up with us all,
even those who for a time seem to be "exceptions to the rule."*

Clogged arteries. Most coronary heart disease is due to blockages in the arteries that supply blood to the heart. Cholesterol and fat circulate in the blood and build up in and along the walls of these arteries. This buildup narrows the arteries and slows or blocks the flow of blood to the heart. This process called "atherosclerosis" may cause chest pain or even a heart attack.

Atherosclerosis is a slow and progressive condition that can begin even in children as young as two years old, but might not produce symptoms until well into the adult years. Most heart attacks happen when a blood clot forms and lodges in a narrowed part of the coronary artery, thus blocking the blood supply to the heart muscle itself.

Elevated levels of serum cholesterol are one of the major causes of atherosclerosis. To completely examine a person's cholesterol as a risk factor, however, we must look at more than just the total cholesterol. Low density lipoprotein (LDL) cholesterol and high density lipoprotein (HDL) cholesterol also figure into the picture.

HDL cholesterol is the so-called "good cholesterol." The higher the level of HDL, the better off you are. In fact, many experts consider the ratio of total cholesterol to HDL cholesterol a more significant indicator of coronary heart disease than total cholesterol alone. This ratio is determined by dividing total cholesterol by the HDL cholesterol; the ideal ratio is 4.0 or lower.

Genetic factors. Coronary heart disease has long been known to cluster in families. Information dating back almost one hundred years has described one family in which three generations were affected by this disease. Close relatives of persons who have had a coronary incident definitely have a higher than average risk of developing coronary heart disease problems of their own.

But this genetic predisposition is also influenced by a number of other factors. With carefully planned intervention and good medical help, many familial tendencies toward heart disease can be eliminated or at least forestalled.

Familial hypercholesterolemia, or the tendency to have high serum cholesterol levels among family members, is the most extreme form of genetic predisposition to premature coronary disease. It occurs in roughly one in five hundred people. In its more severe form, found in about one in one million persons, cholesterol levels can be so high as to cause young children to have coronary heart disease—including severe and even fatal heart attacks—by the age of five.

Another problem with blood lipids stemming from a person's genetic makeup is called "familial combined hyperlipidemia." This is usually characterized by elevated cholesterol and/or triglyceride concentrations. We have helped many concerned and prudent patients take preliminary actions to control fat and cholesterol intakes due to their familial inheritance of heart disease. For some, these preliminary actions were not enough and stricter guidelines still had to be enacted.

One particular story comes to mind. Maydell was a fifty-two-year-old school teacher preparing for retirement. She and her husband had worked hard for many years and were preparing to hit the road in a camper. The last thing either of them needed was poor health. When we told Maydell of her extraordinarily high levels of cholesterol and moderately high levels of triglycerides, she was genuinely surprised. A few years previously, they had been only slightly elevated and she had already begun a self-imposed diet and exercise program.

After analyzing her body composition, diet, and lifestyle habits we could find very little to improve—just a little fine tuning here and there. Maydell reluctantly started on prescription medications for the control of these blood lipid abnormalities. She didn't like the idea of taking pills when it didn't seem to her that anything was wrong. But it is important to recognize that not all developing diseases have noticeable symptoms, and that some can only be handled with the appropriate medications. The drugs that Maydell began taking would probably increase the length and quality of her life.

On her last visit to the clinic before their cross-country trek, Maydell was lamenting the fact that many of her friends who had perfectly normal cholesterol levels ate whatever they wanted. Sharon shared that she had a similar predisposition to high cholesterol levels in her own family of origin. Then she told her, "Maydell, almost everyone is predisposed to something. That's just human nature. I can't think of even one perfect human being. Can you? I think of myself as a total package. Some parts are great, and others—well, others need some special attention and handling. But that's okay."

Don't give up when it seems the genetic cards are stacked against you. Even though Maydell needed the fat-lowering medications, her situation would have been far more complicated had she not developed the personal responsibility necessary to improve her lifestyle choices.

PREVENTING HEART DISEASE

Prevention strategies for heart disease are never carved in stone. They require constant revision to determine if all of the major findings of recent research are included. With regard to preventing cardiovascular disease, we think in terms of two groups of people, each with its own particular needs. The first group is the population at large. For them we need a mass intervention program that can be easily understood. We frequently see these health suggestions at health fairs and even on the back of cereal boxes.

The basic prevention strategies for everyone are these:

1. Keep your total fat intake low.
2. Control your cholesterol intake.
3. Stay close to your ideal body weight.
4. Exercise responsibly.
5. Don't smoke.

Don't give up when it seems the genetic cards are stacked against you.

In addition to the general population, there is also a high-risk population. For them the strategy must be more aggressive and direct. When coronary heart disease has played a major role in family chemistry, these additional prevention strategies become important:

1. Control of hypertension is an absolute must.
2. Eradication of smoking and even passive smoking is necessary.
3. Aerobic exercise should be used to strengthen the heart muscle.
4. Fat intake should not exceed twenty-five percent of total calories, and cholesterol intake should not exceed one hundred mg per day.
5. If the effects of heart disease need to be reversed, dietary restriction to ten percent of the total caloric intake coming from fat will help.
6. Control of diabetes is essential.
7. Frequent monitoring of blood lipid levels at your doc-

tor's office is important. If levels do not normalize with lifestyle intervention, work with your physician to lower blood lipid levels by means of appropriate medications.

The next generation. One large group that is frequently ignored in preventing heart disease are children who are genetically at increased risk. Why wait until they become sick adults to do something, especially when we know they have a genetic predisposition to coronary heart disease in the first place? Intervention can start at any time after age two. Children in high-risk families should be brought up on a healthy diet and should be encouraged to pursue other healthful lifestyle choices, including exercise and non-smoking.

Recent studies have indicated that children who watch more than two hours of television per day are at increased risk of high cholesterol.

Recent studies have indicated that children who watch more than two hours of television per day are at increased risk of high cholesterol, due to the inherent inactivity and to the unhealthy snacking that typically accompanies TV time. Since the average American youth watches about three hours of television per day, this should be a national concern.

If coronary heart disease is in your family background, consider preventive action *now* to avoid or forestall heart problems in your own life and in the lives of those you love.

HIGH BLOOD PRESSURE

Studies show that blood pressure levels have a strong genetic component. In the minds of most people, the cause of high blood pressure is salt in the diet. There is some evidence as to the role of sodium in causing and maintaining high blood pressures. It is clear, however, that excess intake of sodium does not cause elevated blood pressures in everyone. Conversely, sodium restriction will lower blood pressure in many, but not all, persons with high blood pressure.

Interestingly enough, hypertension is what we call an *ecogenic* trait, meaning that primitive populations do not have as much hypertension. That doesn't say much for civilization! Hypertension can even develop in some people when they relocate to a Western environment, where the salt shaker is more free— and where the mind is more stressed.

Owing to genetic factors, hypertension is particularly prevalent in the Black American population. Others also have predispositions to high blood pressures in spite of their efforts to control their weight and other factors. If high blood pressure has been a part of your family chemistry, you should work toward controlling your body weight and limiting salt in your diet. Also, have your blood pressure checked regularly at your doctor's office. If your doctor prescribes medication, take it faithfully.

DIABETES

Medicine has known for centuries that diabetes runs in families. Here again, awareness of your family's medical history is very helpful in recognizing a disease in its early stages—or, perhaps, in avoiding it altogether.

It is a common misconception that if you eat sweets your entire life, you will develop diabetes. This has not been shown to be the case in research studies. However, in our office we will frequently see a diabetic who has developed high blood sugar levels, and perhaps become overweight, as they have become older. Many of these people can reduce their blood sugar levels as they normalize their weight.

There are two basic types of diabetes. Type one usually

occurs in younger people and almost always requires the use of insulin. Type two typically occurs in overweight older people and can often be controlled with oral medication, or even with dietary changes. The genetic components of this second type of diabetes are well established; those with a predisposition to it who become overweight are quite likely to develop the disease.

There is also a genetic aspect to type one diabetes, linked to a specific and identifiable chromosomal disorder, as well as a potential environmental factor if a certain viral illness has been present. There are no measures that can prevent this first type of diabetes. However, those whose family history includes cases of type one diabetes should at least be aware that they are at increased risk, and alert to its possible onset.

With type two diabetes, however, there is a great deal that can be done. If someone in your family has had it, the most important thing you can do is to make every effort to stay as close as you can to your ideal body weight, especially as you get older.

Gestational diabetes (elevated blood sugar levels that occur when a woman is pregnant, and then usually reduce to normal after the pregnancy is over) may provide a window into the future. Studies now show that women with gestational diabetes are more likely to have other forms of diabetes later in life. If you experience this condition during pregnancy, let it serve as a warning to control your diet and weight in the future.

OBESITY

Obesity and weight gain have to be the great dilemma of the twentieth century. How to get excess weight off—and then keep it off—seems to be on almost everyone's mind. One in every two Americans would *like* to lose weight. One in four Americans *needs* to lose weight.

It has been known for many decades that obesity is a familial trait. Most obese patients have at least one obese parent and siblings that are affected, too. We must recognize, of course, that these families share similar environments as well as genes. Still, recent articles in the scientific literature indicate that as much as sixty or seventy percent of obesity is genetically related.

It has been known for many decades that obesity is a familial trait. Most obese patients have at least one obese parent.

In a 1985 study, it was noted that most children of obese parents became overweight, while those of lean parents were thin.[10] In more current research, forty pairs of identical twins were studied, as well as sixty-one pairs of fraternal twins. In this study, an inheritability factor for obesity was estimated at eighty-five percent. Interestingly, identical twins raised in different households tend to have bodyweights similar to one another, rather than to their adoptive families—strong evidence for the genetic aspects of obesity.

Some physicians now believe that the operative factor in obesity is an undersecretion of central nervous system chemicals that turn off the hunger center. That is, chemicals that are normally present in the body are found in lower quantities in the central nervous system of some obese persons. The result is that these people never feel "full." They always remain a little hungry, even when they know they have had a lot to eat.[11]

The thought that your appetite can be an inheritable trait may be a bit overwhelming. But let's not underestimate the environmental factors. In the book, *Love Hunger: Recovery From Food Addiction,*[12] co-authored by Sharon, we talked of the emotional ties people have with food. We asked questions of the reader such as, "Do you eat only when you are angry? Do you eat in times of tension or crisis? Do you eat when you are lonely?" When we eat to fill emotional needs, this is part of the cycle of addiction which we will discuss in the next chapter. Of those who are obese, as many as twenty-five percent might fall into this category. They are eating compulsively.

When considering a genetic predisposition to obesity, keep these things in mind:

1. Most people can weigh within twenty pounds of their ideal weight and maintain that weight with little effort for their entire life.
2. Don't set unrealistic goals, such as extremely quick weight loss or a very low perceived ideal body weight. Instead, look for new habits you can live with.
3. Work with a weight loss program that is not gimmicky, but is informed in the areas of physical and emotional needs for dieters.

With knowledge, patience, and effort,
we can work to overcome our inherited health risks.
Family chemistry isn't final. It can be changed.

No matter which of the problems described in this chapter are part of your family chemistry, *there is hope.* Even where an inherited genetic predisposition exists, that is never the end of the story. With knowledge, patience, and effort, we *can* work to overcome our inherited health risks. Family chemistry isn't final. It *can* be changed.

CHAPTER 3

Addiction: All in the Family?

RUDY WAS THE KIND of person anyone would like— except maybe Rudy himself. Knowing all too well that his many previous attempts at dieting had failed miserably, he came to our office to join one of our group weight-loss classes.

Rudy also knew about other addiction problems from his past. Thinking he had put them to rest, he was to learn that he had really only transferred them into other areas of his life. After he was starting to have a problem with alcohol, for example, Rudy had imposed some drinking restrictions on himself. His drinking now seemed to be under control. Or so he thought, until he found himself in trouble with the law for drunk driving after his usual after-dinner cocktails.

Rudy came from a hard-working, rural family that owned a small farm in South Texas. He was always a big kid, usually the tallest in his class, and played football throughout high school. His athletic endeavors won Rudy a scholarship to college, where he majored in business. He was the only person from his family who had ever gone to college, and probably the only one from his own generation who would have the opportunity to go.

Making ends meet with six children on a limited and fluctuating income had been a real challenge for Rudy's parents.

They were austere, driven folks who instilled the same mentality in their children: *Birthday parties are frivolous and cost too much money. We're too busy for after-school fun and games. When you're not in school, your duty is to be here, working.*

Perhaps because of their austere lifestyle, emotional interactions within the family were also limited. Kisses and hugs were not encouraged. Instead there were handshakes for the boys, pats on the cheek for the girls. Intimacy was an unfamiliar concept at Rudy's house.

The family was very proud of Rudy: the oldest son, the athlete, the scholarship student, the high-achiever. And family members never let him forget it. Rudy felt his performance was inescapably tied to his father's love for him. His dad once boycotted two of his important high school games because he thought Rudy had "let up" at the previous game and been single-handedly responsible for his team's defeat.

When Rudy came to our office, we were unable to weigh him on our scale, which only went up to three hundred fifty pounds. He did not let that deter him, however. He had finally broken through enough denial to allow himself to admit past hurts even before he came to the first class. Over the next year, Rudy lost one hundred thirty pounds, which placed him at a maintenance weight of two hundred thirty. Though this was not thin by any means, it seemed a suitable weight for Rudy, all things considered.

Rudy went through a lot with the group. Coming to terms with his emotionally sparse upbringing was certainly one eye-opener. Feeling like the hero of the family, the one who would lift them out of poverty, was a heavy burden to carry. After he quit drinking, Rudy said he began to "eat like I used to drink." He was beginning to realize that his unmet emotional needs could not be cured with a can of beer or a bag of chips. After talking about some of these issues with his family, Rudy learned that his dad had also had a problem with alcohol. Though his father was rarely drunk, there was frequently a smell of alcohol on his breath.

After working through the twelve step program of Over-eaters Anonymous in our weight loss group, Rudy commented, "Your god is whatever controls you." Interestingly, the Bible makes the same point: "For where your treasure is, there your heart will be also" (Mt 6:21).

Rudy began to realize that his unmet emotional needs could not be cured with a can of beer or a bag of chips.

How about you? Where is your heart? Where is your treasure? Are addictions or other compulsive behavior patterns part of your family chemistry? Are you ready to face them in your own life? Are you prepared to admit the fact that you may be hiding from a problem you already have, or from a hereditary tendency in your family?

Let's look now at the addiction cycle, and at the role that genetics and intergenerational dependency may play in this important area.

THE ADDICTION CYCLE

What is an addiction? Webster's dictionary defines an addict as someone who is "habitually devoted or surrendered to something." The key element in this definition is not the "something," the object of devotion. Rather, it is the devotion itself—the total surrender to that object at the expense of all else. Obviously, this definition leaves open a broad latitude as to the object of our addiction.

We are all familiar with addictions to substances, such as alcohol or drugs. But we can also be addicted to certain behaviors—such as over-exercising, compulsive overeating, shopping, shoplifting, television-watching, or the use of pornography. There is even such a thing as an addiction to relationships. Our society considers some addictions to be good. Few managers complain about an employee who is a workaholic, even at the expense of his or her family. Of course, many of those managers show the same type of unhealthy fixation on work themselves.

Are you addicted? If you answer yes to even a few of the questions listed below, it is likely that you have some emotional ties with food that could be considered a form of food addiction. To check for other controlling actions or substances in your life, just drop the references to eating and food and insert the terms appropriate to your situation.

The bottom line is: What is your motivation? Are your actions based on legitimate, healthy human needs? Or are you trying to cover up pain from your past or present living situation? Are you numbing the hurt instead of dealing with it? Return to Rudy's axiom and ask yourself, "What's controlling me? What am I a slave to? What has become my god?"

Food Addiction Inventory

1. Do you eat when you're angry?
2. Do you eat to comfort yourself in times of crisis and tension?
3. Do you eat to stave off boredom?
4. Do you lie to yourself and others about how much you have eaten or when you ate?
5. Do you hide food away for yourself?
6. Are you embarrassed about your personal appearance?
7. Are you twenty percent or more over your medically recommended weight?
8. Have significant people in your life expressed concern about your eating patterns?
9. Has your weight fluctuated by more than ten pounds in the past six months?
10. Do you fear your eating is out of control?[1]

SIX STEPS TO ADDICTION

Below is shown the six-step downward spiral developed by Drs. Frank Minirth, Paul Meier, and Robert Hemfelt.[2] Although the steps were written in reference to the progression of compulsive eating, they can easily be applied to other addictions.

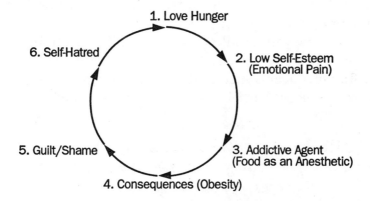

Step one. Many people go through life with a love deficit— what we call love hunger. This might be the result of coming from a dysfunctional family, such as a family where one or both parents had addiction problems. Or it may stem from problems arising in adulthood, such as a difficult marriage, divorce, death of a loved one, severe job-related problems, or a debilitating illness.

Step two. One of the results of love hunger is low self-esteem. Having been told by someone we are unworthy, we believed them. Now we live under that ominous cloud, waiting for it to burst at any second. Nothing we do seems right. If everyone else thinks we're worthless, then maybe we are. If our spouse or parents have told us how awful we are, why shouldn't we believe them? Sometimes we experience precious little evidence or reassurance to the contrary.

As the pain associated with this low self-esteem develops,

most people are tempted to look for anything that can cover up its venomous sting. Think of the last time you had a serious toothache. You probably experienced a very intense, hard-to-control pain. You knew you needed help and needed it quick. And, quite frankly, you were not all that concerned about where the help came from. Anything that would anesthetize the pain was what you wanted. The tooth would still be decayed and in need of repair, but at least the pain would be temporarily numbed.

Is this how you handle pain in your life? Wouldn't you rather be healed once and for all, instead of depending on anesthetizing agents such as the misuse of food, drugs, alcohol, and addictive behaviors for the rest of your life?

> *Wouldn't you rather be healed once and for all,*
> *instead of depending on anesthetizing agents such as*
> *the misuse of food, drugs, alcohol, and*
> *addictive behaviors for the rest of your life?*

Anesthesiologists go to medical school and residency programs for years to learn how to manage anesthesia during surgery. They will be the first to tell you that too much anesthesia is as deadly as poison. We should adopt this view about addictive agents and behaviors in our own lives that are controlling us in unhealthy ways.

Step three. Believe it or not, we willingly choose addictive agents. We look for ways to make the emotional pain bearable. Some choose work, food, or shopping to take their minds off those things that are too painful to deal with. Others choose alcohol and drugs, perhaps due to easy accessibility and the influence of others, including the immediate family. For those with hereditary or chemical predispositions to alcoholism, this is a particularly dangerous time and should be dealt with before the situation gets out of control.

Step four. The consequences of unwise actions are never pleasant, but will inevitably arrive. The consequences may range anywhere from increasing your dress size to losing your home, your family, or your life. Often it is only at this stage that we begin to take action. Perhaps we've been arrested for driving "under the influence." Or a high school reunion shocks us into the realization that we are eating food inappropriately. Whatever the addiction, there will be unpleasant consequences at some point along the road.

Step five. Most addiction is driven by shame. And now, with the new addiction in place, the shame is doubled: the old shame that stemmed from our low self-esteem in the first place, and the new shame resulting from being an addict.

If this is the point you are at right now, keep these important truths in mind. We can only control what happens today. We can always make a fresh start. The past is past. The future is still beyond our reach. But we can always address our problems *today*.

The past is past. The future is still beyond our reach. But we can always address our problems today.

Step six. It is easy to see how self-hatred and even self-destruction are often the last step in this cycle. But this self-hatred can add even more fuel to the fire. Now we have to deal not only with other people not loving us. Now we no longer love ourselves.

IS ADDICTION INHERITED?

What if a mother responded to any difficult situation with a new purchase, or if a father responded to stress by going to work and removing himself from the situation? It is easy to see that the children are learning patterns which they will more than likely carry on to the next generation. This describes the way addictions can be handed down via family environment.

If you are a parent, know that your young ones derive much of their picture of reality from you. They believe what you tell them. They learn by the way you live. As the parents of three young children ourselves, this has served as one of our greatest motivators to clean up our own act and remove unhealthy behaviors from our own lives.

But what about addictions being handed down via genetics? The rest of our chapter will be devoted to substance addictions, facts about genetic predisposition for these addictions, and what we can do to avoid them.

Remember: genetic predisposition is an important factor, but it is *not* all-powerful. You don't have to be an alcoholic just because your mother or father was an alcoholic. As you read this material, *think prevention*. Prevent alcoholism, drug addiction, and obesity from occurring rather than trying to mop up after it has become a reality. This should certainly be our focus for the next generation of predisposed addicts.

ALCOHOLISM

In most Western cultures, as much as ninety percent of the people have at least dabbled with alcohol consumption at some time in their lives. Most will have had their first drink by their thirteenth birthday, increasing the quantities of alcohol consumed to reach maximum intake somewhere in the late teens to mid-twenties.

Alcoholism is one of the most prevalent disorders in our society, affecting as many as one in ten Americans. Sixty percent of all hospital admissions in the United States are related to consequences of drinking.[3] Moreover, if alcohol's role in deaths due to such diverse causes as homicide, suicide, accidents, and certain alcohol-related cancers is considered, it becomes the fourth leading cause of death in the United States today.

Our society still clings to the perception of alcoholics as skid-row bums living in flop houses with no chance of recovery—not now, not ever. In fact, only five percent of alcoholics fit into this stereotype. The average alcoholic probably looks a lot more like your next-door neighbor. Most alcoholics have regular jobs, incomes, houses, community status, and friends.

The average alcoholic probably looks a lot like your next-door neighbor.

Tragically, only five percent of people suffering from alcoholism ever seek treatment.[4] That means ninety-five percent of alcohol addicts in this country are not seeking help! In the process, they are destroying themselves and their families. Perhaps these persons are under the delusion that there is no recovery from this disease. Yet numerous studies have documented that the average middle-class alcoholic who agrees to enter treatment, and who completes a rehabilitation program, has a sixty to seventy percent chance of maintaining abstinence for at least one year.

Even without treatment, there is a twenty percent chance of "spontaneous remission," in which life-long abstinence is achieved even in the absence of formal treatment or participation in self-help groups. The bottom line is: there *is* recovery from alcoholism.

The family connection. Alcoholism's family connection has been known for centuries. Aristotle, Plato, and Plutarch all described the tendency for the drinking behavior of the progeny to resemble that of their parents.[5] The mechanisms for these inheritable family traits were at first attributed solely to genetic transmission. Social explanations for familial alcoholism did not arise until recently. The truth lies in a combination of both factors.

First-degree relatives of alcoholics—which includes daughters, sons, and parents, or what we commonly call the nuclear family—are up to seven times as likely as other people to become alcoholics themselves. A study conducted in 1955[6] also showed a strong degree of familial alcoholism among second-degree relatives, such as grandparents, aunts, and uncles. The risk of illness is consistently greater among male relatives than females. This, however, is not thought to be a genetic tendency, but is attributed to environmental factors including exposure to alcohol, customs, and traditions.

The most compelling evidence linking genetics with the transmission of alcoholism comes from studies of adopted children and their biological parents.[7,8,9,10] These studies eliminate most environmental factors that might otherwise shroud the association between biological inheritance and alcohol abuse. Indeed, such tests indicate an adopted child with at least one biological parent who was alcoholic is two-and-a-half times more likely to develop alcoholism—regardless of the environmental situation with his adoptive parents or the degree of exposure to the alcoholic parent.

Surely this kind of information should motivate us to search for a history of alcoholism in our family chemistry, and to take precautionary measures wherever indicated. Efforts to understand how alcoholism develops, and how it can be prevented, center on the following three major areas of enquiry:

1. *Exposure:* demographic, cultural, and environmental factors such as sex, age, religious affiliation, social group influences, income, availability of alcohol, parental alcohol abuse, etc.
2. *Metabolism:* the mechanism by which alcohol (ethanol) is metabolized and dealt with by the body.
3. *Pharmacological effects:* the effects of alcohol when inside the body.

Family factors may enter in at any of these levels. With regard to exposure, we can readily see that at least some of these factors are controllable and can be kept in check. The metabolism of alcohol seems to be a major area influenced by genetics. Many researchers feel that lack of tolerance for alcohol may actually act as a protective factor against the development of alcoholism—and, to a certain extent, this is an inheritable trait.

It works like this. Two major enzymes are involved in the breakdown of alcohol (ethanol) in the body. Because their systems produce these enzymes in abundance, some people seem not to feel the results of alcohol very readily. This leads to the misconceived "I can hold my liquor" attitude. On the other hand, if a person's system produces lesser amounts of these enzymes—and therefore is less able to tolerate alcohol—this may function as a protective mechanism against continued excessive drinking or alcoholism.

So the next time you become flushed after only one glass of wine, be thankful. This may be your body's way of telling you that ethanol is really not its fuel of choice!

The next time you become flushed after only one glass of wine, be thankful. This may be your body's way of telling you that ethanol is not its fuel of choice.

The key to alcoholism, however, may most likely be found in the effects of alcohol on the brain. One major focus of current research is to determine the role of alcohol in the stimulation of the brain's reward and reinforcement systems. Another key may be that alcohol simply produces dependence by making abnormal states such as irritability, hyperexcitability, dysphoria (general unhappiness), impulsiveness, or stress, seem "normal." If any of these are prevalent in your life, see your doctor, not your bartender.

TREATMENT FOR ALCOHOLISM

How do we define alcoholism? When do a few drinks become "a few too many"? At what point does that evening highball become something more than mere refreshment? When does social drinking extend beyond the party's end?

One diagnostic approach that is clear and easy to use is an evaluation of the occurrence of significant alcohol-related life problems.[11] Alcoholism may thus be diagnosed with respect to various byproducts: a history of marital separation or divorce related to alcohol; multiple arrests related to drinking; physical evidence that alcohol has harmed health, including evidence of alcohol withdrawal; or chronic job loss or layoff related to drinking. The multiplication of such ongoing difficulties usually means that alcohol itself is more meaningful to the person than any of the problems it has caused.

There are as many as eleven different definitions of alcoholism in the scientific literature. However, a large degree of overlap exists among them. For example, someone who is labeled alcoholic because of the excessive quantity and frequency of intake is almost certain to exhibit signs of psychological dependence, serious life problems related to drinking, and physiological consequences as well. The most important point is to spot signs of alcoholism in as many different ways as possible, so that those who are still just "teetering on the brink" can be forewarned and helped.

The three major phases of any alcohol abuse recovery program are *confrontation, detoxification,* and *rehabilitation.* Let's look at each phase of this process to determine how the family might be involved.

Confrontation. Confronting your spouse, child, parent, or even yourself, with the possibility that they may be an alcoholic is a tough job. But it is essential. If such a confrontation seems impossible, you might try to involve an outside party such as a close friend or family physician. The physician can usually help you discern the gray area between social drinking and alcoholism. For example, a simple history of alcohol-related life problems from the patient and another family member will identify most alcoholics. Beyond that, blood tests can also be revealing.

A common response of someone resistant to accepting a diagnosis of alcoholism is the "I'm going to cut down" attitude. The fact is that almost all alcoholics periodically and spontaneously decrease their alcohol intake. The problem resurfaces, however, when they inevitably lose control again. In a gentle way, it may be important to point out that the act of "cutting down" has occurred in the past, but that each effort has ended in a return or even an escalation of previous problems.

Ultimately, remember to keep the doors of communication open and bring in outside parties to help with this phase of treatment.

Detoxification. The heart of the process of detoxification is the first week of total abstinence, in which most traces of the drug are cleared from the body. When alcohol is suddenly restricted from cells that have adapted to its presence, symptoms of withdrawal will occur. The most common of these include tremors in the hands (shakes or jitters), faster pulse and respiratory rate, and increased body temperature. Insomnia, possibly accompanied by bad dreams, feelings of generalized anxiety or "panic attacks," and stomach upset, are other common withdrawal symptoms.

Symptoms may begin within five to ten hours after decreasing alcohol intake. Thus it is easy to understand the typical alcoholic "panic for a drink" that is often portrayed on television and in the movies. The peak intensity for these symptoms will usually occur on day two or three, then taper off through days four and five. However, symptoms of anxiety and insomnia may persist up to six months or more. Unfortunately, the combined occurrence of these symptoms usually contribute to a strong desire to return to drinking.

A physician brought in to help with the detoxification process will first conduct a physical exam and assessment. Nutritional deficiencies may occur even with seemingly well-nourished, middle-class alcoholics.[12] Due to absorption problems in the small intestine, alcoholics may require supplements of multiple B vitamins, especially thiamine, for a week or more.[13] The physician will also be able to administer alternative brain depressant medications (as a substitute for alcohol) to ease withdrawal symptoms.

Alcohol detoxification is often conducted in a hospital. But with rising health care costs and increasing data to support the effectiveness of outpatient programs, more moderate alcoholics with mild symptoms are now being treated at home.[14]

Rehabilitation. The major goal in any rehabilitation program is to provide motivation for abstinence and help for the re-establishment of a lifestyle free of alcohol. There is no conclusive evidence that one type of program is superior to any other.[15] Though outpatient programs are adequate for many, in-patient hospitalization is advisable if the patient has additional medical problems, if there is significant depression, if the patient has had a severe life crisis, if outpatient treatments have previously failed, or if the patient simply lives too far from an outpatient treatment center.

Alcoholics Anonymous (A.A.) offers lectures and support motivation for the patient, spouses (AlAnon), and children of alcoholics (AlaTeen). These twelve step programs focus on personal responsibility, mechanisms for dealing with anger, and handling daily stresses in healthier ways.

Medications are not generally used after detox has been completed and rehabilitation has begun. Though problems with insomnia and anxiety may persist for up to six months, these should be dealt with through education, reassurance, and simple behavior modification techniques such as no napping, avoidance of caffeinated beverages in the evening, and establishing regular retiring and awakening times. It is important not to use sleeping pills or antianxiety pills, lest one addiction be traded for another.

SMOKING AND NICOTINE ADDICTION

Smoking is often considered merely a bad habit, a health risk, or a regrettable character weakness, instead of what it really is: a drug dependency. Consistent use of all forms of tobacco leads to a dependence on nicotine that is indistinguishable from other forms of drug dependence. The diagnostic manual of the American Psychiatric Association classifies tobacco dependence as an addiction in which the drug, nicotine, is needed to maintain an optimal state of well-being. Also, withdrawal symptoms do occur after smoking cessation.

Consistent use of all forms of tobacco leads to a dependence on nicotine that is indistinguishable from other forms of drug dependence.

Cigarette smoking is the major avoidable cause of death in Western society. In the United States alone, smoking is responsible for eighteen percent of total deaths annually—seven times more than the number of Americans killed in the entire Vietnam war. Two researchers have said that "smoking has killed more Americans during this century than were killed in battle or died of war-related diseases in all wars ever fought by this nation."[16, 17] Why, then, do we remain passive about this issue?

Cigarette smoking has dramatically declined among adults since the surgeon general's first report on smoking and health in 1964. However, thirty-two percent of men and twenty-seven percent of women continue to use tobacco daily. Some 1.3

million people quit smoking annually. That's good. But about three thousand people start smoking each day. That's bad—especially since most of these are young people.

Tobacco myths. A popular, but false, belief holds that filtered cigarettes (which now make up more than ninety-seven percent of the market in the United States) are somehow safer than non-filtered cigarettes. In the billboards that line major American thoroughfares, we can see evidence of the massive number of advertising dollars being spent to convince us that low-tar and low-nicotine filtered cigarettes are preferable.

However, studies show that people who smoke these types of cigarettes often make what are called "compensatory smoking changes," in which they inhale more frequently and more deeply to keep up the nicotine levels in the blood. It is like using low-calorie salad dressing, then doubling the amount to make up for lost flavor.

Another myth concerning tobacco revolves around the belief that "smokeless" tobacco, or other forms of tobacco besides cigarettes, are less habit-forming. In fact, nicotine blood levels are similar for cigarette smokers, pipe smokers, and users of snuff, despite the various methods of absorption.

The family that smokes together... One smoking member of a family will affect the health of the entire family. In fact, the effects of tobacco smoke on nonsmokers ("passive smoking") are extremely significant. Almost two-thirds of the smoke from a burning cigarette never reaches the smoker's lungs, but becomes part of the air that everyone else breathes. This "sidestream smoke" is not filtered in any way, and contains a great concentration of toxic substances. A 1979 study found that a nonsmoker who spends one hour in a smoke-filled car or commuter train will inhale toxins equivalent to having smoked nine filtered cigarettes.

We are frequently asked about the influence of a smoking

spouse or parent on other family members. Compared to wives of non-smoking men, non-smoking wives of smoking husbands will usually have an increase of two to four times the likelihood of developing some sort of cancer. The greatest risk is for cancer of the lungs, cervix, or breast. The occurrence of leukemia and lymphoma are also increased. The risk of passive smoking is one-half to one-third that of direct smoking. So if your spouse smokes two packs a day, you are smoking one of those packs as well!

One smoking member of a family will affect the health of the entire family. If your spouse smokes two packs a day, you are smoking one of those packs as well!

It is difficult to relay the unequivocal facts of the effects of family smoking on children without eliciting a guilt attack among smoking parents. However, it is clear that smoking parents are more likely to have children who smoke. In fact, seventy-five percent of those who smoke cigarettes today had at least one parent who smoked. And the likelihood of that child smoking doubles with each additional adult member of the household that smokes.

Children of smoking parents become victims of involuntary or passive smoking as well. They are more likely to have bronchitis, pneumonia, earaches, and increased coughing in direct proportion to the number of cigarettes smoked, especially by the mother. Children exposed to the cigarette smoke of two parents have six times more respiratory infections.

The development of asthma is another major concern for children from smoking families. Small children are particularly victimized by this since they breathe faster, and consequently inhale greater quantities of toxins. They may also experience deficits in growth and in intellectual and emotional development, and may have a higher incidence of behavioral disorders.

Finally, the risk of cancer is increased by fifty percent for children of men who smoke. And the risk of a child developing a cancer of the blood is 4.6 times greater if both parents smoke.

Perhaps you were unaware of these things many years ago when you began smoking. If you have smoked in the past—don't let guilt drive you to despair. Today is a new day! *If you quit smoking now, most of the harmful effects from smoke that you or your family have accumulated can be gone within the next five years.* Health-wise, it will be almost as if you never smoked. So take that first step. Do it now! Here are some tips on what steps to take.

DOUSING THE FLAME

In the mid-seventies, various grass-roots organizations put cigarette smoking on their hit list. Since then, the results have been nothing short of miraculous in terms of the encouragement this movement has given Americans to quit smoking. Even the cartoon strip "Doonesbury" got into the act. A job applicant to a large tobacco company was portrayed as blowing his chances for employment because he could not say "Cigarettes do not cause cancer" without laughing.[18]

One major factor in the drive to curtail smoking is the campaign to protect non-smokers' rights to breathe clean air. Smoking in most public places these days is difficult. You must find a designated smoking area, stay there until you are finished, and leave your companions behind if they are non-smokers. While many people have stopped smoking on their own, the increasing social pressure not to smoke has certainly reinforced if not precipitated this decision.

What of the expensive "stop smoking" programs advertised far and wide? Proposed methods include acupuncture, hypnotherapy, biofeedback, rapid smoking, special filters, diets, self-help books and cassettes, pocket calculators for keeping track of cigarettes, aversive conditioning with electric shock, and a and a slew of chemical remedies including local anesthetic agents, tranquilizers, nicotine substitutes, and nicotine itself in various forms.[19] Except for the nicotine substitutes, most of these programs have insufficient evidence to back up their claims—no matter what the salesperson tells you.

Ultimately, the stop-smoking programs that work are the ones that provide the following elements:

- Encouragement from the entire family. Every smoker in the family should try to quit simultaneously for the greatest chance of success.
- Enrollment in a support group sponsored by the American Cancer Society or some other physician-based group.
- Enlistment of your family physician to help with this effort, especially with the use of prescription medications such as Nicorette gum or Clonidine, which help ease the physical urge to smoke.

Cigarette advertisers and producers, whose livelihoods depend on maintaining the nicotine dependence of more than fifty million Americans—including 1.25 million new teenage smokers each year—are a formidable opponent. Billboards promise freedom, wealth, glamour, manliness, sexual attractiveness, and athletic prowess.

Let's fight this conspiracy as families. If you smoke, stop. Get help in this effort. Then teach your children that smoking is not the cool thing to do, but the stupid thing to do. Don't allow smokers in your house, car, or place of business. Enforce your rights to clean air wherever you are. By adding this extra social pressure, you are helping those around you.

Facts that help smokers stop. We realize that some of these may seem like cheap shots. But if they help you stop smoking, use them.

1. Cigarettes contain cyanide, the substance used in gas chambers.

2. Cigarettes contain ammonia, the substance that gives urine its characteristic smell.

3. Cigarettes contain formaldehyde, the agent used to preserve cadavers.

4. Cigarettes produce carbon monoxide, the same exhaust fumes your car produces.

5. At one pack per day, the average smoker will consume one million doses of the above-mentioned toxins in less than fifteen years.

6. As a smoker, you have a one in seven chance of getting lung cancer. If you have relatives who have had lung cancer, and you smoke, your chances are even greater.

7. Smoking causes wrinkling of the skin and makes you look older.

8. If you are a two-pack-a-day smoker, you could save two Third World children from death and starvation by contributing the money you spend on cigarettes to a hunger fund.

DRUG ABUSE

There seems little doubt about the reality of inherited predisposition to chemical dependency and drug abuse.[20, 21, 22] Children of alcoholics or drug abusers seem to be at higher risk of becoming substance abusers themselves. It is not yet clear exactly how this works. Variations in the way these pschoactive drugs are metabolized by the body, or changes at the receptor sites in the central nervous system, may play a role.

There is also little doubt about the significance of social and environmental factors in the development of drug dependence. Here, as in so many areas of life, children learn what they live. At the most basic level, the mere presence of drugs in the house increases the chances that they will be used— and, perhaps, abused.

Prescription drug abuse. It was about eleven o'clock on Saturday night when the answering service called David about a patient, Stephen, who needed a prescription refilled. It was his weekend to be on call for himself and two other physicians. The patient's name was unfamiliar to him, so he assumed it must be someone who had seen one of the other physicians. David dialed the number the answering service had given him.

Stephen picked up the phone after just a few rings. His voice sounded a little shaky, perhaps even nervous. He said, "Dr. Sneed, I've come to see you every so often for intense headache pain. You gave me a prescription a few months ago, and I've run out of pills. Do you think you could call in a refill for me?" He mentioned the name of a strong pain killer.

David responded, "How long has it been since I last saw you? I'm at home right now, and I don't have your chart in front of me. Have you been in pain for long? What are your symptoms?" Stephen's voice was still shaky as he answered, "I've had this terrible headache for two days and I just can't stand it anymore. But I haven't really been back to see you since that first visit."

David was trying to discern any hidden messages in this latest version of a story he has heard many times before. He told his anxious patient, "You know, the particular drug you mentioned is a controlled substance. Without having your chart in front of me—in fact, without seeing you in the office to evaluate whether or not you have a threatening medical situation—it is our policy to not refill those prescriptions over the phone.

"If the pain gets worse," David continued, "I can make arrangements to have the emergency room physician check you in at the hospital. Otherwise, I'd suggest you take Tylenol tonight and come to our clinic tomorrow morning. We are open on weekends. In fact, we were open all day today. Why didn't you come in today?"

With this question, the phone went dead. David realized that his suspicions were correct: this man was not a patient of his at all. The call had been another attempt by someone desperate to support his drug habit. "Stephen," whoever he was,

was addicted to prescription medications.

Most people are aware that pain medication and tranquilizers are often abused. But amphetamines are also one of the most frequently-abused prescription drugs. In small doses they can produce increased alertness, diminished fatigue, an enhanced sense of well-being, and improved motor skills. But eventually, undesirable side effects appear: anxiety, restlessness, insomnia, abdominal cramping, and general lassitude.

Illegal drugs. It never ceases to amaze us, when compiling patients' medical histories, how many "everyday people" use illegal drugs either recreationally or in an attempt to self-treat such problems as depression and anxiety. These are not just aging hippies left over from the sixties, but bankers, lawyers, teachers—people who look and act just like you or me.

One patient casually mentioned that he was thinking of giving up cocaine because his children had become aware that he used it, and he was embarrassed by their severe criticism. He seemed unaware—or, more likely, unwilling to acknowledge—that he was running an enormous health risk (not to mention the legal ramifications). As he saw it, this kind of recreational behavior from his college days had simply carried on as a convenient means of escape from the troubles of adulthood.

Similarly, many patients who admit to regular marijuana use refuse to acknowledge any problem with what they see as a harmless relaxation tool. We can only wonder how these people will handle the issue of drug abuse with their own children, who have grown up in homes where use of illegal and dangerous substances was openly condoned.

Do the pressures of life often make you feel a need to "just get away"? Many people escape through the use of mind-altering substances, both legal and illegal. Not only are drugs and alcohol potentially both addictive and physically harmful, but their frequent use can also lead to a type of psychological dependency that is itself very difficult to break.

Treatment for drug abuse. Detoxification from drug abuse is often accomplished in an outpatient setting, though many addictions require more intensive inpatient care. Tragically, the availability of treatment is often determined primarily by financial considerations. Who will pay? What type of insurance do they have?

After detoxification has taken place, long-term treatments range from self-help groups to highly structured and long-term residential programs. The twelve step program from Alcoholics Anonymous is usually the hallmark of most self-help groups. There are two drug abuse twelve step programs named the Narcotics Anonymous and Cocaine Anonymous programs.

CHAPTER 4

The Power of
Family Emotions

W HAT FORMS THE basis for your family relationships right now? Are they founded on trust, openness, acceptance, and love? Or are these just fairy-tale memories from the past? We all want happy, loving families filled with care and respect for each other. So why don't we attain this ideal?

The answer can often be summed up in a single word: *stress.* Controlling the stress in their lives seems to be the goal of many of our patients. They expend incredible energy and resources on stamping out the stress-inducing brushfires of life, only to see them revive and blaze to life again in another unprotected area. Left uncontrolled, stress will sap the life from an individual—and, ultimately, from their family as well.

Left uncontrolled, stress will sap the life from an individual—and, ultimately, from their family as well.

Anxiety and depression, seen both alone and together, are occurring in epidemic proportion in America today. The waste of time, resources, and emotional energy is incalculable. Untreated depression and anxiety line the path to the ultimate family tragedy: couples and their children fragmented by physical and emotional pain resulting in separation, divorce, and abuse.

COPING STRATEGIES

There is a clear link between stress and health, both physically and emotionally. Understanding the stabilizing and destabilizing events of life—and learning to cope with them fruitfully—is essential to change. Change comes with knowledge of the cause of the problems, and with treatment of the physical and emotional ills that a person or family may be suffering.

Optimal care of the family requires attention to physical, emotional, and spiritual issues. Intervention can occur at many points in the harmful cycle of stress. A first step is recognizing the enormous array of stressors that bombard the family each day.

Let us introduce you to a family we know. Ted and Jane have been married for fifteen years. They are well liked in the neighborhood, active in church and school activities with their adolescent daughter, Tammy, and preschool son, Jason. From the outside, they seemed solid and secure. But from the inside, they often seemed to be teetering on the brink of destruction.

Why? Ted hears through the grapevine that his company isn't doing too well. He's afraid of being laid off or facing reduced hours, resulting in a cut in pay. Jane has just started coming to grips with an unexpected positive pregnancy test. Meeting the mortgage payment on their house has always been a bit of a stretch. The plan had been for Jane to go back to work after Jason started school, but a new baby on the way and Ted's uncertain career situation toss everything up in the air.

And so the cycle begins—multiple stressful influences piling up on top of one another, depleting a family's physical and emotional resources. We see couples like Ted and Jane frequently. As the fabric of life begins to unravel from too much stress and too many problems, memories of past failures surface and the emotional fear we call anxiety takes over.

How Ted and Jane handle these events depends on a variety of factors: their current physical health, their genetic predisposition toward such illnesses as depression or anxiety, past experiences with problems such as this, and perceived threats to their relationship and personal self-esteem. They must now meet their threatening circumstances with their current resources, learn new coping skills, or call upon others for assistance.

Stress-induced coping failure. Faced with inadequate coping resources, an individual or a family may resort to palliative coping to "buy time" or gain short-term release from emotional tension. Physical exercise, vacations, new hobbies, and sheer denial of reality are just a few of the ways we might respond when faced with overwhelming stress. Clinging to these inadequate solutions often leads to further problems as the source of the stress gets swept under the family's emotional rug and temporarily forgotten.

Failure to develop mature methods of handling stress can lead to further family and personal imbalance. One common outcome of this long-term imbalance is what psychologists call *projection*. That is, people project their difficulties onto someone else: they create a scapegoat. A child with a serious health problem becomes identified as the "real" source of the family's problems.

Failure to develop mature methods of handling stress can lead to further family and personal imbalance.

In Ted and Jane's case, the scapegoat was Jason's asthma. As the stress on the family grew, we saw Jason in our clinic with increasing frequency. Even though Jason was genetically pre-disposed to asthma and did actually suffer from the illness, he was hardly the cause of all the family's problems. Even so, his symptoms worsened with the increased emotional stress.

Another common problem is called *somatization:* con-sciously or unconsciously using physical symptoms to deal with the anxiety of unresolved stress. In Ted's case, an old work-related back injury mysteriously began to flare up, and seemed to worsen with each day as his job uncertainty worsened.

The longer an individual or a family is in crisis, the more difficult recovery becomes, and the more deep-seated become the maladaptive coping mechanisms they use. Thus a vicious cycle is set in motion. Of course, we cannot always see the sources of stress coming. But early recognition of the results of stress—such as anxiety and depression—can lead to earlier recovery with appropriate treatment. Ted never expected to lose his job and Jane was sure she had seen the last of diapers and bassinets. But things changed; the unexpected happened. Now they had some choices to make. Perhaps you do, too.

Some common *overt* examples of stress-induced coping fail-ure include the following:

- Depression
- Anxiety/panic attacks
- Alcohol or substance abuse
- Sexual dysfunction
- Divorce/separation
- Incest
- Abuse of a family member
- Delinquency
- Run-away youth
- School behavior problem
- School failure

More *covert* examples of stress-induced coping failure would include:

- Somatization
- Excessive use of medical care facilities
- Medical non-compliance with prescriptions or instructions
- History of multiple surgeries
- Chronic pain
- Failure to thrive
- Doctor-shopping[1]

ANXIETY

All of life's circumstances impact our equilibrium as individuals. The same can be said for families. One of the major outcomes of stress is the development of varying degrees of anxiety. Untreated, anxiety can become personally debilitating, as well as being a major source of family disharmony. Anxiety can be brief or prolonged. It can serve beneficially as a warning flare, alerting us to present or future dangers. Or it can overwhelm its victims and leave them helpless before the emotional terror of their own mind.

Anxiety is said to be the most common psychiatric problem in our country. As many as two-thirds of all new prescriptions written by doctors today are for the treatment of anxiety. Anxiety disorder is reported in up to four percent of the general population, with one to two percent of all Americans suffering from a more severe form of anxiety known as panic attack.

As many as two-thirds of all new prescriptions written by doctors today are for the treatment of anxiety.

Our friend Jane became increasingly anxious each day after her missed menstrual period. Fear and anxiety about an unplanned third pregnancy mounted until it was confirmed by her obstetrician. Now new fears gave rise to persistent and increasing anxiety. How could she possibly go back to school and complete her degree now? Feeling trapped, uncertain, and angry, Jane's symptoms of anxiety increased in perilous waves.

Anxiety symptoms. Emotional problems such as excessive worry, difficulty concentrating, feelings of nervousness, problems sleeping, and irritability, are often tip-off symptoms that someone is abnormally anxious. People with anxiety may also experience perspiration, clammy hands, nausea, diarrhea or other abdominal problems, hot flashes, chills, frequent urination, and trouble swallowing—like the proverbial lump in the throat. Nervous tension like restlessness, trembling, muscle tension, and easy fatigue are also common symptoms.

A major challenge in diagnosing anxiety disorder is recognizing the often confusing physical complaints and symptoms which are actually manifestations of anxiety itself. Studies consistently show that as many as fifty percent of patients seeking care from a family physician have psychological problems such as anxiety or depression at the heart of their complaints. Initially, the exact cause of a person's distress often escapes both patient and physician due to the process of somatization we alluded to earlier.

Take Jane, for example. Initially, her doctor thought her symptoms—shortness of breath, racing heart, dry mouth, and dizziness—were all related to the early stages of pregnancy. Failing to recognize the real cause of problems often leads to unnecessary medical testing and expense, prescriptions, and sometimes even unwarranted surgery. Anxious patients often need careful examination, judicious testing, and a physician or counselor willing to *listen* to the patient.

Jane's twelve-year-old daughter Tammy almost underwent exploratory surgery in an attempt to explain her frequent episodes of severe abdominal pain, which often caused her to miss school. The pain usually came on in the morning and subsided as the day went on. With unhappy school officials pressuring her parents, Tammy saw a string of doctors, including a gynecologist, gastroenterologist, and pediatrician.

Finally, an astute school counselor recognized Tammy's dread of a certain subject and teacher during the first part of her school day. A schedule change was arranged, and a week later Tammy was "cured" of her stomach ailment. Tammy wasn't faking or malingering. Her pain was very real. She had simply repressed her true feelings and responded to stress in a way she had actually learned from her mother. For years, Jane had avoided anxiety-provoking responsibilities with debilitating headaches.

We certainly do not mean to suggest that all debilitating headaches or stomach pains have emotional origins. But almost any physical symptom can become reinforced when it serves an emotional purpose.

Panic attacks. If anxiety is the thief of peace and harmony, a more intense anxiety reaction, known as a panic attack, is truly the terrorist of the mind. Sudden intense fear, apprehension, even terror—all the symptoms of anxiety heightened and intensified—are the characteristics of a panic attack. These frightening episodes can totally disrupt a person's life and, in severe cases, lead to an increasingly restricted lifestyle.

Panic disorder is twice as common in women as in men. Although the exact causes of this problem remain elusive, there is a definite genetic link. Anywhere from eighteen to forty percent of people with a parent or a sibling who have panic disorder will also have the problem themselves. Recognition of this potential predisposition may allow more rapid diagnosis and treatment in those at risk.

It is abundantly clear that stressful life events—whether a single event or a series of crisis situations—contribute to the development of anxiety and panic disorder. Many people describe their first attack as occurring at the "worst time in their life." If allowed to continue, such episodes can become more frequent and lead to anticipatory dread: constant fear of another debilitating panic attack.

Unrelenting fear and anxiety may cause a person to associate various unrelated events or places with their anxious feelings, and lead to unreasonable fears called phobias and other avoidance behavior. Tammy developed an incredible fear of school and did everything in her power to avoid it.

Many people with severe panic reactions withdraw into the perceived safety of their homes. Without treatment, this can lead to a condition called *agoraphobia,* an intense fear of places or situations from which escape would be difficult or impossible. Without help, the agoraphobic individual may become imprisoned in his or her own home.

Needless to say, anxiety of this magnitude causes everyone in the family to feel as if they are walking on eggshells.

Needless to say, anxiety of this magnitude causes everyone in the family to feel as if they are walking on eggshells. The potential emotional explosion residing within a family member can disable not only the individual, but may impair the rest of the family as well. If you think that you or someone in your family suffers from excessive anxiety or even panic, encourage them to get help. Effective treatment can help prevent anxiety from taking over the life of an individual or family.

TREATMENT OF ANXIETY

A good starting point in preventing anxiety disorder is to address certain behaviors and medical conditions that often "trigger" anxiety. For example, caffeine sensitivity is so great for some people that just half a cup of coffee can cause about fifty percent of people who experience panic attacks to have an episode. Caffeinated drinks and foods such as coffee, tea, chocolate, and cola drinks should be avoided, or at least carefully restricted, by those prone to severe anxiety. Even so-called "caffeine-free" colas may have significant amounts of caffeine, up to thirty percent as much as a regular cola.

Any medical conditions that could potentially be associated with anxiety disorders should be treated aggressively. About fifty percent of those with panic attacks also have problems with depression. In this case, treatment should be directed at both problems.

Substance abuse is at the heart of many problems with anxiety and panic. Some studies have suggested that as many as twenty to fifty percent of alcoholics initially begin drinking in an effort to control anxiety or panic attacks. Others have found that ten to twenty percent of people with agoraphobia also have problems with alcohol.

Do you have a problem with anxiety? The following symptoms may be found to one degree or another in those with anxiety and panic disorder:

- Shortness of breath or a smothering sensation
- Choking
- Dizziness, unsteady feelings, or faintness
- Trembling or shaking
- Heart palpitations or racing heart beat
- Chest pain
- Feelings of unreality
- Sweating
- Nausea or abdominal pain
- Hot flashes or chills
- Fear of going crazy
- Fear of dying

In addition, several medical conditions are frequently associated with anxiety:

- Heart disease: angina, high blood pressure, mitral valve prolapse, heart attack
- Lung disease: asthma, pulmonary embolism, emphysema
- Neurologic disorders: thyroid, low blood sugar
- Anemia
- Substance abuse

Once anxiety disorder has been recognized, and any concurrent medical conditions have been brought under adequate control, treatment should begin as soon as possible. Infrequent panic episodes—which occur in up to one-third of all people—can usually be treated with reassurance and information about the nature of the problem and advice on self-relaxation. More severe and frequent problems may require a combined approach of medication to relieve the immediate anxiety and consistent supportive counseling to help with any underlying issues or established avoidance behavior.

DEPRESSION

Depression is one of the ten most common diagnoses made by primary care physicians. Some days in our clinic, it seems as if every other patient is depressed or has physical symptoms of depression. Individuals, families, and society in general pay a high price for the costs of untreated depression.

Statistics show that the incidence of depression is increasing and that the age of onset is decreasing. At any given time, about four percent of the population suffers from depression. As much as eighteen percent will have at least one episode of major depression in our lifetime. Depression is about two to three times more common in women than in men; women aged eighteen to forty-four have the highest risk.[2]

Absolutely anyone can become depressed. Rich or poor, black or white, blue-collar or white-collar worker—depression affects all equally. Single persons and those who were formerly married are at greater risk of depression than their married counterparts in general, though the very highest rates of depression occur in married individuals not getting along with their spouses. In fact, an unhappy marriage increases your risk of depression by a factor of twenty-five.

Absolutely anyone can become depressed. Rich or poor, black or white, blue collar or white collar worker, depression affects all equally.

Do you remember Jane, from our earlier story? She went through a bout of depression during a rough period in her marriage to Ted. Crying, tired, unable to sleep—Jane felt life just didn't seem worth living. She remembered her mother once acting that way for a few months, but she never thought it might happen to her. The medicine her doctor prescribed helped, but the memory of how awful she felt still haunts her. It is still a mystery to her how she could have felt so bad that she just wanted to die.

Causes of depression. Serious depression is usually related to major life events, especially those involving loss. Depressed people experience three to six times more such events than other people. Those who lack the resources to cope with the serious stresses of life often find themselves depressed. For example, a woman without a close and confiding relationship is three times more likely to become depressed after a stressful life event.

Most people who become depressed suffer a relapse—half of them within two years. Depressions themselves are seldom brief periods of depressed mood, but rather tend to last four to eight months without treatment. In about fifteen percent of all cases, depression becomes chronic, an indefinitely continuing debilitation.

Depression and genetics. A clear genetic link exists in the case of depression. People with a parent or sibling who has had depression are at two to three times greater risk of becoming depressed themselves. Dr. Peter McGuffin, professor of psychological medicine at University of Wales College of Medicine in England, and Dr. Randy Katz, professor of psychology at the University of Toronto in Canada say that, "genetic studies are widely accepted as providing a firm foundation for the notion that there is a biological basis to depression."[3]

Their studies indicated strong genetic links for such problems as manic-depressive illness. Of special interest was their finding that depression not only runs in families, but that some families seem to be more likely than others to encounter stressful life events. Their research suggests that depression occurs more often in these "hazard-prone families."

Recognizing the potential genetic transfer of a tendency toward depression can help identify a problem that is often masked by its accompanying physical complaints. Twenty-five percent of depressed psychiatric patients have a clear family history of depression. Interestingly, what is known as "assortive mating" is high among depressed people: that is, depressed men tend to marry depressed women, and the cycle continues and deepens.[4]

Depression and medical illness. Depression and medical illness interact in complex ways. Depression can coexist with another illness, or it can be a by-product of the illness itself. People suffering from chronic illnesses are more likely to also have depression. Failure to recognize this causes much unneeded suffering.

There are many illnesses that can actually *cause* depression: diabetes, thyroid disease, liver disease, vitamin deficiencies, infections such as the flu and mononucleosis, kidney failure, cancer, and hormonal changes associated with childbirth, to name several. Studies have shown that as many as twenty percent of those persons believed to have depression are eventually found to have an undiagnosed medical condition. This simply underscores the need for careful physical examination and physician involvement in all cases of depression.

As many as twenty percent of those persons believed to have depression are eventually found to have an undiagnosed medical condition.

A significant number of common medications, including birth control pills, some blood pressure medication, steroids, and sleeping pills can have depressant side effects. Some medication used to treat ulcers, Parkinson's disease, and even anxiety, are known to cause depression in some people. Several of our patients have had remarkable improvements in their mood when they stopped using birth control pills.

Chemical or clinical depression. One of the great advances in the understanding of depression and its treatment was the realization that—regardless of the effects of life stresses, losses, or other potential precipitating events—many people are depressed due to chemical changes in their body. These changes are specifically located within the central nervous system and are due to fluctuations in substances known as neurotransmitters.

More than thirty years of research has led scientists to believe that specific chemicals in the brain, such as dopamine, norepinephrine, and serotonin, play a significant role in the illness we know as depression. Either an oversupply or an undersupply of these hormonal chemicals contributes toward depression.

A greater understanding of the role that "chemical depression" plays is often helpful in accepting the diagnosis of depression as an illness in need of treatment. It is easy to see how a genetic tendency toward chemical imbalance could promote the inherited tendency toward depression. Anti-depressant medication works to correct these imbalances and restore normal functioning of the neurotransmitter system. After taking these medications for several months, your doctor may try to reduce or stop these medications while at the same time carefully monitoring you for any signs of recurrent depression.

Recognizing the "chemical" nature of depression makes it easier to understand how women, with their complex hormonal interactions, are twice as likely to become depressed as men. Menopause, pre-menstrual periods, and the period after childbirth are times of intense hormonal fluctuation—and, not surprisingly, times of increased symptoms of depression.

Although it is often assumed that menopausal women have more depression than other women, this is not the case. In fact, a woman's highest risk for depression is between the ages of twenty and forty. Cyclic depressive symptoms are a common feature of depression in women, correlating with their menstrual cycle. Depression lasting all month and increasing as menstruation approaches probably requires anti-depressant treatment—as opposed to more focused monthly mood swings, which suggest a need for treatment of premenstrual syndrome (PMS).

Though some people seem to doubt its reality, post-partum "blues" is a well-recognized problem. The very disturbing symptoms of sudden crying, sadness, mood swings, and anxiety at what should be a happy time can obviously disrupt the whole family. Treatment should be considered for symptoms which are prolonged, but post-partum depression usually lasts only a few days, with peak symptoms occurring four to seven days after delivery.

TREATING DEPRESSION

Recognizing depression is the first step toward successful treatment. Symptoms of depression are clearly defined; anyone having a sufficient number of these symptoms is, by definition, depressed. It is amazing to us how many patients who have some serious health concern reject the diagnosis of depression as the root of their problems. Many people cling to physical complaints, which are a result of the underlying problem of depression, as if to legitimate their ailments.

Failure to diagnose depression for what it is—or refusal to accept the diagnosis—may lead to expensive and unnecessary testing and painful delays in getting the needed treatment to control this tragically common problem.

Are you depressed? Here is a simple test you can take to assess whether or not you are suffering from depression. If you answer yes to two or more questions, you should consult your physician about depression.

- Do you feel sad and depressed most of the time?
- Have your sleep habits changed?
- Has your weight or appetite changed?
- Are you having problems with concentration and memory?
- Do you feel worthless and guilty about your sad feelings?
- Do you feel tired all the time, for no apparent reason?
- Have you lost interest in the things you once liked?
- Have you thought about harming yourself?
- Have you lost interest in sex with your spouse?
- Do you have any chronic painful conditions?

Not every person shows all symptoms of depression, nor will every symptom necessarily be of equal severity. However, where there's smoke, there's probably fire. Depression is highly treatable once recognized for what it is. The sooner effective treatment begins, the easier in general the control of the depression.

If you suspect that you or a member of your family suffer from depression, seek help right away. Your doctor can help assess your problem, rule out other illnesses, and begin treatment or refer you for appropriate treatment. Don't let stubbornness or pride stand in the way of getting the help you need.

Antidepressant medication. Many people are reluctant to take medication for depression. For some, it is an admission that something really is wrong, and they resist that idea. Others are afraid of becoming dependent on the medication, fearing addiction and its control over their life. You will be relieved to know that antidepressant medications used today are not addictive. They work to correct the chemical imbalances that are causing the depression to occur.

There are several prescription medications available, no one of which is right for all people. Your physician can help prescribe the best medication for you. Be patient when you begin this treatment as it can take from two weeks to two months for the full effect to be noticed. Don't make the mistake that many people make, quitting your medication once you begin to feel better without consulting your doctor. Stopping too soon can cause a severe rebound depression.

What about counseling? Most evidence suggests that using antidepressants in conjunction with insightful counseling is the most effective way of treating depression. While antidepressant medication is very effective at relieving many of the troublesome effects of depression, good counseling is important in resolving the damaged interpersonal relationships and addictive behaviors that often accompany depression.

Counseling is important in resolving the damaged interpersonal relationships and addictive behaviors that often accompany depression.

Unfortunately, everybody is not always in agreement on the issue of counseling. We frequently see depressed couples where only one partner will agree to counseling. This can be frustrating. But as one person is helped by the therapy, sometimes the other partner will recognize the helpfulness of the treatment and join in.

Depression in a family is a difficult burden to bear. Failure to recognize and get help for this highly treatable illness is tragic and, no doubt, a leading cause of family disintegration in today's high-stress world. Depressive disorders are genetically-inheritable, environmentally-learned, and extremely common. Watch for the warning flags of depression if risk factors are part of your family chemistry. Correct minor problems right away and work to eliminate any avoidable causes of stress in your life where possible.

PERSONALITY AND TEMPERAMENT

Have you ever wondered how children from the same family manage to turn out so differently? How many times have parents said to themselves, "I raised them all the same!" Yet they look different from each other, think differently, dress differently, have different values, and even different personalities. It's not hard to understand some variation in physical attributes, but surely growing up in the same home environment will yield basically similar personalities and temperaments.

As much as fifty percent of some personality traits may be genetically determined.

Yes—and no. Though the field is still in its infancy, the research so far indicates that as much as fifty percent of some personality traits may be genetically determined. Thus the same home environment will have different effects on different individuals, depending on their genetic inheritance.

Once upon a time, parents had the major role in deciding

whom their children would and would not marry. It seems clear from historical records that while financial considerations were uppermost, consideration was also given to family chemistry. What were the prospective in-laws like? Was there a family history of physical or mental illness?

Nowadays we pride ourselves on considering each person's worth apart from his background and inheritance. We certainly do not want to return to a system in which many fine individuals were no doubt judged unfairly. But our ancestors may have had an intuitive sense of what modern science is beginning to teach us: that family chemistry has a profound effect on why we are the way we are.

Genetic factors. Environment and social learning certainly play a major role in molding personality and temperament, but not the only role. Even a brief glimpse at the animal kingdom helps us see that genetic factors are also important. Selective breeding of dogs has consistently demonstrated the remarkable degree to which certain desired stable patterns of behavior (personality) can be fostered.

Many children who endured seriously adverse experiences seemed to have emerged unscathed, while others whose circumstances seemed far less traumatic developed severe emotional problems.

We typically buy certain breeds of dogs precisely because we know that their docile nature tends to make good household pets. Try as you might, it is very difficult to train a golden retriever to be an attack dog. But other breeds typically make excellent attack dogs. The difference lies largely in the genes.

A similar principle holds true for people. Studies conducted over the past twenty years indicate that personality can be passed along genetically in human beings. In 1977, two doctors began to feel that the adverse experiences children suffered were inadequate to explain why some developed behavioral and emotional disorders and others did not. Many children who endured seriously adverse experiences seemed to have emerged unscathed, while others whose circumstances seemed far less traumatic developed severe emotional problems. There appeared to be something in the makeup of these young people that rendered them either vulnerable or invulnerable to environmental influences.[5]

These doctors also came up with a concept that many families can identify with—the "good fit" theory. How did a particular child, given his or her unique personality, fit into that particular environment? No doubt all of us can think of particular children who just don't seem to match up well with the family they were born into. They might have done quite well in other environments, with other standards for what is acceptable. But as things happened, there was not an especially good fit.

The existence of this kind of "poor fit" does not mean that "all is lost"—not at all. Rather, this insight helps us grasp the concept of the *family system,* and to see the importance of helping both children and parents understand their respective roles in the overall mix.

In recent years, a great many studies have been conducted on the inheritability of personality traits. One journal stated the results rather starkly: "Genetic variation for… personality is significant, and the influence of rearing in the same family (shared family environment) is negligible."[6]

Now before you get upset and throw this book across the room, note that this does *not* mean that the home life you provide is not important. It simply means that it is important in different ways for different children. It also helps explain the mystery we described at the beginning of this section: why children who grow up in the same environment can have such different personalities. There are other factors involved.

PERSONALITY TYPES

According to the dictionary, personality and temperament have to do with these variables:

- The quality or state of being a person.
- The complex of characteristics that distinguishes one individual, group, or nation from another.
- The totality of an individual's behavioral and emotional tendencies.

Medical studies that have examined the relative importance of genetic versus environmental factors in the development of personality traits have determined that certain traits may be as much as forty-five percent genetic in nature. Genetically inheritable personality types may include:

Neuroticism: emotional instability, perhaps deriving from a nervous disorder.

Extraversion: needing to be at the center of attention, driven to stand out.

Impulsiveness: acting in the heat of the moment, without thought of the consequences.

Monotony avoidance: having a low level of tolerance for tedium and sameness; often bright and creative individuals who are extremely bored with repetitive work.

Social introversion: predominantly concerned with one's own life, not feeling a need for other people. There is an extremely high genetic link for this trait.

Type "A" personality. The "isms" that drive us—either to success or to suicide—are often related to what has become popularly known as the Type "A" personality. It is clear that this temperament can be learned and passed from one generation to the next through environmental factors. But studies of twins and of adopted children have shown that the Type "A" personality may be *genetically* determined as much as forty percent of the time.[7]

With how many of the following statements would you agree? The more these statements describe you, the more you can be described as a Type "A" personality.

1. I want to be the best at everything.
2. I am sometimes described as domineering.
3. I often take the words out of other people's mouths.
4. I prefer to do one thing at a time.
5. I do not like to compete.
6. I eat too quickly.
7. I demand a great deal of myself.
8. I am punctual.
9. I am ambitious.
10. I often feel "stressed."
11. I have often felt stressed at the end of the working day.
12. I often think about work away from the office.
13. I feel mentally and physically exhausted after work.
14. I often feel uncertain, worried, and dissatisfied with my performance at work.
15. I get impatient when I have to wait.

Type "A" personality has been the subject of a lot of study, because it relates closely to longevity and to incidence of heart disease. Interestingly, research shows that the assertiveness and hostility that sometimes accompany this particular temperament are not as strongly linked to genetics; they seem more affected by environmental factors. There is good news here for parents with hard-charging kids: bringing them up to understand compassion and gentleness *will* pay dividends.

There is good news here for parents with hard-charging kids:
bringing them up to understand compassion
and gentleness will pay dividends.

Many years ago, a very wise man had this to say about bringing up children: "Train a child in the way he should go, and when he is old he will not turn from it" (Prv 22:6). Note what this Bible verse does *not* say. It does not say, "Try to change your child's basic personality type." It does not give us permission to turn a basically introverted person into a replica of his or her Type "A" parent. It does not give us permission to try to make an engineer out of an artist, or a salesperson out of a withdrawn individual.

It does, however, urge us to take a "hands-on" approach to bringing up our children. We should train and counsel them, and not leave this job to someone else. We should bring them up to understand the meaning of right, wrong, and personal responsibility in an age of moral relativism and situational ethics. We should give them thoughtful advice about life-shaping decisions. We should help them set clear boundaries —and, when they cross those boundaries, help them connect the negative consequences to their actions.

The important thing to remember is that *any* temperament can be a good one. A loving family and friends help us to amplify what is healthy and helpful and overcome negative aspects. The bottom line is simple: love the kids you've got. Love them for who they are. Don't try to make them into what they are not. If you allow them to be their own persons, they will grow into adulthood secure in the value system they have received—whatever personality type they may have.

CHAPTER 5

Especially for Women

J OANNE WAS THE MOTHER of three teenage girls. Her oldest daughter, Leslie, seemed to favor Joanne's side of the family with her dark thick hair and lithe body frame. Suzanne described herself as "the sandwich material" since she was the middle child. She was a happy fifteen-year-old more like her father, who was a good tennis player and an avid jogger.

The youngest daughter, Beth, had just turned thirteen and was both enjoying and coping with the joys and traumas of being a teenager. She loved her new-found freedom with friends and extracurricular activities, as well as extended curfews and later bedtimes. But, in her heart, she was frightened by the approach of womanhood. Beth had felt moody most of the time over the last six months, and that scared her, too. Where was that blissful, simple life she had known before bras and feminine hygiene entered the picture?

Joanne and her daughters were tight. She had always been involved with their lives, though she was careful to allow them room to grow and mature by themselves. Her husband, Burt, was a good father and faithful husband. So why, amidst all this harmony, did something akin to World War III break out several times a year?

Joanne had always suffered from premenstrual syndrome

(PMS), and was looking forward to the cessation of these symptoms when she went through menopause. Not long after Beth began her periods, Joanne noticed that she and all her daughters began cycling simultaneously. Maybe that was the answer. Could she and her daughters all be suffering from the effects of PMS at the same time? Was this the source of the ugly words, tensions, and disputes?

Why did something akin to World War III
break out several times a year?
Could Joanne and her daughters all be suffering from
the effects of PMS at the same time?

Joanne spoke with her family physician about this question. He encouraged her to chart her premenstrual symptoms and those of her daughters. There is no standard blood test to diagnose PMS, only a timetable chart like the one on page 95 to help diagnose PMS.

In this chapter, we will talk about two specifically feminine health issues: premenstrual syndrome and menopause. Since these conditions and their symptoms affect the whole family, we felt they warranted a chapter of their own. Understanding the family chemistry of these normal occurrences can help you cope more effectively with changes in yourself, and in the lives of those you love.

PREMENSTRUAL SYNDROME

Premenstrual syndrome (PMS) is a collection of symptoms that occur anywhere from ten days prior to the onset of a woman's period to a few days after it ends. These symptoms usually recur on a monthly basis, though some months may be better or worse than others. Despite the fact that some symptoms are more common than others, PMS can appear totally different from one woman to the next. Since there are no definitive blood tests to determine the presence or absence of PMS, diagnosis is difficult and can be frustrating for both the patient and the physician.

Symptoms of PMS. More than a hundred possible symptoms of premenstrual syndrome have been listed in research articles from nations around the globe. These can usually be divided into two general classes: emotional symptoms and physical symptoms, as explained in a previous book, *PMS: What It Is and What You Can Do About It.*[1] The most common and significant symptoms are shown in the list below. Check off the ones that seem to be a particular problem for you and other female members of your nuclear family. Do you see any similarities?

PMS can often accompany other problems such as depression, anxiety, or even panic attacks.

It's important to note that PMS can often accompany other problems such as depression, anxiety, or even panic attacks. The added stress of premenstrual tension can often push a woman over the edge of what she might otherwise be able to deal with. For example, depression may be kept under control through self-will on most days, but become an unbearable burden to carry on PMS days. In cases such as these, treatment for both depression and PMS should be sought.

If you are suffering PMS-like symptoms that are not cyclical in nature—that is, they come and go, usually with two to three weeks between episodes—then it is *not* PMS. You should consult a physician for a complete medical evaluation.

In the tables below, we have provided an exhaustive list of PMS symptoms reported by other researchers and seen in our own practices.[2] Some of these symptoms affect almost all women at various times, while others may be rare even among PMS patients. Also, since so little is known about PMS, and since the specific cause is undiscovered, the symptom lists are probably incomplete.

You may well find yourself described in this list. One word of caution: *don't let PMS become a catch-all diagnosis for your ailments.* If your symptoms don't go away for at least one week following your menstrual period, it is *not* PMS. You should seek medical treatment for some other condition (which may or may not be serious, of course).

As you read the lists below, mark the symptoms you most often experience during the premenstrual days. We will use this information in the next section. Identifying your symptoms will help you to know what to do about them when treatments are discussed.

Physical Symptoms of PMS

- abdominal bloating
- fullness in the lower abdomen
- aching in the lower abdomen
- generalized swelling of the body
- tightness of rings
- tightness of shoes
- tingling in the fingers (parasthesias)
- carpal tunnel syndrome (numbness of the hands related to swelling in the wrists)
- breast tenderness
- headaches
- acne
- skin rashes
- irritation of the eyes (conjunctivitis)
- irritation of the eyes not caused by infection
- outbreaks of herpes (including fever blisters of the lips or herpes of the vulvar area)

- sinus congestion (due to increased fluid production from the sinuses)
- increased vaginal secretions (a woman may think she has a vaginal infection)
- increased problems with pre-existent epilepsy
- increased problems with asthma (PMS does not cause asthma, but symptoms may worsen)
- backache
- muscle-spasms and pain in the arms and legs, especially the joints
- passing-out episodes (syncope)
- tiredness and fatigue
- dizziness
- lack of coordination
- clumsiness
- heart palpitations
- poorly-fitting dentures
- easy bruising
- increased problems with hypoglycemia or with feelings of hypoglycemia
- increased problems with ulcerative colitis
- increased problems with pre-existent heart disease
- ulcerations of the mouth

Emotional Symptoms of PMS

- tension
- irritability
- depression
- anxiety
- mood swings
- outbursts of temper
- shouting
- throwing things

- paranoia
- forgetfulness
- self-blaming
- desire to withdraw from other people
- suicidal feeling
- compulsive activity
- change in sexual interest (usually increased at the time of ovulation and decreased afterward)
- aggression
- lethargy
- sleeping disorders
- insomnia
- nightmares or unusual dreams
- unnatural fears
- increased use of alcohol and other mood-altering drugs
- argumentativeness
- inability to initiate activities or accomplish work at the usual pace
- indecisiveness (or making poor decisions)
- marital conflict
- food cravings
- increased appetite
- difficulty in concentrating

Charting the symptoms

Use this type of calendar to record your *five worst symptoms.* Two sample months are shown on page 96.

Examples of coding:
A: Anxiety
AB: Abdominal Bloating
BT: Breast Tenderness
H: Headache
M: Menstruation

A PMS Calendar*

Use this type of calendar to record your five worst symptoms. Two sample months are shown on page 96.

Examples of coding
A–Anxiety
AB–Abdominal Bloating

BT–Breast Tenderness
H–Headache
M–Menstruation

	Month 1	Month 2	Month 3
1			
2			
3			
4			
5			
6			
7			
8			
9			
10			
11			
12			
13			
14			
15			
16			
17			
18			
19			
20			
21			
22			
23			
24			
25			
26			
27			
28			
29			
30			
31			
32			
33			
34			
35			

* From *PMS: What It Is and What You Can Do About It* by Sharon M. Sneed, Ph.D. and Joe S. McIlhaney, Jr., M.D. (Grand Rapids: Baker Book House 1988) 52-53. Used by permission.

In chart "A" the woman is diagnosed as having PMS. In chart "B" the timing of symptoms does not have a clear relationship to the menstrual cycle; this woman's symptoms may have another cause that should be investigated.

	Chart A	Chart B
1		
2		*a*
3	*h*	A
4		
5		*a*
6		
7		
8		H˙
9		
10		
11		
12		
13		
14	A	
15	HA 6+	H
16	*a*	*a*
17	*a*	
18	A	A
19	Ah	
20	Ha AB	
21	H A B	
22	HA B Ⓜ	Ⓗ
23	A B Ⓜ	
24	Ⓜ	Ⓜ
25	Ⓜ	Ⓜ
26	Ⓜ	Ⓜ
27		Ⓜ
28		Ⓜ
29		h
30		
31	H	A
32		
33		
34		
35		

WHAT CAUSES PMS?

The symptoms associated with premenstrual syndrome affect as many as ninety-five percent of all menstruating-age women to some extent. Thus, to some degree, PMS may simply be part of what it means to be a woman. However, there may be disease patterns at work in those who persistently experience the most severe symptoms. Some estimates indicate that as many as ten percent of the female population may have experienced such severe PMS symptoms that they were disabling or altered their daily routines.

Below, we have briefly listed the major proposed causes of PMS. It is apparent that any of these could be linked to inheritable traits, passed on from one generation to the next:

1. progesterone deficiency
2. estrogen deficiency
3. abnormalities of the estrogen/progesterone ratio
4. subclinical thyroid deficiency
5. increased progesterone-type androgens
6. abnormal fatty acid metabolism
7. neuro-transmitter abnormalities
8. altered carbohydrate tolerance

Other factors that may contribute to PMS but are *not* inheritable traits include:

1. decreased levels of vitamin B6 in the body
2. decreased levels of vitamin A in the body
3. decreased levels of vitamin E in the body
4. decreased levels of magnesium in the body

Hereditary factors. Simply from scanning the brief list of possible causes of PMS, it is clear that hormones play into the grand scheme of things in some way. Knowing that hormone production is an inheritable trait, we can easily surmise that heredity plays a key role.

In 1971, a study was conducted to examine this very issue. Results showed that sixty-three percent of the daughters of symptom-free mothers were also symptom-free.[3, 4] Likewise, if the mothers were experiencing PMS, nearly seventy percent of the daughters had similar symptoms.

We might ask what part of the family chemistry is most important in causing this correlation? Was it the hormonal factors? Or did the mothers teach their adolescent daughters that this is how one should act when they are premenstrual? The authors of the original research article have commented on this question as follows:

The comparison of the mother/daughter menstrual patterns indicated that the symptoms of pain, or the lack of them were obviously repeated from mother to daughter. Both genetic factors and unconscious imitation may play an important part in the etiology of both dysmenorrhea and premenstrual tension. The correlation coefficient of menstrual patterns between daughters and their mothers was highly significant, a finding which to some extent speaks in favor of a genetic influence.[5]

Knowing that you might have a predisposition to PMS based on genetic factors will make it that much easier to take precautionary measures and to seek appropriate treatment at the first signs of problems.

As we have noted before, twin studies are an extremely useful method of determining the genetic element of a disease. The incidence of PMS among identical and non-identical twins has also been examined. Out of fifteen sets of identical twins, both twin siblings suffered from PMS in every case except one. Among the non-identical twins, both siblings suffered from PMS in only seven out of sixteen sets.[6]

Knowing that you might have a predisposition to PMS based on genetic factors will make it that much easier for you to take precautionary measures and to seek appropriate treatment at the first signs of problems.

TREATING PMS

Treatments for PMS can be divided into two categories: steps you can take on your own, and those that can only be undertaken with a physician's help. Note that any help you may get from a physician will be more effective when the self-help program is already in place.

1. Reassure yourself that you are not going crazy! If your family is like Joanne's, you may think all the family females have become deranged—at least some of the time. PMS is nothing to be ignored. It can be an underlying cause of depression, marital conflict, divorce, family unrest, child abuse, even suicide. Ignoring the monthly SOS that your body sends will not make this situation miraculously disappear.

For many women, the more comfortable times of their monthly cycles are so refreshing that there is almost an amnesiac effect. Perhaps you had decided that this time you really would go to see that specialist for help. Then during the hormonal lull, you ask yourself, "Did I really feel that bad? I feel okay now. Maybe I should just cancel my doctor's appointment." Education is essential. Reassuring yourself that PMS is normal for many women, and that even the more severe cases are treatable, makes it easier to think about seeking help.

2. Exercise is a hallmark of any PMS treatment program. As you will read in other chapters of this book, exercise helps relieve symptoms of moderate depression, fatigue, and other medical problems including high blood pressure, diabetes, and elevated levels of serum cholesterol and triglycerides.

The major benefit that exercise may hold for PMS sufferers is that it can promote a "peaceful, easy feeling" due to the release of endorphins. These are naturally-occurring opiates produced in your body, which are released as a response to strenuous exercise, laughter, eating, and sexual excitement. They are nature's way of relieving tension and making you feel good. And who couldn't use more of that?

3. Avoiding obesity is another way of improving PMS symptoms. When you are more than twenty percent over your ideal body weight, hormone levels may begin to differ from those of normal-weight women. Fatigue and hypoglycemic feelings may also be worsened by this situation. Additionally, obesity sometimes contributes toward feelings of low self-esteem, which may already be exacerbated by the PMS. If you need to lose weight, get on a sensible, lifestyle change diet.

4. Eat a sensible diet—especially during PMS days—but also all month long. Don't let your calories fall off too dramatically in dieting, or eat an over-abundance that will contribute toward fatigue. Consume somewhere between 1200 and 2200 calories per day, depending on your energy needs and level of activity. Avoidance of certain dietary items—including caffeine and excess sugar and salt—may be of limited help for some individuals. *PMS: What It Is and What You Can Do About It* provides an appropriate PMS diet plan.[7]

5. Controlling sources of stress, instead of letting them control you, is also a key in PMS treatment. For many busy mothers, a normal day may include housework, childcare, volunteer work, errands, and dealing with the butcher, the baker, and the candlestick maker. If you are involved in either a full or part-time career, add that on top of everything else.

Before long your brain begins to flash the **TILT** signal.

"Hold everything," your body says. "You can't push this machine that hard." One helpful tool is to keep a precise calendar of your responsibilities and monthly cycle. Then if you need to cut back on your commitments around your monthly PMS, you will know when and how to do it. One firm rule may be helpful: Never make any major decisions three days before your menstrual period!

GETTING HELP FROM YOUR DOCTOR

Finding the right physician to help female members of the family with premenstrual tensions can be a challenge in and of itself. Your daughters may still be seeing a pediatrician. You may be seeing the same obstetrician/gynecologist who delivered your babies. While these physicians are undoubtedly skilled in their profession, that is no guarantee of their level of competency in treating PMS.

Premenstrual syndrome has almost become a specialty in and of itself. There are PMS clinics and individual specialists located throughout the country that focus on this area exclusively. The fees at such clinics may be high—but it may be a worthwhile investment if your symptoms have not been controlled by other means.

Here are some various ways in which a doctor can help.

1. Accurate diagnosis. This is the crucial first step. Whether you seek this information for yourself or your daughter, a physician can help you rule out other disorders and verify that PMS is the problem.

2. Prescription medications. Medications treating water retention (diuretics), muscle and skeletal pain (non-steroidal anti-inflammatories), breast tenderness, anxiety, and other general symptoms are commonly prescribed by physicians for PMS patients.

3. Physicians can act as an intermediary within your family. They can help explain female biology to spouses and can help mothers and daughters cope with compounded situations where female members may cycle simultaneously.

MENOPAUSE

Menopause is often spoken and written about as something negative. It is often referred to as "the change of life," which sounds rather fatalistic and final. The fact is that menopause is *welcomed* by millions of women who no longer desire to bear children and are weary from dealing with PMS and menstrual periods. We must understand menopause as a life event, not a disease.

Menopause, of course, is marked by a woman's final menstrual cycle. But it is not clearly evident that this has occurred until twelve months after the fact. Menopause does not occur "all at once." Body changes may be very subtle, and as many as ten percent of all women will experience no menopausal symptoms at all.

We must understand menopause as a life event, not a disease.

The great majority of women, however, *will* experience symptoms, and some fifty to sixty percent will require a physician's care to make life easier through this event. Considering these figures, it is easy to understand how the process of menopause can affect family chemistry—especially when everyone, even the woman herself, is caught off guard.

The average age of menopause, across at least four ethnic population groups, has been found to be fifty years. There does not seem to be any sort of genetic link regarding the age at which menopause occurs or the severity of the symptoms.

Though other conditions exacerbated by estrogen deficiency —including osteoporosis and cardiovascular disease—*are* inheritable, the actual mechanics of menopause are the same for virtually every woman.

Family chemistry does come into play, however. A mother unable to cope with life due to severe menopausal problems can affect the entire family. Perhaps she becomes a less tolerant parent. Or, perhaps self-image or sexuality issues become so difficult that marital problems arise. Remember, family chemistry is a complex mixture of genetics, emotions, and physiology, coming together to affect family members in different ways.

Effects of menopause. Around the age of forty, frequency of ovulation begins to decrease for most women. This is accompanied by a decline in the production of estrogen and other hormones. The major symptoms are summarized in the chart below.

Estrogen Deficiency Timetable
A schematic representation of the climacteric as one syndrome occuring over time*

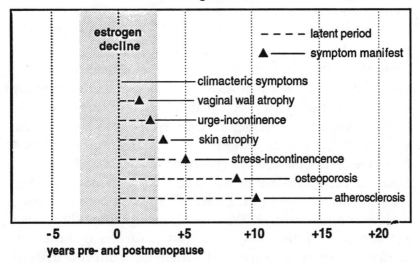

years pre- and postmenopause

* Reprinted by permission from Wyeth Laboratories information, 1988. Original research from W. Utian, *Menopause in Modern Perspective* (New York: Appleton-Century-Crofts 1980), 108.

(We should point out that these symptoms are representative of the menopausal woman who has *not* chosen to take an estrogen supplement. More on this in a moment.)

With all of these physiological changes taking place, it's easy to see how nurturing family systems might be altered. For example, if self-esteem problems, menopausal depression, and vaginal problems arise simultaneously, the sexual relationship between a woman and her spouse might well be in jeopardy. Ignoring these issues will not make them go away, but will only give their long-reaching effects an even greater control over your life.

HORMONE REPLACEMENT THERAPY

After initially being hailed as a panacea for all mature female ills, the use of estrogen supplements was questioned in the seventies with increased reports of its association with uterine cancer. With later changes in the formulations, usage, and recommended dosages of both estrogen and progesterone, it is now clear that the emotional and physical advantages of this therapy far outweigh any risk factors.

Of all the symptoms associated with menopause, the "hot flash" is the one most commonly mentioned by women to their physician. Some eighty percent of all women report uncomfortable flush symptoms, which may occur intermittently over a period of as long as a year. Estrogen therapy can substantially reduce the incidence of this symptom. Women being treated for hot flashes with estrogen therapy show significant decreases in insomnia, anxiety, and irritability as well.

Other consequences of the maturing woman's changing body chemistry may include decreased sexual desire, anxiety, and poor self-esteem. These may ultimately affect the sexual performance of the spouse and lead to further dysfunction. Urinary urgency, frequency of urination, painful urination and incontinence can also be among the problems resulting from hormone deprivation, which can be helped by hormone supplements.

In other areas of health, carefully controlled studies have shown that estrogen therapy has beneficial effects on psychological function. Women receiving replacement hormones report improved memory and an improved sense of well-being. Keep in mind that it is not normal to feel depressed, anxious, and irritable most of the time. If this *is* the way you feel most of the time, see your physician for evaluation.

It is not normal to feel depressed, anxious, and irritable most of the time. If this is the way you feel most of the time, see your physician for evaluation.

Physically speaking, protection against cardiovascular disease is the most important benefit of estrogen therapy, and one that adds further weight to the importance of long-term —possibly lifelong—estrogen therapy for women. One researcher has estimated that estrogen therapy may reduce the risk of cardiovascular disease by as much as fifty percent.

With heart disease being the number one cause of death in the United States—and markedly on the rise among women— we should be motivated to do whatever we can to prevent it. You should especially consider estrogen replacement therapy after menopause if osteoporosis and heart disease are a part of your family's genetic background.

Potential risks of hormone therapy. Even as we begin to discuss potential risks of estrogen therapy, bear in mind that by the time you read this information, it could already be outdated. More research is being conducted in this area constantly.

One of the major concerns regarding hormone therapy is the increased development of endometrial cancer. The endometrium is the lining of the uterus. If estrogen is administered to a patient without the simultaneous use of progesterone, there is an increased occurrence of abnormal cellular build-up in the uterus, leading to early cancer. However, recent research has shown that administering estrogen in lower doses along with progesterone, virtually eliminates the threat of endometrial cancer for postmenopausal women.

Most physicians and national physician groups recommend hormone replacement therapy.

The effect of estrogen therapy on the development of breast cancer remains controversial. Some studies have shown no association at all, while others indicate slightly increased risk after prolonged therapy. Other data have been reported on the *combined* use of estrogen and progesterone and breast cancer. But much of the research is inconclusive. Most physicians and national physician groups still recommend hormone replacement therapy, and suggest mammograms and early detection as the best way to prevent breast cancer.

There are occasions when the potential negative effects of doing something outweigh the good that might be done. Estrogen replacement therapy is to be avoided in cases involving pregnancy, undiagnosed abnormal genital bleeding, previously diagnosed or suspected breast or uterine cancer, active thrombophlebitis or thromboembolic disease (blood clots), and acute liver disease. Estrogen replacement therapy *may* be considered unwise in cases involving chronic liver disease, obesity, preexisting uterine fibroids, endometriosis, history of thrombophlebitis or thromboembolism, hypertension (high blood pressure), migraine headaches, and smoking.

CHAPTER 6

Stages of
Family Life

EUGENE HAD ALWAYS BEEN a compliant and relatively problem-free child despite his diabetic condition, which had been diagnosed several years before. When he turned fifteen, however, his parents became upset with him. They felt he was not eating properly according to the diabetic diet guidelines and was not taking his insulin in a reliable way.

These problems seemed compounded by Eugene's own frustration with his parents, who suddenly seemed to him to be overly strict and critical of everything he did. Family harmony and chemistry, which had before been easily maintained, were suddenly threatened.

Louise and Vincent got married when they were twenty-four. Now, seven years later, they were ready to have children. Or so they thought. They had looked forward to the excitement of childbirth and to the prospect of hearing "the patter of little feet." What they hadn't counted on was the tremendous loss in income, increase in expenses, and overall lack of freedom they were now experiencing.

Vincent's short temper, once under control, now seemed like a lit firecracker ready to explode at any minute. He and Louise began to have marital problems. They had never dealt with some underlying issues in their relationship. Under the new and different stresses of parenthood, the camouflage of success and career no longer worked.

Hank had been brought up in the Depression years. The oldest of eight children in a poor, rural family, he had experienced the weight of the world on his shoulders his entire life. His father had put a lot of pressure on him to help support the family. Hank had been a good husband and father for more than forty years. But now, suddenly, he felt like a child again. His father had come to live with them and the silent flak between the two was deafening.

Though Hank had previously kept his weight, blood pressure, and cholesterol level under control, he had recently found himself returning to old habits, such as potato chips and brownies with lots of rich ice cream. Sometimes Hank didn't even know why he was eating these foods. It did occur to him once that it felt somehow defiant of his father. He had never admitted the extent to which his father had intimidated him. Now that they were under the same roof once again, the old wounds were festering.

Fred hit his thirty-ninth birthday like someone slamming into a brick wall. *What's happened here?* he wondered. *How is it that I've worked my entire life but I still don't feel like I know what I want to be when I grow up?*

Fred's wife had gotten a little nervous when she noticed her husband suddenly starting to wear some new and unusually "stylish" items of clothing. He had indeed noticed that the world suddenly seemed full of attractive women. Several of Fred's divorced friends told him it was time to "live a little." At the same time, his counselor told him that while making some changes could add gusto to his life, he should be careful to hold onto what was really dear—his wife and children. Fred was confused. He didn't know what to believe about himself or about the world around him.

Fred had never considered himself an alcoholic. He always

felt he was in control of his drinking. He told himself, "I can hold it to just a few." But increasingly, "a few drinks after work" was turning into "a lot of drinks any old time." Fred vaguely began to realize that he was drinking for emotional reasons, and was finding it increasingly difficult to stop.

STAGES OF HUMAN DEVELOPMENT

Human beings pass through many stages in their development that have a profound influence on their health and relationships: childhood, adolescence, young adulthood, middle adulthood, old age. In the same way, the family also goes through recognizable stages: newlywed couples, families with young children, families with adolescents, families with career or college-aged children, and families in old age.[1]

Change is a major cause of stress,
and the human and family life cycles
exemplify change in the extreme.

Change is a major cause of stress, and the human and family life cycles exemplify change in the extreme. Families who were once on an even keel may be temporarily swamped by the waves of change. Let's consider a more complete listing of life changes in the classic Holmes and Rahe Social Readjustment Scale, found on the following page. These researchers have created a standardized method for assessing the impact of stressful life events on an individual's health. Note that ten of the first fifteen items on the list involve family issues. Follow the instructions underneath the scale to determine your own level of stress.

Holmes and Rahe Social Readjustment Scale

Life Event	Stress Value
Death of a spouse	100
Divorce	73
Marital separation	65
Jail term	63
Death of a close family member	63
Personal injury or illness	53
Marriage	50
Fired from a job	47
Marital reconciliation	45
Retirement	45
Change in health of family member	44
Pregnancy	40
Sex difficulties	39
Gain of a new family member	39
Business readjustment	39
Change in financial state	38
Death of a close friend	37
Change to a different line of work	36
Change in number of arguments with spouse	35
Mortgage over $50,000	31
Foreclosure on mortgage or loan	30
Change in responsibilities at work	29
Son or daughter leaving home	29
Trouble with in-laws	29
Outstanding personal achievement	28
Wife begins or stops working	26
Beginning or end of school	26
Change in living conditions	25
Revision of personal habits	24
Trouble with boss	23
Change in work hours or conditions	20
Change in residence	20
Change in schools	20
Change in recreation	19
Change in church activities	19
Change in social activities	18
Mortgage or loan less than $50,000	17
Change in sleeping habits	16
Change in number of family get-togethers	15
Change in eating habits`	15
Vacation	13
Christmas	12
Minor violations of the law	11

BASIC NEEDS ACROSS THE LIFE SPAN

In 1963, Eric Erikson[2, 3] was the first to systematically examine the psychosocial development of individuals over their entire life span. In Erickson's model, each stage of development is distinguished by a specific issue that seems universal for people at that age or stage. In this section, we will summarize these stages, their distinguishing characteristics, and the unique problems and needs associated with them. Later, we will describe how they can affect the family.

Stage one: trust vs. mistrust (birth to eighteen months). In the first stage of life, infants learn basic trust or mistrust of themselves and others, depending on the treatment they receive from their parents. If an infant feels love and comfort, this will usually allow them to develop trust.

Stage two: autonomy vs. shame and doubt (eighteen months to three years). Toddlers either learn autonomy or shame and doubt, depending on how parents handle failure experiences during this stage. Failures might revolve around toilet training or behavioral choices. This age group is beginning to experiment with self-control and self-determination. Stubbornness, refusal, and temper tantrums are all common during this stage. Parents should above all be supportive and encouraging of appropriate behaviors. If parents are excessively critical or punishing during this time, they may teach their children to be ashamed, self-doubtful, and self-critical.

Stage three: initiative vs. guilt (three to six years). During this stage, young children are beginning to take their parent's rules and ways to heart. Initiative is also developing. Children who are made to feel guilty, and are thus discouraged from exploring and experimenting, during this stage may lack initiative and instead be overly dependent on others.

Stage four: industry vs. inferiority (six to twelve years). As the child enters school, the focus turns to productivity and development of social skills. During this stage a sense of industry (instead of inadequacy) develops in children who are doing well in school and getting along with their peers. Parents can remain actively and appropriately involved during this phase by supporting their children in homework, projects, and extracurricular activities, as well as by serving as a sounding board.

Stage five: identity vs. role confusion (puberty and adolescence). In this very important stage, self-identity begins to take shape—defined as a consistent, continuous personality and self-concept. This is something the adolescent must actively pursue. As a natural part of the developmental process, teens become increasingly concerned with peer pressure and their own views on clothing, music, sex, friends, parents, school, drugs, alcohol, dating, language, and general behavior. Role confusion can be devastating at this age.

Stage six: intimacy vs. isolation (young adulthood). In this stage, the young adult must develop a sense of intimacy (as opposed to isolation) in relationships. Intimacy is defined as the ability to develop and maintain close, enduring relationships. In most cases, these relationships require compromise and sacrifice. The peer group begins to lose some of its glamour during this stage of intimacy. Courtship and marriage emerge as issues.

Building on the other stages, a personal or self-identity is a prerequisite for a sense of intimacy. Problems may often arise in new marriages when one partner continues to be preoccupied, after adolescence, with others' opinion of him or her.

Stage seven: generativity vs. stagnation (middle adulthood). By this stage, the individual hopes to "have his or her act together," to use a familiar cliché. The key seems to be, are we creating or are we stagnating? Erickson calls it *generativity*, defined as productivity and creativity, especially as these qualities contribute to the growth of *other* people.

It is not enough that we should just produce. We must also have opportunities to create something for the good of others besides ourself. Healthy individuals in this stage nurture others and become invested in their growth rather than only looking after themselves. Those who do not reach this stage of generativity face stagnation, or the termination of further psychosocial development.

It is interesting for us to observe this stage of development among our clinic patients. Once considered as something akin to folk medicine, it turns out that performing acts of generosity and kindness toward others—rather than living a life of self-centeredness—really *is* "good for what ails you." When we think only of ourselves, nothing is ever good enough and life always falls short of expectations.

Stage eight: ego integrity vs. disgust and despair (older adults). "Ego integrity is defined as the successful integration and appreciation of one's own life experiences as well as acceptance of the inevitability of death."[4] To truly age gracefully, we must have succeeded in the previous stages. Six out of seven won't do. These developmental stages are meant to build upon one other, with the apex being a fulfilled senior citizen who is a joy to be around. Ego integrity is characterized by wisdom, maturity, independence, spirituality, and leadership.

MID-LIFE CRISIS

We certainly don't mean to suggest that people jump smoothly and imperceptibly from one stage to another, with no snags and no entanglements. In fact, there are well-noted transitional periods, characterized by the end of one stage or life structure and the beginning of a new one. These transitional times have been referred to as "predictable life crises."[5] Have you ever noticed that at different ages in your children's lives, things sometimes got worse right before there were dramatic changes? Perhaps these were transitional times.

The most publicized transitional stage is the "mid-life crisis." This occurs somewhere between the young adult and middle adult stages, and is a time of asking oneself, "What's it all about? What does it all mean? Where is the purpose in it all?"

Alice couldn't understand what was happening to her. Her hands trembled and she shook her head in disbelief as she contemplated the risks she was taking. Didn't she have it all? Two beautiful children, a considerate husband, a lovely home? Why then had she accepted a lunch invitation from the salesman in the office next to hers? And why was she considering meeting him again?

The "mid-life crisis" occurs somewhere between the young adult and middle adult stages.
It's a time of asking oneself, "What's it all about?
What does it all mean? Where is the purpose in it all?"

Uncomfortably close to her fortieth birthday, and increasingly unsure of her physical attractiveness, Alice was at a turning point. Yes, her husband was kind and thoughtful. But when was the last time they had gone on a date, just the two of them—not at a "family restaurant" with all the kids, but a real evening out? She loved her kids, but her teenage daughter's moods were so frustrating.

Things had happened so fast. Where had the years gone? What happened to all those dreams she once had? The days just kept racing by, and Alice felt trapped—trapped in a world that didn't seem to care that she existed. Well, if the world didn't care, why should she? Maybe she would go out to lunch with that salesman again. What could it hurt?

Her husband, Rick, was angry. Passed over once again for a promotion he had been sure would be his, he stopped on the way home at the overlook by the lake. When they were first married, he and Alice used to come here often to talk and dream and plan for the future. Looking out over the blue expanse of lake with his true love had made anything seem possible.

Was he unhappy now with Alice? No, not exactly. He wasn't unhappy with his wife, but with his marriage. Did that make sense? They seemed so distant. The kids! The kids kept them so busy. And the stress of work, making the payments on the new house—sometimes it was just more than he could handle.

Rick was in a crisis, too, but he didn't even realize it. Increasingly alienated from his wife and children, all he could think to do was to work harder, and longer, and maybe that next promotion would finally be his. It never entered his mind to discuss his feelings with Alice. As he shifted into gear and drove away from the lake, he thought to himself, "Alice and I ought to come here again... someday..."

Risk factors for mid-life crisis. Who is at risk for mid-life crisis? Just about everyone. We see couples like Rick and Alice frequently in our clinic. Physically ill from stress-induced sickness and poor lifestyle choices, they are indeed in a crisis.

Mid-life is a vulnerable time. Without a clear understanding of the potential dangers, there is great risk of an individual or a couple being overwhelmed by the magnitude of problems they cannot even name. Had Rick and Alice been aware of some of the common symptoms and risk factors of mid-life crisis, they might have been better prepared for what came upon them.

Here is a list of common risk factors for mid-life crisis.[6]

1. Unrealistic modern cultural expectations for men and women.
2. An unhappy marriage, or being single against one's choice.
3. A spouse's mid-life crisis.
4. Increasing demands from children, and their growing independence.
5. Career priorities out of proportion to other life priorities.
6. Accumulation of tragic losses, such as death, illness, or aging of loved ones.

7. Urgency from "inner clock" to accomplish life's dreams.
8. Need for time to review the past and plan for the future.

Where are you in your journey through life? Do several of these risk factors for mid-life crisis apply to you? If so, give yourself some time to consider where you're at in life, and where you're headed. Are you accomplishing the goals you set for yourself? Can you see ways in which those goals need to be modified or adjusted? Sharing your hopes and dreams can be just as important as sharing your hurts and disappointments. It's always easier to head off a crisis now than to salvage the pieces of a shattered relationship later.

THE FAMILY LIFE CYCLE

Not only do individuals have predictable stages within the life cycle, but so do families. Marriage, birth, illness, and death are major transitional events that can affect emotional and physical health within the family unit. In most family life cycle models, it is believed that families fulfill important emotional needs for their individual members, and that these needs change at each stage of the cycle. Similar to the life-cycle models for individuals, the transition stages can be met with confusion and intense stress. And, when the needs at each stage are not met, development within the family is stunted and problems arise.

Not only do individuals have predictable stages within the life cycle, but so do families. Major transitional events can affect emotions and health within the family unit.

The model we will describe over the next few pages was designed by Carter and McGoldrick in 1980.[7] Knowing what to expect at each of these stages can help you understand why certain times are difficult, as well as shed light on possible solutions.

Stage one: between families (the unattached young adult). The period between leaving your parents' home and entering into a long-term and intimate relationship—marriage and the start of a new family—is an important time of developing values, ideas, behaviors, and skills that will carry on into new roles as a spouse and parent. It is also an important time of separating from the family of origin. Differentiation, career development, and pursuit of personal goals and dreams are key during this stage.

Most young adults consider "falling in love" the next step. But what do we mean by love? Jack had just moved to Austin from a small town in west Texas. Three years out of high school, he had a great job with a manufacturer of computer chips, plus a new car, new friends, and a new freedom he had never known before.

One day, when Jack had come to see us for a bad cough, he mentioned that he was considering marriage. Mentioning the many people he knew at work who were divorced or just unhappily married, he was concerned about making a good decision. The more we talked, the more it became clear that Jack was unsure of just what he was looking for, either in marriage or in a wife. Yet he was thinking of proposing to a woman he had known for only two months.

We usually think of marriage as the logical expression of the commitment that naturally develops when a couple falls in love. But for Jack and many others like him, the line between mature, committed love and romantic infatuation is blurred. Inexperience, impatience, and lack of self-confidence frequently propel young adults into marriage before they are ready for such a serious commitment.

Ultimately Jack did get married, though not to the girl he had first told us about. He and his wife are happily expecting their first child. His earlier "near miss" added to his maturity and helped shape his values about relationships—so that he was able to recognize the right woman when she came along.

"Mature love (versus romantic love) is defined as an unselfish commitment to another person's growth and development, or the willingness to care about another person as much as one cares about one's self."[8] Romantic love, conversely, is associated with physiologic and sexual arousal and excitement. People in romantic love tend to idealize each other, seeing their partner as they wish them to be rather than how they truly are.

The period between leaving your parents' home and entering into a long-term and intimate relationship —marriage and the start of a new family— is an important time of developing new values, ideas, behaviors, and skills.

We do not want to minimize the need for both types of love in a stable marriage. Too often we hear wives complain that their whole life has gone from "moonlight and roses to daylight and dishes." Romance is important. Nevertheless, it is mature, unselfish love that creates the foundation for strong families.

Research has actually shown that for couples sharing only romantic love, the average relationship lasts only two years.[9] By the end of this time, the novelty has faded and there is no longer any reason to continue. "Many individuals confuse romantic love with mature love. By doing so, they may experience confusion, disappointment, and disillusionment when they no longer feel the intense feelings of romantic love for their partner."[10]

Stage two: the joining of families through marriage (the newly married couple). The newly married couple is the beginning of a new family system that is linked to their individual pasts, but also forms another union that is even stronger. The key in this system is *commitment.* It is a "leaving-and-cleaving" attitude (leaving your parents and cleaving to your spouse) that will help the young couple face adversity and conflict with strength.

Paul and Rita had been married just fourteen months when we first met them. Rita had come in for an annual exam and to renew her prescription for birth-control pills. We discussed her medical history and wrapped up the exam. As she was preparing to leave, Sharon sensed a hesitancy in her and asked if there was anything else we needed to talk about. Almost immediately Rita choked up, then started to sob.

"It's really nothing," she said after composing herself. "I'm just afraid that maybe my husband's not too happy with me." Sharon replied that such a concern was far from "nothing" and encouraged her to explain. It seemed that during the first months of their marriage, she and Paul had been very active sexually. Now, according to Rita, the passion had waned a bit. As they talked further, it came out that Paul had recently been promoted at the office. His work load had increased and he was under more stress.

As is not uncommon, Rita had never discussed her concerns with Paul. She had simply begun to imagine that he was dissatisfied with her—even that he wished he had never married her. Sharon urged her to discuss her feelings with her husband, and she reluctantly agreed. A few months later we saw Rita again. She said somewhat sheepishly that she and Paul had talked, and admitted that her fears had been totally unfounded. Communication, trust, and acceptance were simply new marital skills that Rita and Paul had needed to learn.

Unless the attitude that "there's no turning back" is assumed, when physical and emotional stress arises, the temptation will be to bail out. No doubt this is a major reason for such a high divorce rate. "Commitment requires that each member of a couple be willing to compromise self-centered beliefs and behaviors for more collaborative attitudes and actions."[11] When both partners are working to this end, success is far more likely.

There are many adjustments that must be made in the newly married couple. These include areas of finance, career goals, lifestyle, recreation, friendships, sexuality, and in-laws. The popular bridal magazines would have us believe that the whole marriage process is a fairy tale. They show beautiful color spreads of what a couple's first apartment might look like. When real life doesn't match up with these unrealistic targets, we are naturally disappointed.

When those first disagreements come along (as they inevitably do), we may panic. Thinking that perhaps we chose the wrong person, we then begin to "contemplate our options." The grass back in our parents' yard, or in seemingly carefree days of single life, begins to look greener and greener.

Secrets of success. So, what are the secrets of marital success? Not so secret, actually. First, marital satisfaction has been shown to vary over the life cycle. We love the words in John Denver's song, "Some days are diamonds, and some days are stones." Those diamond days are certainly spectacular. But even on the stone days, there still can be a sense of solidarity within the couple even if outside stresses seem to be closing in from all sides. Learning to accept reality and make the best of each day—good or bad—is part of this maturing process. Those who choose not to master this will not progress to maturity.

Learning to accept reality and make the best of each day—good or bad—is part of this maturing process.

Another secret of marital success is based on the simple concept of rewards and punishment. Not surprisingly, surveys show that marital satisfaction is highest in couples who consistently reward each other rather than punish their spouses. There is not a person we know who doesn't enjoy a compliment, a pat on the back, or a gift for a job well done.

The same principle holds true in happy marriages. Here the rewards come as compliments, physical affection, or special favors. Contrast this with common marital punishments such as "the silent treatment," name-calling, and threats. No wonder happy marriages place an emphasis on rewards.

Without a doubt, one of the most emotionally charged areas of a newlywed couple's life is sexual intimacy. As many as fifty percent of happily married couples have some concerns about their sexual relationship.[12] Specific concerns about sexual matters often go uncommunicated due to embarrassment, lack of fundamental information, and the sense that somehow everyone is supposed to intuitively know everything there is to know about this subject.

Not wanting to hurt their partners' feelings, many newlywed couples suppress their dissatisfactions about sexual intimacy, which may ultimately lead to a disinterest in sexual activity altogether. Very few of our patients initiate discussions about sexual matters. But when asked directly, there are frequently many questions and issues to be dealt with. Achieving long-term sexual intimacy is a function of good communication, accurate information, and a willingness to be sensitive to the needs of your spouse.

Starting a family. A decision critical to the couple's identity is the decision to start a family. Pregnancy seems to bring out both the best and the worst in a couple. But despite the many problems that can arise, literally millions of couples successfully navigate these emotionally and physically demanding nine months.

We still remember one young couple that David cared for during his residency training. Early in the pregnancy, the doting behavior of the father-to-be was almost comical. Later, as the novelty wore off and as his wife became increasingly un-comfortable in the hot, humid South Carolina summer, he seemed to become somewhat less compassionate. At the same time, his wife became more and more demanding—to the point that David began to wonder whether they might end up in divorce court!

Sobered by the difficulties that had cropped up, the young couple welcomed an appointment with a counselor. As it turned out, they had each brought some emotional "baggage" and expectations into the marriage. The woman had seen her own mother abandoned by her father during pregnancy. Knowing of this, the young husband had tried to compensate early in the pregnancy, but eventually found himself unable to cope with the increasing stress.

When they eventually had a healthy baby boy, you never saw a happier couple. David later learned that they had twins in their second pregnancy, with no recurrence of the stormy emotional issues that had plagued them earlier. Fortunately, they had learned their lessons the first time around.

Both the husband and the wife experience significant changes during this nine-month wait. Adjustment to changes in body image, hormonal fluctuations, and the physical dis-comforts of pregnancy are but a few of the challenges encoun-tered. Major psychological adjustments also occur in the areas of relationships with family, friends, the doctor's office, and the work place. The well-adjusted couple grows closer together. By overcoming any physical or emotional difficulties arising dur-ing the pregnancy, they enter the third stage of family develop-ment with anticipation and determination.

Stage three: married with children. Marriage after children is many things, but it is above all *different* than the couple's previ-ous relationship. Therein lies the challenge presented to the family: to adjust and go forward. Parenthood can be highly sought after. But the infringement on a couple's privacy, per-sonal time, sleep, and intimacy as a couple is great. Failure to address these matters is one of the reasons that many married couples report a decrease in marital satisfaction during this time of life.

Marriage after children is many things, but it is above all different.

Bill Cosby says, "My wife and I used to be intellectuals. Then we had children." It does seem that children can tax any couple's ability to cope. Difficulties that arise at this time could easily be misinterpreted as "proof that he really doesn't love me," or that "we were really never meant for each other." Many divorces spring from a failure to recognize the tremendous stress and change placed on a marriage by the arrival of that little bundle of soft, cuddly innocence that looks just like you.

Attractive, intelligent, eager to better themselves—John and Sally looked like the all-American couple. But as nice as they were, David did not look forward to seeing their two-year-old daughter, Jenny, in his office. She was almost uncontrollable during the examination. And after she left, the office staff would have to completely reconstruct the waiting room. All the while, her mother sat quietly by as Jenny tore the place apart.

After several months, David asked about John and Sally's home life. How did they feel about being parents? Sally acknowledged that Jenny was quite a handful. "But, then, aren't all two-year-olds?" she smiled. John, on the other hand, noted that discipline was an area where he and Sally frequently differed. Sally had come from a very rigid family, with high standards and severe disciplinary practices. John's parents had been far more relaxed. Both John and Sally expressed doubt about their parenting techniques. "Jenny didn't come with a training manual," they laughed.

David suggested they attend a parenting seminar at a local hospital. A few months later they remarked on what a difference the seminar had made. Just talking with other parents had bolstered their confidence and encouraged them in a consistent approach to discipline that they both felt comfortable with.

What does every school child learn to do before crossing a street? "Stop, look, and listen." These principles can apply to families during this stage of development. *Stop* arguing and feeling bad or guilty long enough to *listen* to what you are saying to each other. *Look* carefully at your relationship. Are you communicating, listening to each other's needs, saving a little bit of your energies just for each other? Don't forget you are still a couple and need to act like one.

Effective parenting requires two basic elements:
love and organization.

As if maintaining your marriage relationship is not enough, you also have to become effective parents. Effective parenting requires two basic elements: love and organization. *Love* promotes individuality, easy expression of emotions, and a sense of belonging. *Organization* encourages a balanced awareness of the realities of life in a safe and nurturing environment.

Children need protection from physical and emotional harm. They need to be surrounded by unconditional love and acceptance tempered with the boundaries of an organized home. Like carefully-tended young plants, your children can blossom and grow in ways that would make any parent proud and happy.

Stage four: the family with adolescents. Adolescence is the time between ages twelve and eighteen. As everyone knows, it is typified by change and, often, turmoil in family relationships. In order to cope with the teenager's need to establish autonomy and independence, the family must increase flexibility and soften boundaries. Some of the best advice we have heard is that whenever you *can* say yes, do so!

What happens to those cute little girls and cheerful little boys that so often changes them into sullen, distrustful, rebellious teenagers? I asked that question of a father who had two teens. Without hesitating, he replied, "The teenager's emotional veneer is so thin that most teens would rather crack than confront the shallowness of their experience." How often have we seen big, strong young men and proud young women break down in tears when the painful circumstances of life threaten to overwhelm them. The little boy and girl are still there, but hidden, only to appear at awkward moments.

Perhaps it is the very nearness of childish emotions that makes teens so stridently seek adult acceptance and, at the same time, resist the most reasonable attempts to negotiate a middle ground of compromise in the family. A close friend noted that when he married his wife—who already had two teenage children—he was suddenly plunged into the world of "sex, drugs, and rock-and-roll." It's easy for parents to be overwhelmed by the issues facing today's teenagers. Perhaps a bit more understanding is in order for these developing individuals who will follow our footsteps into the harsh reality of the adult world.

In the functional family, the adolescent will be integrated and incorporated into the family in such a way that the whole family will grow and enjoy those teen years. In an unstable family, however, the teen's changes in behaviors and attitudes will disrupt the family to such an extent that others feel alienated, confused, and threatened by this new contender for power.

---

*Perhaps it is the very nearness of childish emotions that
makes teens so stridently seek adult acceptance and,
at the same time, resist the most reasonable attempts to
negotiate a middle ground of compromise in the family.*

Successful family relationships at this stage are dependent on having successfully completed the other developmental stages, both individually and as a family unit. Relationships, character, trust, and love are built in stair-step fashion. If there were unresolved problems earlier in life, they do not simply go away. Difficulties usually don't spontaneously "get better." Functionality, stability, and family development must be pursued in earnest, despite all the obstacles in your path. If there are moderate to severe problems at this stage, it may be wise to bring in an outside counselor.

Stage five: "What's next?" (launching the children). The launching phase of the life cycle begins when the first child leaves home and takes up permanent residence elsewhere. This can be a traumatic event. But as a friend who had been through this phase once told us, "When you consider the alternative (their not leaving), it ain't half bad." This stage ends in the proverbial "empty nest," when all the chicks have flown the coop.

Alex was a fifty-four-year-old man whose youngest child had just graduated from high school and was leaving for college soon. Another son was in his third year of college. Alex's wife was looking forward to the freedom that life without the kids would offer—especially the chance to travel. He, on the other hand, was concerned about cutting back on his work. After all, there were tuitions to pay. Besides, Alex had never really looked forward to traveling with Lisa. He preferred to stay home and play golf.

It turned out that Lisa had been very involved with the local PTA. She was now feeling a bit at sea, with time on her hands, and eager to rekindle the romance in her marriage. In recent weeks, she had taken to calling Alex at work and "pushing" him for luncheon dates. Her husband felt irritated by these intrusions into his busy day.

In the end, Alex and Lisa worked out their new lifestyle. They got used to not always doing something with the kids.

They started meeting for lunch once a week. They even took a trip to Hawaii. Alex played golf while Lisa drove the cart. Letting go of the kids was easy—once Alex and Lisa learned to adjust their own relationship.

As the children leave their parents' home, personal growth within the children begins to soar as they start new, individual stages of life. Parents, too, can sense a time of refreshing when they can once again be "just a couple." It is an exciting time for many who have nurtured and protected the special relationship of husband and wife. For a married couple who have not grown together over the family life span—but only stayed together "because of the kids"—there can be some rude awakenings, perhaps even divorce.

> *For a couple who have not grown together*
> *over the family life span,*
> *but only stayed together "because of the kids,"*
> *there can be some rude awakenings.*

It is also an important time to consider and reassess personal pursuits. For women who have exclusively devoted themselves to children and homes, this can sometimes be a time of difficult introspection. If you are one of them, we want to assure you that many people in your own community need you today, whether in a volunteer or wage-earning capacity. And believe it or not, business people are actively seekly employees just like you—mature, stable, and willing to work. Or try going back to school for some updated training. Sometimes the most difficult step is making that first call.

Though we are not personally of this age group yet, many of our friends experiencing this phase come to it with happiness. They begin to look forward to time together as a couple, much as honeymooners would. They also relish the new, more adult relationships they are enjoying with their children. With these kinds of healthy attitudes, they anticipate the retirement years with a sense of fulfillment.

Stage six: the family in later life. During this last stage of the family cycle, the older generation must learn to accept the shifting of family roles. Having left their parents, the children have often created their own families. If they are to have a healthy family, they must cleave more tightly to their spouse and their own children than they do to their parents. The couple in this stage of life may note a gradual reversal of dependency roles as their children start "looking out for" their parents.

Couples who were able to let go of their children and become more independent during the launching years will probably enjoy this new phase of retirement to a greater extent. Freedom from work and child-rearing often provides a renewed spark of romance and intimacy.

This transition is not without its difficulties. Consider Ron, a retired engineer who is a patient of David's. "Merry Christmas," David greeted him. Unfortunately, Ron didn't view this Christmas as a merry occasion. Not only did he have a bad case of bronchitis, but he said that his ungrateful daughter and son-in-law had called to inform him they wouldn't be coming for the holidays after all. Something about "the kids needing to spend Christmas in their own house." Ron couldn't understand it. Why didn't they want to come and visit like always? David asked if he and his wife had considered driving to their daughter's house instead. "It just wouldn't be the same," he grumbled.

In recent years, an increasing number of our patients have requested help in caring for their aging parents. Some have had to consider nursing home arrangements, while others have had to help pay for their parents' recurring hospitalizations. Almost all have expressed difficulty adjusting to a more dominant role in their parents' lives.

Still others have faced the death of their parents—or even

their own siblings—and have been overwhelmed by the stark reminder of their own mortality. The death of a spouse during this phase can still upset the family chemistry. Statistics show that women are four times more likely to be widows than are men.

With a heritage of healthy family chemistry from previous years, the last stage of the family cycle can be the most rewarding of all.

Grandparenthood also characterizes this stage of life for many. If a strong sense of security and confidence has previously been attained, grandchildren are usually a great blessing. It provides older adults an opportunity to enjoy children without the responsibility and conflict involved in parenthood. With a heritage of healthy family chemistry from previous years, this last stage of the family cycle can be the most rewarding of all.

CHAPTER 7

Fussing and Fighting: the Family in Turmoil

A NYONE WATCHING TODAY'S television depictions of the "typical" family would think that fussing, fighting, and feuding are more common among family members than loving, sharing, and accepting. We hope these caricatures of American family life seem as bizarre and foreign to you as they do to us. Unfortunately, judging from the soap opera-like lives of troubled people we see in our office, it seems that the TV-sitcom family may be all too real.

If individuals are the product of genetic and environmental influence, then families certainly feel the impact of these same factors. These powerful biological and circumstantial forces are actually intensified in the context of the family unit. We have personally observed many cases in which the impaired family—burdened with physical and emotional illness—spirals downward into the permanent wreckage of separation and divorce.

Other families are healthier in all respects—physically, emotionally, and spiritually. Its members seem strengthened by each other. They draw more tightly together with each passing year no matter what the circumstances. Many families are in emotional and spiritual flux, wavering between health and sickness, triumph and defeat. Some never fully regain their balance. Others correct their course to make a change for health and happiness. What state do you find your family in now?

FAMILY FEUDS

Ruth and Jim had long argued and fought over almost every aspect of their lives. During the two years they had been our patients, they had separated on two occasions, had at least one knock-down, drag-out fight (resulting in a broken nose for Ruth), and suffered the effects of various psychosomatic ailments. Their lives were in constant turmoil. You could almost say they suffered from battle fatigue.

You could almost say that Ruth and Jim suffered from battle fatigue.

David learned more about their background while treating Ruth for depression. They lived in a two-bedroom house with their two teenage daughters, and recently Jim's parents had come to live with them. Initially this was supposed to be just a "long visit" while they looked for a home of their own. But the in-laws had taken up residence in Ruth and Jim's converted screen porch, and showed no signs of leaving any time soon.

Ruth couldn't remember a time when she and Jim hadn't fought about things. Even their wedding reception had been marred by a brawl when Jim's brother got into a fracas with her uncle. She and Jim both worked, but always seemed to run out of money before payday. Finances were a constant source of conflict, as were discipline issues with their daughters.

They had both come from homes where violence was a more or less accepted means of imposing one's will on others. In fact, this was a major reason why Ruth married and left home at such an early age. But marriage to Jim only provided more of the same. Scarcely a week went by without a major altercation. They had considered divorce but "wanted to give the girls a good home."

After so many years, this approach to dealing with conflict had come to seem almost normal to this couple. Ruth admitted that she wasn't really all that interested in trying to change things: she just wanted to find new ways to "get back" at her husband. For his part, Jim was unwilling even to discuss the possibility that there was a problem.

They are still married as we write these words. Every other month or so Ruth's depression flares up after an especially bad fight. We seldom see Jim, though he did come in to get his eye stitched up once after his wife threw a drinking glass at him. They seem simply to have accepted their lifestyle, even with its dysfunctional and dangerous aspects. Change is inconceivable to them. Ruth and Jim seem to prefer the familiarity of their violent routine.

All families fight. Very few are like Ruth and Jim. But all families at least have occasional disagreements, differences of opinion, disputes, arguments—conflict of one form or another. Sometimes it's rather mild: differences over where to go on vacation this year or what kind of new car to buy. Sometimes it's more serious: disagreements about the family budget or personality clashes among various individual family members. Sometimes it's extremely serious: major conflict resulting in rupture of relationships, physical or other forms of abuse, separation and divorce.

All families face certain basic tasks in interacting with the world around them. Some families handle them well, some not so well, and some seem to fail miserably. Arguments inevitably ensue when reasonable discussions about differences of opinion disintegrate into heated battles for dominance over a certain issue.

Is fighting and conflict an inevitable fact of life for families? Not unless we let it be. Recognizing the common causes of family conflict—as well as taking corrective action—may help prevent tragic consequences, which may even include abuse and divorce.

Is fighting and conflict an inevitable fact of life for families?
Not unless we let it be.

Family members fight over many issues, but four basic reasons seem to lie at the heart of most family battles. Understanding why we fight may help us to avoid this traumatic breakdown, with its inevitable emotional consequences for all involved.

Pursuit of dominance. The name of a popular television program laughingly asks, "Who's the Boss?" Unfortunately, in many families, power struggles are not at all humorous. The struggle for power and dominance within a family can be a constant source of arguments. Who's going to have the final say? Arguments over who's right and who's wrong, leading by intimidation and domination, unwillingness to negotiate, and assumption of a false sense of infallibility all lead to family strife.

Forced dominance weakens the parental coalition necessary for a strong and unified family. Dominance also tends to isolate and distance an individual from other family members. Children may be afraid to approach a domineering father who rules from a lofty pedestal of power and fear.

Dominance can lead to distorted family interaction. An overpowering family member snuffs out attempts at negotiation, encouraging violent confrontation or sullen acceptance of "imperial" decrees. If one person makes all the rules and decisions, other family members may shirk all responsibility, further adding to the confusion of the family.

Constant dominance leads to personal intrusions, speaking

for another, and other "mind-reading" statements. Boundaries are thoughtlessly abused and arguments become inevitable. Dominance tends to repress feelings, leading to potential explosive outbursts of pent-up frustration. Unable to express themselves, dominated family members may become cynical and pessimistic. Although conflicts appear to have been easily solved, in reality there are numerous unresolved issues that are a constant source of conflict in the family.

Release of emotional frustration. Many arguments are simply the release of bottled emotions that can no longer be contained. Indistinct boundaries between family members are a common source of emotional frustration. Ineffective negotiating skills, confused feelings, and lack of receptiveness to an individual's ideas are some key points of emotional frustration.

Resentment and hostility, along with unresolved conflict, usually lead to frequent arguments. Families that are insensitive to or unable to acknowledge the feelings of their members are especially vulnerable to arguments due to emotional frustration.

Lack of basic communication skills and unwillingness to assume personal responsibility for one's actions are often generalized family traits.

Transference of guilt and responsibility. For many people, arguing is a way of easing personal guilt or responsibility, at least temporarily. This vocal, and sometimes physical, purging of emotions has a positive (though self-centered) effect for some individuals who lack appropriate communication skills. Blaming another is somehow easier to do after assuming a demeanor of righteous indignation.

Typically, this lack of basic communication skills and unwillingness to assume personal responsibility for one's actions are often generalized family traits. Thus, the attempted transfer of guilt or responsibility by one party is vigorously blocked by the other party—leading to further escalation of tension and distress.

Learned or habitual means of communication. "We don't really mean anything by it, it's just the way we talk." This excuse often follows a knock-down, drag-out battle of epic proportions over something as trivial as which television show to watch. Sometimes families learn to fight as a means of "talking." Unfortunately, the emotional price tag on this inefficient way of handling problems is quite high. The cost can even be dissolution of the family unit.

Did you grow up in a family where every question was like the opening shot of a war? Were you fearful of asking questions—and even more fearful of the answers? Was it necessary to launch an argument just to get a simple point across? Are these same harmful methods of dealing with problems now being established in your own family? Consider this possibility the next time you're tempted to raise your voice to someone around the house.

Solving family confrontation. Whether your arguments take on the appearance of open warfare or more covert skirmishes, the harmful effects of constant bickering add considerable stress and strain to family life. Here are some effective ways of deflecting arguments and conflict:

- Consider shared leadership between parents, depending on the circumstance.
- Form a tight parental coalition on family policy and decisions.
- Respect individual differences within your family.
- Be specific and goal-directed in your discussions.
- Be clear about your needs and expectations.

- Encourage personal responsibility.
- Be receptive to the ideas of other family members.
- Encourage healthy expression of feelings.
- Attempt to resolve conflict over issues.
- Be sensitive to the feelings of others.

STOPPING THE CYCLE OF ABUSE

Child abuse, spouse abuse, even elder abuse, have reached epidemic proportions in the United States. It is likely that many of you reading this book are victims of abuse yourself, or know of someone who is. Tragically, at our clinic we regularly see cases just like the ones you read about in the newspaper or see on television. Sometimes the physical injuries are minor, sometimes not. But the emotional scars are always serious.

*Abuse has a devastating and lingering effect
on a family, one that can continue for generations.*

In our years of medical practice, we have encountered every form of abuse that we discuss in this chapter. The statistics may speak for themselves, but nothing can speak for the frustration and outrage you experience when you face the consequences of abuse first-hand. Abuse has a devastating and lingering effect on a family, one that can continue for generations.

Abuse cases most often turn up in the emergency room. Often the victim and the abuser slip past unnoticed in the hustle and bustle. When we were stationed in Japan with the Navy years ago, one little girl died from the beating she had received at the hands of her serviceman father. He was arrested, but the authorities didn't seem to know what to do with him, so few were cases of child abuse in Japan.

Many abuse victims accept their fate in silence, either

refusing medical help or building such elaborate bulwarks of denial that the central issues get lost in the shuffle. Time and again we have seen women who have been beaten almost senseless by their husbands come in for treatment of their wounds. They express concern about the possibility of facial scarring and then return to their terrifying home environment—without ever taking action either to deter their husbands or even to protect themselves.

Janice was a scared, disheveled young woman who had been married only four months, but was already in the emergency room seeking treatment for the third time. Her eyes were swollen shut and encircled with deep bruises. Her mouth, too, was swollen so that she could barely talk. Even sipping water was painful because of the cuts in her lip.

No, we told her, her nose was not broken. The stitches would need to come out in about a week. Was she sure she didn't want to notify the authorities? And, by the way, we said, your pregnancy test was positive.

Thanks, she said.

Not yet twenty, already horribly disfigured, and pregnant with her abuser's child. We can only wonder whatever became of Janice. After she left that night with her sister, we never heard from her again.

Child abuse. The United States is second only to Northern Ireland in the number of child homicides, most often due to violence within the family.[1] Infants, due to their physical vulnerability, are at greatest risk for severe injury. Those at especially high risk tend to be premature infants, those with congenital defects or chronic health problems, and twins.

Abusive parents tend to have low self-esteem, a sense of being unfairly burdened by parenthood, and a history of personal abuse in their own lives. Family characteristics predisposing individuals to abuse include increased isolation, stress, and cultural acceptance of violence.

When child abuse occurs, the child must be separated from

the abusive parent until appropriate therapy and counseling can occur. While this often seems severe, remember that the child is almost totally defenseless. Without intervention, the cycle of abuse will invariably repeat itself. The risks of continued physical or emotional harm to an abused child are simply too great.

Abusive parents tend to have low self-esteem, a sense of being unfairly burdened by parenthood, and a history of personal abuse in their own lives. But continuing the legacy of abuse is not *inevitable.*

One of the primary ways to prevent child abuse is to recognize whether it happened to you or your spouse as children. Continuing the legacy of abuse is not inevitable, but a history of personal abuse *does* increase your vulnerability to falling into this tragic pattern of behavior. Education, improvement of self-esteem, prenatal care with an emphasis on parental readiness training, and counseling, are all potential helps in preventing child abuse from occurring in your family.

Sexual abuse. Sexual abuse is a form of child abuse, typically without violent injury. Cloaked in secrecy, denial, and taboo, this form of abuse often goes undetected and unreported. Still, it appears to occur at an alarming rate. Some studies suggest that as many as sixty-three percent of women have been abused sexually before the age of eighteen.[2, 3]

The harmful consequences of sexual abuse extend far beyond the potential for physical injury. Long-term emotional harm is very likely. Sexual abuse has been linked to increased incidence of suicide, mental illness, substance abuse, sexual problems, criminal behavior, and an incapacity for intimacy.[4] Many problems within families today may stem from unresolved issues of childhood sexual abuse. In many cases, failure to deal with and acknowledge these wounds make the possibility of fully satisfied lives impossible.

Spouse abuse. Although technically this could involve either a wife or a husband, well over ninety percent of spouse abuse is committed by husbands against their wives. Spouse abuse occurs in more than eleven percent of married couples each year.[5]

Some researchers have proposed that men abuse women simply "because they can."[6] For many men, the cost of their violence is relatively low. Helping to encourage the abuse may be their wives' inability to retaliate physically or economically, compounded by callous indifference by authorities reluctant to get involved in "domestic quarrels." The man finds he can settle any argument, win any debate, vent his frustrations, and get just about whatever he wants, through the threat of physical violence.

One often wonders why spouse abuse occurs, and why it is allowed to continue. Why do the abused not speak up? The women we have seen with blackened eyes, bruised ribs, and even broken bones do not enjoy being battered. Nor do they seek to be abused. Typically, the pattern of abuse occurs only after both partners have developed a deep emotional investment in each other that would be difficult to abandon. Often the first episode comes as a complete surprise to both the victim and the aggressor, who expresses deep remorse.

Typically, the pattern of abuse occurs only after both partners have developed a deep emotional investment in each other that would be difficult to abandon.

Unfortunately, however, the aggression tends to escalate over time. At first the injuries may be so minor that the victim's commitment to the marriage outweighs the pain. Later, as the pain and injury escalates, so does the fear of abandonment—as well as the fear of even worse punishment if the abused party "squeals."

Wife-beaters share certain common characteristics. Low self-esteem, sex-role attitudes that place the woman in a totally subservient position, and sudden shifts in personality typify an abusive husband. They also demonstrate a tendency to blame others for their own problems, use sex as an act of aggression, cope with stress by drinking and rowdiness, and deny responsibility for their actions.

As you might expect, many long-term problems are common in abused women beyond the physical effects of the beatings. Fear, confusion, depression, chronic fatigue, anxiety, and nightmares are frequent results of spouse abuse. Even mental changes occur that could be mistaken for severe emotional disorders such as schizophrenia, rather than as stress reactions to chronic abuse.

Elder abuse. Increasing numbers of elderly people—who often require assistance during their final years of life—are also facing the effects of physical, emotional, material, and financial abuse. It is estimated that as many as two million elderly Americans suffer from some kind of abuse. Lack of close family ties, a history of family violence, lack of financial resources, and lack of community support are all contributing factors.

The most common form of elder abuse may actually be a form of spouse abuse. The most common perpetrator in some studies has been the husband of the aging couple.[7] Careful attention to the needs of our elderly relatives will undoubtedly reduce the incidence of this tragic end to so many people's lives.

DIVORCE

Divorce is not just an isolated event, but a transition that continues for years, casting its shadow over family members in various ways. Millions of people—our friends, family, and neighbors—are affected directly and indirectly by this upheaval in family life. Although the divorce rate appears to be leveling off, it is still extremely high. Fifty percent of all first marriages end in divorce.

Divorce is not just an isolated event,
but a transition that continues for years,
casting its shadow over family members in various ways.

It is never just the adults who suffer the consequences of marital disintegration. Up to sixty percent of all divorces involve children, and more than fifty percent of all children in the United States will be affected by their parents' divorce or separation during their childhood.[8] Half of all children will live in a single-parent home for at least a while, and more than twenty-five percent will have to assimilate into a stepfamily at some point.[9] Divorce and remarriage are becoming so common as to be considered almost normal—part of the expected family life cycle.

What happens to a family after a divorce is somewhat predictable, with inevitable transitions from breakup to post-divorce to remarriage. What is not so predictable are the individual experiences of family members. According to Rakel's *Textbook of Family Practice*, "Most research indicates that, in general, being married is associated with better outcomes and fewer health problems than being divorced or single."[10]

The initial decision to divorce almost always triggers extreme emotional distress. We have seen women who were in a horribly abusive marriage—one that threatened their health and the health of their children—still become emotional wrecks at the mere thought of leaving their husbands.

Factors predisposing to divorce. Any number of life stressors have the capacity to prompt a couple to think about divorce as the solution to their unhappy life. The key seems to be either the intensity of the stress factor—such as an extramarital affair—or the number of stressors involved. A couple may be able to handle a single traumatic event. In some cases, they may even grow stronger because of it. But too many stressful events can overwhelm anyone's coping capacity.

In tough economic times, it is not uncommon for a husband or wife to lose his or her job and be unable to find work for months at a time. Financial hardship begets other problems: loss of self-esteem, arguing, fighting, potential for abusive behavior, denial of central issues. Even role reversal is not uncommon, in which the wife assumes the role of breadwinner and head of the house. Unemployment, by itself, might be manageable. But the addition of a host of other problems can be dangerous to an already-strained relationship.

Cultural influences also play a role. Individuals from divorced homes may more readily look to divorce as an acceptable alternative to working out problems. On the other hand, a background of divorce can make an individual vow that "it will never happen to me." We often see both influences at work in the same marriage.

Frequently, one member of the couple is influenced in favor of a divorce by a friend or relative. In one couple we tried to counsel, the husband—disenchanted with the responsibilities of marriage after two years—was being encouraged by a recently-divorced coworker who extolled the virtues of "being single again."

Post-divorce distress. After divorce, family members experience reactions that frequently surface as physical complaint—such as headaches, ulcers, depression, and anxiety. More than fifty percent of newly divorced men and women experience problems with work, sleep, and/or health. Children typically experience problems with school, anger, anxiety about the future, and loyalty conflicts.

Post-divorce or bi-nuclear family relationships are often very confusing and difficult. It is reported that as many as fifty percent of fathers stop visiting their children after a divorce. But even though he is no longer present, the absent father continues to affect the children. This influence could come in the form of a child having to pick a side in the divorce dispute, financial support used as a tool of leverage for negotiations, or a child's idealized perception of the absent parent.

In the United States, mothers are the custodial parent in eighty-five to ninety percent of divorces. Sole custody, joint custody, and legal wrangling by parents, grandparents, and others, contribute to the immediate confusion of post-divorce families.

It takes about two years for a new "steady state"
to develop after divorce.

Emotional reactions to divorce. Most adults see the first post-divorce year as highly stressful, with divorce recognized as the single most powerful predictor of stress-related illness.[11] Separated couples have thirty percent more doctor's visits and acute illnesses than married adults, as well as increased rates of suicide and admissions to mental hospitals, more major and minor illness, and an increased risk of being a victim of violence. Statistically, it takes about two years for a new "steady state" to develop after a divorce.[12]

Many factors influence the effects of divorce on children. Boys seem to have a more difficult time adjusting than girls, although girls seem to have more difficulty with remarriage than do boys. Different reactions occur at different ages. Children under the age of three tend to regress in their behavior. Preschoolers may regress and even show some developmental delays.

School-aged children often become sad and upset, and frequently fantasize about reconciliation between their parents.

Older children may show resentment, anger, and behavioral problems. These problems often continue for years, with vivid memories of the divorce and its problems reported ten years or more after the fact by children of divorced parents.[13]

A central issue for many divorced parents is "role overload," as duties that were formerly shared are now the sole responsibility of just one parent. Cut off from family and friends, divorce can lead to increased social isolation, even the possibility of moving as a consequence of the separation. Economic hardships are not unusual in single-parent homes with issues of child support causing further distress.

Families of remarriage. A friend of ours who married a woman with teenage children described, with a knowing smile, the difficulty of suddenly transitioning from single life into the world of "sex, drugs, and rock and roll." Reaction to this creation of an "instant family" is as diverse as the individuals who make up this new family. This new step in the life cycle is becoming increasingly common: at least one child in six will likely become a member of a stepfamily at some time.

These three tasks are essential in establishing a reconstituted family:

- Achievement of integration of the two families and their members.
- Establishing marital and familial cohesiveness.
- Consolidation of the stepparent into the new family.

It should be recognized from the outset that it may take two to four years for a stepparent to be accepted by the children. The stress of divorce may gradually ease as the family pulls together, but frequent reminders of their post-divorce status are common—especially intrusions by the noncustodial parent, who often fails to meet his or her responsibilities and obligations.

One key to bonding and cohesiveness in families of remarriage is the development of strong couple bonding. Strong bonding can help weather the feelings of jealousy and competition between child and stepparent, loyalty conflicts with the absent parent, anger, guilt, discipline issues, and the inevitable stresses of change.

HOW TO HELP

Those who have friends or family in the midst of marital difficulties often don't know how to respond to their needs. Bear in mind that getting divorced is seldom a snap decision. It usually occurs at the end of a long run of stress and emotional turmoil. Recognizing and helping friends and family members who are undergoing severe stress is, in the long run, the best way to help endangered marriages. Ignoring their problems may only encourage them to contemplate divorce as "the only way out."

Common indicators of relational stress include anger, disillusionment, dissatisfaction, hopelessness, and separation from friends and family. People under severe stress often develop physical complaints such as headaches, depression, ulcers, and sexual dysfunction.

These are just a few of the "red flags" that may signal marital distress. Not every couple displays such clear warning signs. Some studies have found that as many as thirty percent of couples report no intense conflicts prior to their divorce. Instead, they just seem to drift into a loveless relationship with increasingly divergent mutual interests.[14]

Often the most helpful thing we can do for a friend in marital crisis is simply to *listen.* It has been estimated that less than ten percent of children in a divorcing family have any meaningful discussion with an adult about their feelings.[15] A sympathetic ear and diligent prayer will go far in easing at least some of the stress faced by those who find their lives shattered by divorce.

There is often a tendency among those viewing the disintegration of a marriage to say and do nothing. Most people feel such matters are "none of their business." At the same time, however, those in the midst of marital crisis often find themselves feeling isolated and desperately alone. Most of the couples we deal with are often reluctant to "bother others" with their problems. They are nevertheless grateful for other people's concern and welcome opportunities to talk.

Often the most helpful thing we can do for a friend in marital crisis is simply to listen.

If someone you know is clearly in trouble, take a chance and offer them an opportunity to open up to you. If *you* are in a troubled marriage, seek out a trusted friend or relative who may be able to extend a listening ear.

Helping Families in Conflict:

- Encourage discussion of personal feelings.
- Acknowledge the confusion of conflicting feelings that occur in a family in turmoil.
- Facilitate discussions about problems based on facts, rather than on speculation about what someone *may* be thinking or feeling.
- Realize that different stages of conflict require different approaches.
- The stage of actual physical separation is usually the most stressful.
- Children typically view separation as a crisis, and fantasize about parental reconciliation.
- Encourage professional help for those couples who continue to experience conflict, whose problems seem to repeat over and over, and whose communication continues to deteriorate.

CHAPTER 8

Charting a New Course

Life is too short to waste
In critic peep or cynic bark,
Quarrel or reprimand:
'Twill soon be dark;
Up! mind thine own aim, and
God speed the mark!

Ralph Waldo Emerson

MOST PEOPLE LOVE facing a challenge, pursuing a goal, and gaining the prize. Consider the popularity of Rubik's Cube, crossword puzzles, mysteries, jigsaw puzzles, and computer games. Without a challenge, humans wither and fade—both physically and mentally. But for many people, the challenges of life may seem like insurmountable difficulties. They feel paralyzed. Their outlook is one of resignation in their very soul.

If you are looking to improve your family chemistry, we trust you have been informed and challenged by the preceding chapters. Understanding the complex environmental and genetic influences on your own life and that of your family is the basis for formulating a plan of action for optimizing your family's health and well-being. Now it is time to actually develop that plan and begin putting it into effect.

As we shall see, one of the crucial factors is *acceptance*, the subject of the next chapter. By acceptance we do not mean a fatalistic resignation to our fate, but a calm understanding that undergirds our efforts toward improvement. Acceptance of our genetic heritage and environmental influences highlights the areas of our lives that need attention, either through remedial or preventive measures.

Communication is another area that is crucial to optimal family chemistry. We'll look at this in detail in the next chapter as well. Open and clear communication of our desires requires that we have a goal or purpose in mind. This could be physiological in nature, such as getting a thorough physical examination each year. Or it could be directed at our emotional or spiritual needs, such as carving out a few minutes of daily quiet time from our busy schedule. Goals that involve our families require that we clearly communicate our desires to the family members involved, and perhaps seek their input on these issues.

---

*The setting of realistic goals,
and planned efforts aimed at attaining them,
are a tangible sign of an effective and functional family.*

Recognizing the emotional and spiritual status of our family is essential to developing goals. As we'll see, families fall into varying levels of function and dysfunction. No one plans for their family to become dysfunctional. It just happens, as families without a clear definition of their goals drift deeper into chaos and confusion. The setting of realistic goals, along with planned efforts aimed at attaining them, are tangible signs of an effective and functional family.

TAKING STOCK

One of the most basic of all human needs—which is therefore of prime importance to families—is the promotion and maintenance of optimal health. Who among us hasn't heard or made the statement, "If you haven't got your health, you haven't got anything?"

It is amazing how little knowledge most people have about the health problems of their ancestors.

Such a statement is relative, of course. The fact that a person has diabetes or high blood pressure doesn't mean his or her life isn't worth living. But taking stock of the health status of your family, identifying any genetic predispositions toward illness, and practicing sound preventive medicine are worthwhile family goals that enhance both the quantity and the quality of life.

We frequently see men and women who come in for complete health evaluations because they have reached a certain age, noted some increasing problems, or just thought it was "about time for a checkup." Whatever their reasons or yours, good health is a foundational element for any family seeking to make changes in their lives.

In general, all women and men over forty should have annual examinations. Children and men under forty need to be seen less frequently. Sometimes, a *family* health checkup is a good starting place for significant family change if this has not been done in a while.

Family physicians have long recognized the importance of taking an accurate and detailed family health history. It is amazing how little knowledge most people have about the health problems of their ancestors. This lack of knowledge usually becomes glaringly obvious when we take down a family medical history in the course of giving someone a physical exam.

There are many reasons for this high level of unawareness. Often there is reluctance on the part of some families to openly discuss health problems. There may be an inadequate understanding of the exact nature of certain problems. There may even be an unconscious choice to deny the existence of health ailments in close relatives. Most of the time there has simply been little effort expended in gathering potentially important family medical information. Let's learn a simple method of mapping your family health tree, called a *genogram.*

THE FAMILY HEALTH TREE

Genealogy is a popular subject in community education classes throughout the country. Each year, thousands of people seek to learn more about their roots. It can be very interesting to find out where your ancestors came from and learn more about their lives. But knowing more about your family's health history could be of even greater, more tangible benefit.

The purpose of a genogram is to provide an overview of the physical and emotional problems that may be prevalent in a particular family. The best part is, it's easy for you to learn how to chart this important information yourself in the form of a self-administered genogram.[1]

By charting the health of your relatives, you will be made more aware of any health problems that seem to occur frequently in your family. This could very well encourage you to take corrective steps, or to be more aware of the need for preventive measures with regards to these family health issues. Not only physical problems, but emotional ones as well should be noted and evaluated for increased risk to yourself.

Here are the steps to developing a genogram of your family's medical history, with sample illustrations to show you what your genogram should look like.

Step one. Gather all the basic information about your spouse, parents, and grandparents if possible, including:

- names of all family members
- age or birth year for these members
- deaths, with age at death and cause
- significant diseases or problems
- names of those who live together in the same household
- dates of marriages and divorces
- sequential listing of the siblings in a family

Use squares for men and circles for women throughout your chart. Follow the basic example below to get started.

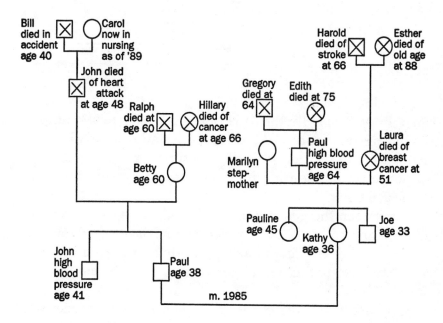

Step two. Now add your children below you and your spouse, including names, birthdates, and health problems. List your children in birth order from left to right, with your firstborn on the left. Then add brothers and sisters for both you and your spouse, along with the same information as for your children.

Follow the example below to complete step two.

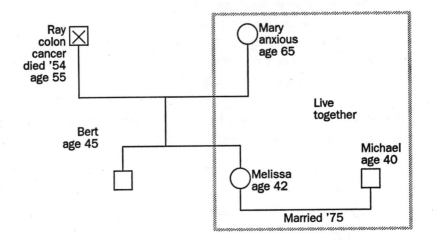

Step three. Finally, list the dates of any marriage relationships, including separations and divorces. Relationships with extended family, especially in divorce situations, become very important when considering how family members interact with each other.

Remember, the genogram includes all family ties, whether the relationship is genetic or just by marriage or adoption. Clearly the health issues would apply primarily to your genetic relationships, but all family bonds may have an emotional impact.

Finally, add any life events that seem to be of particular importance to you or your family. Examples might be job changes, major moves, or the dates of children leaving home. Follow the example provided to complete your personal family health tree.

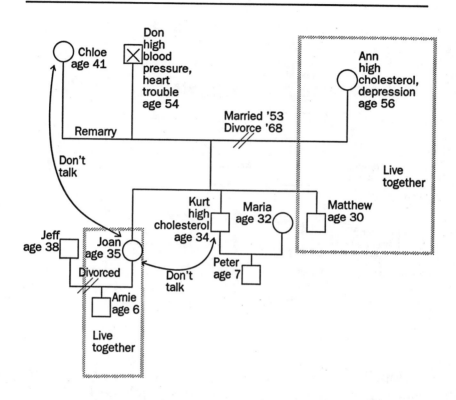

WHAT DOES IT ALL MEAN?

Remember there is no such thing as a "perfect" family tree, or a perfect family for that matter. Your record is simply a tool, a way to highlight any recurring medical or emotional problems. Interpreting the chart is a way of evaluating your possible risk, encouraging preventive health practices, and assessing the family's resources to handle various life stresses.

Sharing this information with your physician will enhance the interpretation of this information. It will also help your doctor better appreciate the complexities and various relationships that exist in your life. Consider the following example of a completed family health tree.

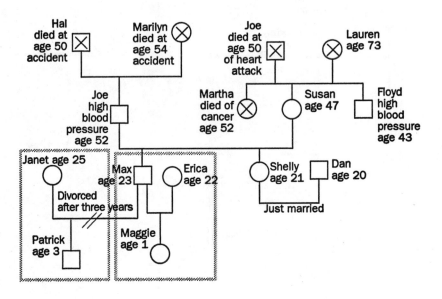

Hopefully you have uncovered all the significant facts about your family—including, perhaps, some family health "skeletons" left forgotten in closed memory closets. Have most of your immediate relatives lived long and healthy lives? Are there diseases that seem to run in your family? Are there emotional or relational problems that seem to recur regularly?

Most importantly, what action can you take to improve the future health of yourself and your family? Armed with the information contained in your family health tree, you and your doctor can target areas of particular concern during your checkup.

THE FAMILY CIRCLE

Any evaluation of personal goals would be woefully lacking if the emotional needs of the individual and his or her family were not considered. Most of the patients we see have only vague, ill-defined ideas about their emotional goals. "I just want to be happy," or "Nobody seems to understand me," seem to be recurrent themes. Personal happiness and better personal relationships are certainly appropriate goals. But first we must assess our specific emotional needs and our relationships with those closest to us.

One way to do this is to draw a family circle.[2] This simple device can help you visualize your relationships with others in terms of closeness and importance to you. First list all those who are highly significant in your life. Typically this would include close family members such as your spouse, children, parents, siblings, close friends, and anyone else who is especially important to you.

Now draw a large circle, placing your own name in a circle at the center. Now place those on your list in circles of varying size (depending on their importance to you) at distances from your circle corresponding to the degree of closeness you feel to that person. Here is an example of what a "family circle" might look like at this point:

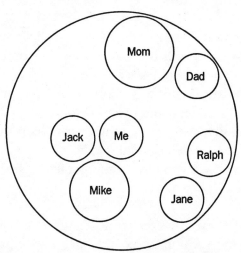

When you have completed this circle, study it and the relationships you have indicated. This personal assessment will better enable you to establish some clear and workable emotional goals. For instance, you may find your father's name in a large circle, but far from your own circle. This indicates that you consider him a significant person in your life, but that you feel distant from him. One of your goals might be to establish a closer relationship with your father. Or if one of your children's names is in a relatively small circle compared to the others, you might want to consider why such a disparity exists.

FUNCTION AND DYSFUNCTION

Another tool to help identify emotional needs and formulate personal goals is the Family APGAR inventory.[3] APGAR is an acronym for Adaptation, Partnership, Growth, Affection, and Resolve. Answer the following questions adapted from the APGAR Test with answers of "almost always" (two points), "some of the time" (one point), and "hardly ever" (zero points).

The APGAR Inventory

- I am satisfied that I can turn to my family in times of trouble.
- I am satisfied with the way my family communicates with me and shares problems with me.
- I am satisfied that my family considers my wishes with regards to change and new activities.
- I am satisfied with my family's expression of affection and response to my emotional needs.
- I am satisfied with the way my family and I spend time together.

A score of seven to ten points suggests a highly functional family situation. Four to six indicates moderate dysfunction, whereas zero to three shows a high degree of family dysfunction. This is only a rough estimate, but highlighted areas of dissatisfaction may provide us with a starting place for formulating emotional goals for ourselves and our families. In the following chapters we'll talk about how to go about reaching those goals.

ESTABLISHING SPIRITUAL GOALS

Failure to address our spiritual needs often explains why efforts at implementing family change are unsuccessful. Where are you now in matters of the spirit? How effectively does your family communicate in this important area of life? Without considering spiritual needs, treating the whole person or the whole family is difficult, if not impossible.

Go back to the family circle drawing you made earlier and locate God in perspective with your other relationships. Follow the same rules as to relative size of God's circle and its distance from the center of your life. Is it where you want it to be? Is God on the outside or inside of your life circle?

Now, just as you did with your family and friends, establish some spiritual goals based on your current relationship with God. As you prioritize goals for you and for your family, consider this passage from the Bible: "One thing I do: Forgetting what is behind and straining toward what is ahead, I press toward the goal to win the prize for which God has called me heavenward in Christ Jesus" (Phil 3:13-14).

THE RISK OF IMPROVEMENT

Who among us could not stand a little polishing? Everyone occasionally needs to take stock of their lives, of where they and their families are headed. For many of us this only occurs in times of crisis: a friend about your age has his first heart attack, your child announces she's quitting high school, you lose your job, or perhaps you celebrate a milestone birthday. Suddenly you see life in a different light, and feel the need to reassess.

We all experience some hesitancy when evaluating goals for our future. Whether it is the fear of change itself, concern about what we might find out if we get a checkup or a mammogram, or possibly the apprehension of leaving life goals unmet—we all risk something in our attempts to improve.

The rewards of clearly established life and family goals far outweigh the perceived risks.

Fortunately, in almost every case, the rewards of clearly established life and family goals far outweigh the perceived risks. Yes, there is some expense and inconvenience associated with having regular physical checkups. But what if a potentially serious health problem is found early on, when a simple and effective cure can be applied? This is often the case with many diseases. Careful attention to increased genetic predisposition and the practice of sound preventive medicine can greatly increase the quantity and quality of life.

Just as some physical testing is painful, so too is some emotional probing into those sensitive areas of life that we have so often swept under our emotional rugs. Shedding light on our true feelings and relationships with others is the first step toward effecting real change in the quality of our relationships at home.

Many times we hear someone say, "What I wouldn't give to have a happy home." Well, what *would* you give to have good relationships with your family, to keep or regain your good health, to feel free to express your needs to God? Consider the words of Jesus himself: "What good would it be for a man if he gains the whole world, yet forfeits his soul? Or what can a man give in exchange for his soul?" (Mt 16:26).

There may be a sense of urgency in our need for change. In many cases, we feel as if we needed change *yesterday!* But fortunately, in most cases, today is still not too late to implement our carefully considered goals.

Evaluate your present situation. Seek help if you need it to meet your physical, emotional, and spiritual needs and those of your family. The remaining chapters of this book will help you make the crucial first steps. But whatever you decide to do, act *now*. Why wait another day?

CHAPTER 9

First Steps
Toward Change

J ANIS AND PAUL looked like a couple that had it all. A successful insurance salesman, Paul had eventually begun a new brokerage firm. He owned it—lock, stock and barrel. He was his own boss, his own man. The family lived in a charming house in the suburbs outside a major city. Their two children, Kate and James, made good grades in school. They belonged to a country club, had maid service on Wednesdays, owned two new cars, a cat, and an American Express card.

Things couldn't have been better. Or could they?

Janis and Paul had been deeply in love twenty-two years earlier when they exchanged "'til death do us part" marriage vows. Full of the lofty dreams that only newlyweds can share, they talked of children, career goals, and the way their life together would be.

Many of their dreams did indeed come true. But by the end of their first year of marriage, a few battle scars were already evident. The heaviest artillery seemed to be Paul's bad temper, which he believed he had inherited from his father. Paul loved his wife and kids; he just didn't know there was any other way to respond to life's stresses than to "blow off steam." He also didn't realize that for this type of warfare, there were no protective flak jackets or havens of safety. The bullets of family cruelty cut straight to the heart and exploded on impact.

When Janis graduated from college, she had begun a promising career in high school teaching and administration. Everyone thought of her as cooperative, pleasant, and always ready for a new assignment. But when her first child was born, Janis "retired." This was partly at Paul's urging, though she agreed with the decision as long as the children were young. Now that Kate and James were well on their way, however, Janis was feeling restless. She found herself asking hard questions about her feelings of self-worth and her role in life.

Kate, their first child, had been named for Janis' grandmother. Janis had virtually been raised by this loving lady, since her own mother had been seemingly unable to cope with life. Kate was seventeen years old, made good grades, and never seemed to argue or contradict her parents. She went with the flow... didn't make waves... accepted what was before her unquestioningly. Kate might have appeared to be every parent's dream, but Janis sensed an inner frustration on her daughter's part that was almost unnerving.

Their son was thirteen and openly rebellious. He and Paul got into major confrontations talking about even the simplest matters. James felt the deficit of love in his family, but instead of crying out, he decided to make a joke out of everything. "Who cares, anyway?" was his standard line. He turned to the only things he felt he could trust: friends, fun, sports, humor. Eventually, the boy dabbled in drugs.

We all know families that continue to "just exist" in this kind of condition, failing to realize—or simply denying—that they are teetering on the edge of a precipice... that the slightest jolt could make them fall to extinction. This is exactly what was happening to this family. Once the dominoes began to fall, there seemed to be no way of stopping them.

Once the dominoes began to fall, there seemed to be no way of stopping them.

Paul was the first to have trouble. His business began to falter in a sour economy. He could still squeak by on his mortgage payment, but just barely. And how long would it last? Vacations and frills of all sorts were a thing of the past. His reserve of self-esteem seemed to dry up as the walls caved in around him. Paul's answer to all of this was to work harder, and be angry while doing so. When his workaholism and anger came out in full force, he was the only one who did not see it.

What about Janis? Faced with family squabbles, diets that would not work, premenstrual syndrome, career regrets, and impending menopause, she slid into a severe depression. Where were those wings that once helped her to soar? How could she ever have anticipated so many disappointments? Was she held captive by her own mother's legacy of depression and inability to cope? We became involved when Janis came to us for help.

Change didn't come easily to this family. They had a great deal of resistance to acknowledging their need, and spent vast amounts of emotional energy looking for someone or something to blame for their troubles. It took a long time for them to realize that their current emotional distress was a result of past failures to address important family needs, compounded by outright denial of their current state of reality.

Eventually, however, they were able to pull together as a family. If you asked them about it now, they would say they are stronger for having gone through their struggles. They have healed family wounds and grown in personal strength as well. Their first step was *acceptance*. This should be your first step as well.

ACCEPTANCE

Peace of mind, fulfillment, happiness, a sense of security—these are all part of the feeling we call serenity. Serenity flows from acceptance. Acceptance of who we are as an individual made in the image of God. Acceptance of our particular role in that most intimate of emotional relationships we call family. Acceptance of our uniqueness in the midst of a world that constantly tries to produce a bland sameness in everyone.

Acceptance is freeing both for the individual and for the family. It frees us to feel, to love, to hope, to fulfill the God-given potential within us. Denial of reality promotes a never-ending search for a self-constructed version of "truth"—one that can never be achieved because it is not based on what is real in our lives or even in the world around us. Acceptance leads to peace of mind and personal happiness.

Perhaps the Serenity Prayer by Reinhold Niebuhr says it best:

God grant me the serenity
to accept the things I cannot change,
the courage to change the things I can,
and the wisdom to know the difference.
Living one day at a time,
enjoying one moment at a time;
accepting hardship as a pathway to peace;
taking, as Jesus did,
this sinful world as it is, not as I would have it;
trusting that you will make all things right
if I surrender to your will;
so that I may be reasonably happy in this life
and supremely happy with you forever in the next.
                                                      Amen

Recognizing the exact nature of your present circumstances, both personally and in your family, can certainly be a challenge. Acceptance is *not* a "woe is me," life-will-never-get-any-better attitude. That is fatalism. Acceptance is the careful consideration of ourselves as the sum total of our life experience, the insightful recognition of inherited potential molded by the varied environmental circumstances of our lives.

Rejection of reality—and thus lack of acceptance of ourselves and of others—can lead only to life in a shadow world that promotes false assumptions about ourselves and those around us. If we continue to deny the truth, how can we ever expect to appreciate who we really are?

A life based on denial rather than acceptance leads many to unhappy personal quests for "fulfillment" or to addictive behavior as a means of escape. Eventually we become unable to distinguish fact from fiction, truth from lies, and the real from the unreal.

STEPS TO ACCEPTANCE

How do we grow in our ability to accept life as it is, to escape the shadow world of denial? Here are some important steps.

Reality orientation. Acceptance starts with facing reality—not reality as we might wish it to be, or reality as seen through the biased filters of denial and self-deception, but accepting circumstances as they really are. This requires honest inspection of ourselves, of past issues, and of family relationships. Honest self-appraisal may seem easy enough when things are going great. But it's not so easy when our life, or our family's life, seems to be spiraling toward destruction. But it is precisely at these times that facing reality is most crucial.

Accepting reality isn't so easy when our life, or our family's life, seems to be spiraling toward destruction. But it is precisely at these times that facing reality is most crucial.

Start with yourself. When was the last time you took a careful look at yourself? We find that people are much more likely to periodically check under the hood of their car for potential problems than they are to take a personal inventory. It takes time to do this. Such quiet time is a rare commodity for most of us. Besides, there is always the possibility we might discover something we don't like, or become aware of some inner feelings that might force a painful reevaluation of our lives.

Begin with your origins. What messages about life, and about yourself, did your parents leave with you? Then analyze your current situation. Are you happy? Are things going the way you planned? Do you have a plan for your life beyond next year? The next month? How do you feel about your life? Are you satisfied? Still searching? Are your personal relationships in good order? How could they be better?

This is just a start. As you keep at it, you'll become more comfortable with your feelings and be able to make real headway toward honest acceptance of yourself and others. Here's an example of one man's attempt to take an honest look at himself:

"I used to think I married the wrong girl. For years I held back my attentions and affections trying to punish her in some way for even marrying me. In fact, I was punishing myself and not making the most of what could have been a great marriage and relationship.

"We have two kids now. It's still not always easy. But once we accepted the fact that we were married, had a responsibility to each other and our children and that divorce was not a viable option for us, we were almost immediately happier. It was like sink or swim. Now, we can't imagine life any other way. Troubled friends even look to *us* for help!"

Check for past issues. Does the specter of past hurts, failures, and disappointments still control certain aspects of your life? Do you have unresolved grief? Issues of personal loss that have never been dealt with? Does the weight of the past crush you and prevent effective progress forward?

Acceptance of the past—both good and bad—is essential if we are to deal effectively with the here and now, to say nothing of the future. Denial of past hurts and mistakes is often at the root of many self-destructive behavior patterns. For example, the child who was continually humiliated and shamed may become a chronically depressed adult. Due to inappropriate self-guilt, such people often never allow themselves to be happy.

Accepting your family. Consider all the members of your family and identify those who are closest to you. This would, presumably, include your present spouse and children, as well as your family of origin: parents and siblings. It could include extended family members such as in-laws, and even close friends. Remember, neither you nor others will be perfect at all times. Acceptance is the realization of this imperfection and forgiveness of yourself and others for acts of human selfishness.

What does acceptance mean to you? Think of the following phrases, as found in a dictionary, and compare them with your view of acceptance:

- to receive with consent
- to be able or designed to take hold
- to endure without protest
- to regard as inevitable
- to receive as true
- to receive into the mind
- to undertake responsibility for
- to receive favorably something offered

Meditate on these definitions. Examine your present and past life where unpleasant situations arose because you were unable to be accepting, or times when you exhibited these qualities during times of acceptance.

Identify risk factors. When we counsel people about their risk of having a heart attack, we concentrate on risk factors that increase the likelihood of heart disease. Understanding a person's genetic history is an important part of this. But as we tell our patients, you can't pick your parents. A strong family history for heart disease simply points out the need for greater attention to other, correctable risk factors such as smoking or a high-fat diet.

If you have a family tendency toward certain problems, don't roll over and wait for the other shoe to fall. Instead, *use* this information to modify or eliminate correctable risks. Accept your heritage, but change what can be changed. Personal change can be inspiring to other members of your family who may lack motivation. Self-help leads to help for others. Personal acceptance leads to family acceptance.

Identify specific goals. "I just want to be happy." "I wish I felt more fulfilled." "I wish I felt better about myself." These are laudable goals, but they are not specific enough. Being more specific about your goals allows your actions to be focused and results better defined. Acceptance of the need for change will stagnate without a specific idea of where you want to go.

Be specific about your goals so your actions can be focused and results can be defined.

Make a list of personal desires. Let's say you feel bored with your current job and realize that change is needed. Okay, what career change could you make? How much are you willing to do to make this change? Do you have family support for this decision? You can't become a neurosurgeon in your spare time, but you could start night classes to learn a new skill. Accept the possibility for change, be specific and realistic in your goals.

Recognize that others may need to change as well, but may be at different levels of acceptance. Resist the temptation to become obsessed with success or failure. As the Serenity Prayer notes, it is God who grants serenity and the courage to make changes. Here's one woman's reassessment of her personal goals:

"I was never pretty or popular in school. That was hard for me to accept as a child. I don't really think my parents liked me much either in those days. Who knows? Maybe I was just disagreeable.

"One day (this may sound ridiculous), I was driving in my car and the song, 'Don't Worry, Be Happy,' came on the radio. I had already been working on the issue of acceptance and it was like a lightning bolt. I thought, Why should I make myself miserable just because I'm not as attractive or perhaps vivacious as some other young women? I want to enjoy life just as much as they do—maybe even more, since I've known what it's like not to enjoy life.

"That was five years ago. Now I not only accept who I am, but have discovered a whole slew of wonderful qualities that are also the real me. I accept me—I love me. And now that I don't feel sorry for myself, I have loads of friends—*true* friends."

Change what can be changed. "God grant me the courage to change the things I can." Remember, acceptance is reality-based. We accept what is real and reject what is unreal. Recognizing what we can change—and taking the first halting steps toward *doing* something about it—is crucial to acceptance of ourselves and our families.

Kids are sticklers for fairness and equality. A shared blueberry muffin had better have the same number of berries in each half. Sound familiar? Yet we "mature" adults apply this same reasoning all the time. "The boss sure likes him better." "I've worked for everything I have. Why does she still ask our parents for money?"

Life isn't always fair. We live in an imperfect world, populated by imperfect people, including ourselves. Accept these realities and concentrate instead on what you can do to improve justice and inequality.

We live in an imperfect world,
populated by imperfect people, including ourselves.
Accept these realities and concentrate instead
on what you can do to improve justice and inequality.

Acceptance of the gifts, attributes, and personal qualities given us by God will go far toward gaining us peace of mind. Consider those words, "God grant me...." Cast aside the blinders of human perspective and consider the possibility of a loving, all-powerful God who truly sees the "big picture" as we cannot.

See yourself as a creation of God, endowed for a purpose and equipped for the tasks which face you. Accepting yourself and those around you as individuals, as members of a family, as persons of unique genetic and environmental heritage, is an essential step toward personal serenity. "I praise you because I am fearfully and wonderfully made; your works are wonderful, I know that full well" (Ps 139:14).

COMMUNICATION

It was a hot, muggy day in the delta. The sun was sinking toward the hazy western horizon, obscured by the heavy growth of the jungle. At a time when most of his friends were half a world away, cheering their college football teams to victory, David's friend and eventual medical school colleague was slogging his way through a rice paddy in Southeast Asia. A medic with Bravo Company, Ken had four months down and eight to go in one of the longest years of his life.

Without warning, small arms fire broke out in the trees, along with the ominous rattle of heavy caliber automatic weapons. Ken and the other soldiers took cover as Bravo Company returned the fire. It was over as suddenly as it had begun. The afternoon calm was broken now, not by gunfire, but by the screams of wounded men calling for help.

Ken rushed forward. He found one Marine dead and two badly wounded. They moved the injured men, who were cursing with pain, to the relative dryness of an earthen dike in the middle of the paddy. Their wounds were serious. Fortunately, med-evac helicopters were only minutes away—if they knew you needed help and how to find you.

The radio had been on the blink all day. Now, at this critical moment, it failed completely. Wounded men lay dying while another Marine tried desperately to repair the radio. A few minutes later—it seemed like hours—the radio crackled to life and help was finally on its way.

Shielding his eyes from the blazing sun, Ken watched as the life-saving choppers lifted the wounded men to safety. Turning to his sergeant, Ken shook his head and remarked on their good fortune in getting the radio fixed. His sergeant was a thin, young Alabama farm boy made older and wiser by war. He just smiled and said, "If you ain't got commo, you ain't got nothin'."

Good communication is definitely a required skill for healthy families. Those that function poorly—described as *dysfunctional* families—experience any of a number of common communication deficits. They explain away difficulties by blaming a person or condition outside the family. They "scapegoat" one particular family member, who is blamed for everything. These families do not negotiate. They cannot work together and children do not learn to solve problems. Hostile, attacking feelings flow freely, but most other feelings cannot be expressed. The family mood is hostile and conflict appears relentless and endless.[1]

Just as dysfunctional families display less effective communication, healthy families in contrast excel at communicating with each other. There are several distinct characteristics of good family communication.

Clarity of expression. Good communication relies on individuals' ability to know what they want and effectively convey that idea to others. Lack of clarity leads to frustration and misunderstanding. Clear, direct communication avoids the use of deception and ploys to trick another into agreement or compliance.

Permeability. Good communicators recognize communication as a two-way street. Listening and responding to the ideas of others is just as important as expressing your own thoughts. A good communicator is permeable to the ideas of others, acknowledging both verbal and non-verbal communication.

Goal-directed negotiation. The way a family solves its problems puts communication skills to the acid test. Successful negotiation employs the exploration of each family member's opinions and feelings on a subject. Good negotiators search for a consensus of opinions and exhibit the ability to compromise when appropriate.

Ease of emotional expression. Communication encompasses not only utilitarian verbal messages like "When do we eat?" but also offers the opportunity for expression of feelings. "I'm hurting so bad inside it feels like I might burst." Families that hinder communication of emotional needs will soon squelch any attempt at emotional expression, even under desperate circumstances. Dysfunctional families are at high risk for stress-induced anxiety and depression—or worse. One patient, discussing the recent suicide of her sister, lamented, "We never even knew she was unhappy."

Empathy. The empathetic family responds to family members' feelings with genuine understanding. "I know how it feels to be sad." Less functional families have no ability to relate or accept emotional displays. The Oscar-winning film, *Ordinary People*, depicted a family whose members simply could not share the feelings they were experiencing, let alone support one another in their trials. This stifling atmosphere forced them into hostility, suicide attempts, and divorce.

GROUND RULES FOR EFFECTIVE COMMUNICATION

Everyone has a biological need for expression. Just as we must be able to convey our physical needs to survive, so the ability to express our emotional needs is vital to good mental health. Even the smallest babies have the ability to express their needs and get their point across succinctly. Babies don't hedge or make you guess what they really want. And they don't stop expressing themselves until their needs get met.

Just as we must be able to convey our physical needs to survive, so the ability to express our emotional needs is vital to good mental health.

But somehow, many families either forget how to express their needs, or they just quit trying. It is possible for people to lose the ability to communicate effectively, or to be inappropriate in the communication of their needs. We have patients who communicate their emotional needs through physical symptoms. We discussed this earlier when we talked about somatization. This is an extremely inefficient and evasive way of expressing needs.

Perhaps communication in your family is not what it should be. Besides, who couldn't use at least a tune-up? Perhaps understanding the basics of human communication can help.

As with other areas we have discussed, restoration of effective communication begins with a careful self-assessment of our present communication skills. We must also recognize that while families tend to be similar in many areas, individuals are not always functioning at the same level.

It is essential for everyone to play by the same set of rules. Consider the following ground rules for effective family communication:

- Recognize each person's need for expression.
- Allow uninterrupted opportunity for each person to talk.
- Encourage clear and direct expression.
- Avoid interrupting or telling others what they think.
- Be open to the ideas of others.
- Attempt to resolve conflicts in a goal-directed manner.
- Try for greater understanding and empathy.
- Recognize the need for closeness among family members.

For some, even attempting to implement these ground rules will be a major undertaking. It may be necessary to have an outside counselor mediate while members are determining if these ground rules are being followed. Wherever you find yourself or your family in the area of communication skills, there is no time like the present to initiate efforts at improvement.

Certainly there will be setbacks along the path toward improved communication, possibly reversions to old habits when faced with stressful circumstances. Don't lose heart. Just ask forgiveness if you have offended another, and continue to work on this essential area of successful family functioning.

FIVE LEVELS OF FAMILY COMMUNICATION

Level one: talk to each other. While it may seem redundant to say that we must talk to each other in order to communicate, we feel it essential to establish this as a basis. A family must be able to convey factual information such as, "The washing machine is broken," or, "The kids need to go to the dentist." Remember Officer Friday on the old *Dragnet* television series? "Just the facts, Ma'am."

It may be difficult to imagine, but there are families who drift through life totally oblivious of each other, without ever substantially talking to one another. These families usually don't stay together long. They see no need to.

If your family is not talking, the first step is to try and establish at least elementary, utilitarian communication—quickly. If you don't, there will soon be no one to talk to at all.

Level two: "We Are Family." The Pointer Sisters sang "We Are Family" to the top of the pop music charts in the eighties. We also must sing this lyrical expression to each other. We all want to belong, and the family is our first opportunity to do so.

At this point, people begin to realize that all these individuals living under the same roof are connected in some significant way. Individuals who view themselves as radically independent begin to explore the possibility that belonging to a family might provide potential allies and support in times of stress.

At this point, people begin to realize that all these individuals living under the same roof are connected in some significant way.

While family relationships are being recognized, at this level they tend to be more *functionally* oriented. Communication is still self-centered, with little or no empathy. Negotiation is difficult and conflict is high. Emotional needs are not discussed and family members express little personal responsibility for their actions, preferring instead to blame and use scapegoats. There is frequent interrupting and "speaking for others."

Although these families have a long way to go, they are not on the brink of destruction. They have at least an interest in change for the better. For example, awareness of a need for intervention in major family dysfunction can occur at this level. Even if not the result of a heartfelt concern for another, at least an awareness is dawning that one individual's problem is unsettling the delicate family balance.

Level three: sharing feelings. We have now reached the critical juncture between recognizing a problem and taking corrective action. Feelings and emotion-laden issues are frequently discussed at this level of communication. Family members recognize an intense need for emotional release, and they desire change. But they are unsure how to proceed.

Families at this level tend to be better at expressing their own needs than at perceiving the needs of others. Although needs are expressed strongly, they are still not always expressed clearly and directly. Hidden agendas and problems with closeness are still present.

The following areas can present special challenges:

Stress. Families at this level need to take an inventory of the stresses being applied against their family. They should consider life cycle stresses, such as those associated with the birth of the first child. Acute or chronic illness can act as a significant stressor as well. Stresses such as financial or job pressures should be explored. By examining any such issues, families can come to better appreciate individual needs to be more empathetic, less judgmental, and more open. They can negotiate ways of dealing with their common problems.

Adaptation. Some experts in family therapy say the key to family coping is family adaptability. Are you rigid or flexible in the face of new challenges? Level three families are interested in *exploring* their problems, but are often reluctant to begin making changes.

The key to family coping is family adaptability.
Are you rigid or flexible in the face of new challenges?

A good example occurs frequently in our medical practice. A couple who is having marital problems agree to some short-term counseling. We typically ask them when the last time was that they went on a date together—no kids, no friends along, just themselves. Many times the husband and wife just look at each other and shrug their shoulders. Willingness to make a change—even one as simple as deciding to go on a date—indicates whether they are stuck here or have progressed to the next level of family communication.

Cohesion. Cohesion is an important indicator of the level of family communication. It is also evidence of a well-balanced family. A cohesive family supports each other emotionally and physically while holding on to an adequate degree of separateness. Too much cohesiveness can lead to harmful *enmeshment.* Overprotective and overreactive to each other's feelings, the enmeshed family frequently interrupts each other, speaks for other family members even when they are present, and are often unwilling to adequately discuss problems for fear of "hurting someone's feelings."

The other extreme is the *disengaged* family, in which individual family members go their own way. Disengaged families tend to be emotionally unreactive toward other family members. Achieving cohesive balance is a critical function of the healthy family who seeks to improve communication.

Triangulation. One pattern very damaging to effective communication between parents is the establishment of a parent-child coalition against the other parent. This triangulation quickly becomes a struggle for control in which honest communication becomes all but impossible.

Variations on this theme may take the form of the oldest child being thrust into a parental role with inappropriate responsibilities, or an alliance with a grandparent rather than a parent. Children quickly learn to play one parent against the other. Even therapists who are seeking to help the family may be drawn into "siding" with one parent against the other.

Such harmful triangles block clear and direct communication in a variety of ways. A father may find himself blocked from communicating with his daughter except through his wife. Parental communication may be severely impaired because of the influence of a third party such as a grandparent, sister, or even a close friend.

Education. Families frequently get themselves into trouble when facing unfamiliar situations. Families who were once communicating on a much higher level may regress to less sophisticated communication when stressed. Family education about new issues is frequently a way of improving communication. This can be accomplished in many ways, such as reading and discussing books like this one. Outside information sources such as pastoral counseling, family therapists, or your family physician may be helpful.

Prevention. Understanding the various stresses you are likely to encounter at various stages in your family's life may help you prepare for what lies ahead. Exploring options in advance may prevent communication problems due to sudden needs which may arise. For example, one of the most consistent findings in family research is that the average couple often experiences a decline in marital satisfaction following the birth of their first child.[2] Recognizing this possibility may encourage new parents to continue to focus on their needs as a couple as well as those of the new baby.

Support. Some families just need a little encouragement and support during difficult times. There are many resources available to today's family. Support and counseling is offered within many churches. Many companies offer emotional support counseling for their employees. Numerous private counseling resources are available in almost every community.

The challenge of change. The family that is not challenged to change is unlikely to do so. Those seeking change must be challenged to consider that their current view of their family's health may be just an illusion, a myth ready to be exploded at the first ill wind of life. Those families who have adapted very rigid ways of facing problems must be challenged to consider more flexible responses.

The danger for families at this level is believing that simply discussing a problem leads to its solution. They "cuss and discuss" until they are emotionally worn out—but no steps toward change ever occur. This is much like the family who constantly says, "What are we going to do about Dad?" Everyone knows he's an alcoholic, everyone laments the obvious decline in his physical health, his wife mourns their lost relationship daily—but nobody ever takes a step toward confronting him with his disease and need for treatment.

---

*Families sometimes believe that simply discussing
a problem leads to its solution.
They "cuss and discuss" until they are emotionally worn out
—but no steps toward change ever occur.*

Level four: time for change. The critical difference at this point is that problems are not just recognized and discussed, but real steps toward resolution of the issues occurs. These steps may be small, "testing the water" type efforts, but at least change is occurring.

Families usually waver between levels three and four as they experiment with change—probing forward then retreating into the relative safety of inaction. Often a person attempting this type of action-oriented communication for the first time will be reluctant to raise their hopes and expectations too high for fear they will again be disappointed.

Read over the issues addressed in level three again, but develop concrete strategies for implementing the necessary changes. Perhaps it's time to quit talking about attending a marriage seminar and actually go. Don't just continue to patronize your spouse about the family budget, stick to it this month. Find someone in your family who has expressed a definite need and make an honest effort to help that person. Don't just sit there, *do* something!

Level five: truth, honesty, and love. At this level, family interactions are open, direct, and efficient at solving problems. Members show appropriate empathy, but are neither enmeshed nor disengaged from one another. Emotional needs are easily expressed and different ideas from each family member are treated with respect. As a result, these families are warm, affectionate, humorous, and optimistic. Who wouldn't want this kind of family life?

Change and grow, give up the mistakes of the past, and look forward to improved family relationships in good times and in bad.

The key is successful communication between members, with no unhealthy coalitions or alliances. They are truly "all for one and one for all." The difference between levels four and five is not just that change is taking place, but that there is a willingness to grow. Change without growth is never permanent. The same issues are worked on over and over. Change and grow, give up the mistakes of the past, and look forward to improved family relationships in good times and in bad.

These are but suggestions of ways to improve communication—a template to lay over your family in evaluating strengths and weaknesses. Change is never easy, we are often reluctant to change even when our present situation hurts. Large companies spend fortunes trying to teach effective communication skills to their employees so they can work more effectively together and relate better to consumers. Shouldn't you be investing at least some effort in improving communication in your family? Remember, "If you ain't got commo, you ain't got nothin'."

CHAPTER **10**

Hope and Healing, Today and Forever

WHEN WRITING A BOOK like this, it is difficult not to focus too heavily on problems. To some degree, such is human nature. One psychologist has pointed out that if you ask the average person to tell you what's wrong with them, or with their spouse or children, or with their family of origin, they will be able to provide an exhaustive catalog of weaknesses, failings, and faults. But if you ask those same people to tell you what's *right,* they are likely to stammer and shuffle their feet and have little to say.

By the same token, many of us are adept at describing what an unhealthy person or family looks like, but we have a hard time portraying what *health* looks like. We are all more attuned to our problems than to what is going well in our lives. And those who pick up a book like this are much more likely to turn to those sections that discuss areas they are presently experiencing as problems. Why bother to read about an aspect of life that's already going just fine? As the old saying goes, the squeaky wheel gets the grease. People go to the doctor when they need someone to "fix what's broken," not to strengthen what's already working well.

With all of this in mind, our effort has been to zero in on potential problem areas as the quickest way to offer you some meaningful help. The danger in this approach is that we can focus so much on potential problems that we don't give enough attention to hope and healing—to the promise of soul-mending from both a temporal and eternal perspective.

Thus, in this chapter and the next, we propose a spiritual recovery process that can help with the physical and emotional problems we have outlined. Our desire is to point the way to happy, healthy, joy-filled living—both for individuals and for families.

The danger is that we can focus so much on potential problems that we don't give enough attention to hope and healing—to the promise of soul-mending from both a temporal and eternal perspective.

WHAT WE HAVE IN COMMON

To set the stage, let's consider four facts that we believe to be true of every person in every family, both children and adults.

1. Each of us is born with God-given needs: not just physical needs, but emotional and spiritual needs as well.[1] In alphabetical order and not necessarily importance, we all need the following elements in our lives:

- *Acceptance:* To be loved no matter what we do or do not do. To be liked for who we are, with our own unique qualities, is also very important.
- *Affection:* Non-sexual touching—holding, caressing, hugging, kissing.
- *Affirmation:* Verbal expression of our intrinsic value and worth, and verbal expressions of appreciation for our good performance or effort.
- *Attention:* Sustained time with significant people, devoted

to what we want to do or talk about.

- *Belonging:* To be included in a group of people who are significant to us.
- *Celebration:* Encouragement to keep our sense of humor and wonderment toward the world.
- *Comfort:* Warm, caring responses to our pain.
- *Communication:* Clear, unambiguous talk, and focused listening to what we have to say.
- *Competence:* To be able to do age-appropriate tasks, to be good at something.
- *Discipline:* Clear boundaries for our behavior and attitudes, lovingly set and enforced.
- *Forgiveness:* Our wrongdoings are not held against us over time.
- *Guidance:* Wise, sensitive direction in every dimension of life.
- *Nurture:* Consistent provision for our physical, emotional, and spiritual needs, communicating love and security.
- *Protection:* Age-appropriate sheltering from potentially harmful objects, environments, and people.
- *Stimulation:* A variety of opportunities for challenge, change, curiosity, creativity, and fun.
- *Structure:* A predictable, reliable environment where people consistently keep their promises.
- *Understanding:* For significant people to enter our world, seeing circumstances from our perspective.

2. God intends for families to be the primary agency for meeting these needs. God intends for parents to be a representation of his unconditional, infinite love for us. He intends for us to experience a balance of love and limits, of affection and discipline.[2] Indeed, there is no other context even remotely equipped to provide the sustained effort necessary to meet these needs.

3. We all had imperfect parents, so we all grew up with some of these legitimate God-given needs going unmet. Some parents are more imperfect than others, but even excellent parents occasionally fail. No parent can meet all our needs all the time.

4. When our needs were met, we felt loved and cared for. When our needs were not met, we felt hurt and angry. We also may have felt afraid that these needs would continue to go unmet, and thus that the hurt would continue or get worse. Or, we may have become jealous of others who seemed to have their needs met. We may have felt depressed, despairing that no one would ever meet our needs.

OUR RESPONSE TO UNMET NEEDS

We believe that these four statements hold true for every person in every family, everywhere and at all times. Now let's consider three ways in which we can respond to these realities of family life.

1. Denial. Some of us refuse to acknowledge—even to ourselves—that we are feeling pain, or that our hurt has adversely affected us. We refuse to admit that we have unmet needs, or we contend that these unmet needs do not bother us. If anything, we rationalize that we are stronger because of our difficult childhood environment. This response pattern is called *denial.*

Let's consider an example of someone stuck in denial. As an associate pastor of a large suburban church, Mark headed several ministries, including counseling. For years he maintained that his chaotic, turmoil-ridden family of origin had not affected him. Mark admitted that he felt distant from his mother and sister, and he grudgingly admitted that they had "let him down." Yet he believed that he had forgiven his alcoholic stepfather and that the past should be forgotten.

Ordinarily, Mark was adept at "tuning in" to the feelings of those he counseled and of others on the church staff. But he was often unaware of his own feelings. When Mark felt hurt or angry, he would usually deny these feelings or turn them inward. Because he did not consciously feel hurt, sadness, or anger from his childhood experiences, this pastor assumed he had no unresolved emotional problems.

In fact, however, Mark was very "bottled up" emotionally, a fact that expressed itself in ways he was only vaguely aware of. He found it difficult to counsel chemically-dependent people, for example. Mark couldn't understand why it was so hard to be his usual warm, patient self with such people.

Do you identify at all with Mark? Do you find yourself thinking, "Sure, my childhood was hard. But I'm a stronger person because of it. My parents did the best they could, and I didn't turn out so bad. So what's the big deal?" Do you deny your true feelings about present struggles, pretending they are not there?

Mark was adept at "tuning in" to the feelings of those he counseled and of others on the church staff. But he was often unaware of his own feelings.

---

2. Blaming parents, spouses, or others. If some of us deny our unresolved hurt, others of us prefer to blame it on someone else. In particular, we may believe that our parents failed, that they are to blame for all the problems we experience. We focus on how they wronged us and are unwilling to acknowledge anything they did was right.

The result of blaming others for our problems is that we have difficulty taking responsibility for our own lives. Instead, we look for others who are willing to take care of us. When we blame others for our problems, we evade both personal responsibility and reality.

Bill responded to his unmet needs in this way. Thirty-five

years old and married with two children, he had recently lost his job, largely because he just wasn't performing. He had spent significant work time talking to fellow employees about his depression and his vague, but strong, feelings of worthlessness. When Bill told his supervisor that it wasn't reasonable to expect much from him because he was in a lot of pain, the supervisor had reasonably concluded that Bill needed to find another job.

Bill's problems were compounded by his struggle with compulsive eating and television watching. He would stay up all night watching TV and consuming large amounts of junk food. Dead tired the next day, he would excuse himself from looking for work or giving focused attention to his wife and children. Not surprisingly, financial pressures constantly threatened to inundate him. He had neglected needed maintenance of his home and had fallen behind on his property taxes. Compulsive spending habits had him deeply mired in credit card debt.

All this time, Bill attended two support groups, saw three different counselors, and actively pursued several relationships for emotional and spiritual support. He spent hundreds of dollars on self-help books, tapes, and seminars. He frequently expressed frustration that these efforts did not make him feel better.

Bill blamed his problems on his family background. His father had kept his emotional distance, spending every waking hour overseeing the family's west Texas ranch. His mother had tried to control his every thought and action. Bill knew he could not change the past. However, he believed that until his past hurts of rejection and shame were healed, he could not take responsibility for his own life.

Meanwhile, Bill's family struggled to survive. His wife remained continually exhausted from carrying the load of responsibility. Not surprisingly, his children felt the same feelings of worthlessness and depression Bill did.

Do you identify with Bill? Do you find yourself thinking,

"I've got so many problems. If my parents had only treated me right, I'd be so much better. There is nothing I can do about it. I'm stuck. And it's all my parents' fault!"

Many of us, especially victims of abuse, blame not only those who abused us, but we blame God as well. We ask, "Where was God when I needed him? Why didn't he help me? Why did he let it happen?" We may believe we were not good enough to merit God's protection. Yet all the while, we may also hold God responsible. "After all," we think, "he could have stopped it." It is not hard to see why abuse victims have trouble responding to God in a meaningful way. Their pain is only increased because of spiritual estrangement from God.

Many of us blame not only those who abused us,
but we blame God as well.

---

3. Blaming ourselves. Even if we avoid blaming God or others for our problems, we are still left with one other available target—ourselves. We may develop a deep-seated belief that something is inherently wrong with us. Our reasoning is, "If I had just been smarter, or better, or prettier, my parents would have loved me and met my needs. The fact that they didn't meet my needs proves that I am no good, ugly, and worthless. It must be my fault." Psychologists call a deep sense of worthlessness *shame.*

Why would anyone blame themselves for others' shortcomings? This approach seems more plausible when we remember that children are egocentric: they believe everything revolves around themselves. Such a response springs not so much from arrogance as from a reasonable, perhaps even an inevitable, worldview. According to developmental experts, it is the only worldview children are capable of in their early years.

From their limited perspective and experience, kids can only conclude that they really *are* the center of the universe.

Thus their perception is, "If something bad happens, it must be my fault." If their parents don't meet their needs, the most obvious explanation is that they are responsible for that failure. Sometimes parents reinforce this false belief by blaming the child for whatever goes wrong. When this happens, a powerful sense of shame becomes deeply rooted in the child's self-perception.

This shame usually persists into adulthood. What we learn to believe in childhood resists adult objectivity. Even when we become able to think objectively and realize that we were not the cause of our own unmet needs, we somehow continue to think, feel, and react as though we were.

Even when we become able to think objectively and realize that we were not the cause of our own unmet needs, we somehow continue to think, feel, and react as though we were.

Rita was burdened by this kind of deep shame. Her mother was an alcoholic. Her father was a workaholic who was seldom home. As the first-born of three children, Rita became a substitute parent for her younger brother and sister. Meanwhile, no one met her own basic needs for nurture, attention, discipline, acceptance, or celebration. Rita's efforts to take care of her two siblings submerged the hurt she felt as a child.

Today she admits that very few of her needs were met, but Rita believes that she just simply wasn't good enough to deserve anything from her parents. At age forty, she has never married. She is sure she would not be good enough to satisfy a husband. She struggles daily with a pervading sense of failure and low self-worth.

Moreover, Rita still feels responsible for helping her brother and sister. Her brother is an alcoholic and her sister married an abusive husband. She is sure she could be doing more for them and her parents. She even blames herself for not knowing what to do.

Do you identify with Rita? Are you aware that you have unhealed hurt due to unmet needs? Do you assume that if you had been a better child, your parents would have met your needs?

Each of these faulty responses to unmet needs inevitably leads to further problems. For example, when we deny that we have any hurt, we get out of touch with our own emotions. We also find it difficult to take other people's feelings and needs seriously, and thus have trouble forming intimate relationships.

When we blame others for everything, we have difficulty accepting responsibility for our own lives. This type of response also impairs our relationships. Why? Healthy people avoid us because they do not like to be blamed for our problems.

If we blame ourselves, we become slaves of chronic low self-esteem. We feel responsible for everything that happens. We blame ourselves for everything that goes wrong.

THE FUNCTIONAL FAMILY

These three ways of responding to unmet needs can characterize anyone, regardless of their family of origin. But some families *are* better than others at consistently meeting the needs of their members—or at least at positively responding to the hurt and anger when they *don't.*

These are what we call *functional* families. Though not perfect, they nevertheless function in a way that meets the basic God-given needs of their members most of the time. When the family does not meet these needs, the right people notice and respond in ways that resolve the anger and heal the hurt. Let's review some of the key characteristics of the functional family.

Meeting basic needs. A functional family is one where the parents (or a single parent) are free to be aware of, and concerned about, how the children are developing physically, mentally, emotionally, socially, and spiritually. These parents are free to love each other and their children unconditionally.[3] They accept imperfection in themselves and their children. They don't take everything personally. They don't give up when conflicts occur.

Responding to unmet needs. In a functional family, when parents hurt their children or when their children hurt each other, they work together to acknowledge both the wrong and feelings about the wrong. They comfort the hurt ones and achieve reconciliation. They forgive, and they work with their children to encourage them to forgive. They strive for justice in family relationships, but they also extend mercy.

Above all, functional parents recognize the challenge of meeting their children's greatest need— feeling loved and accepted, no matter what.

The greatest challenge. Above all, functional parents recognize the challenge of meeting their children's greatest need— feeling loved and accepted, no matter what. Understanding the importance of this challenge, they work hard to see life from their children's perspective. This helps them determine what will most help each child to feel unconditionally loved. They help their children identify both positive and negative feelings. They then invite the children to express these feelings appropriately.[4]

The primary goal in a functional family. Functional parents work to encourage each family member to maturity. Because they are not seriously needy themselves, the parents are free to give whatever is necessary to help their children mature.

FUNCTIONAL FAMILY RULES

What rules do functional families consistently follow? Popular family author and speaker John Bradshaw has defined several rules of functional families.[5]

1. Problems are acknowledged and resolved.
2. All members are free to share their perceptions, feelings, thoughts, desires, and fantasies.
3. Each person is of equal value as a person.
4. Communication is direct, congruent, concrete, specific, and behavioral.
5. Family members can get their needs met.
6. Family members can be different.
7. Parents do what they say. They are self-disciplined disciplinarians.
8. Family roles are freely chosen and flexible.
9. The atmosphere is fun and spontaneous.
10. Mistakes are forgiven and viewed as learning tools.
11. The family system exists for individuals.
12. Parents admit when they are wrong.

Betty: case number one. Betty got up from the dinner table. She was pleased that everyone had enjoyed the meal, especially since she got a late start on the soufflé. Somewhat tired from her part-time job at the local bank, she decided to ask her eleven-year-old daughter Mary to help with the dinner dishes.

Mary was in no mood to be helpful. "No way! You always ask me! Besides, you didn't let me rent the movie I wanted!" She stomped down the hall to her room and slammed the door. Betty waited a few minutes. Then she walked down the hall to her daughter's bedroom and knocked on the door.

"Go away! I don't want to talk to you! Leave me alone!"

"I'd really like to talk to you," Betty said through the door. "Can I come in?"

"All right." Betty found her daughter sitting on her bed, staring at the wall.

Betty began, "Honey, I can tell you're upset, not only about me asking you to help with the dishes, but also about not getting to rent your video earlier. Am I right?"

With a frown on her face, Mary responded, "I guess so… I never get to rent what I want! You always let Jill get those old ones. I hate them!"

"I guess I hurt your feelings when I said no today to your video choice without more explanation. I wonder if maybe you are feeling unimportant, because we didn't agree with what you wanted. Am I close?"

Mary began to cry. "You never listen to me! All my friends have seen *Lost Lovers in Paradise*. I feel so left out when they talk about it!"

Betty gave her a tissue and said tenderly, "I can see how not letting you see it would hurt your feelings." She reached over and put her arms around her daughter. "I'm sorry I hurt you. I don't want you to feel hurt. Thanks for telling me about it. Will you forgive me for not being more sensitive?"

---

*"I'm sorry I hurt you. I don't want you to feel hurt.
Thanks for telling me about it. Will you forgive me?"*

Mary hugged her mother tightly. "Sure, I forgive you." Betty hugged her back. Then she calmly said, "Honey, we probably won't rent that particular video right now, but I promise that the next time we go, we'll rent your choice of an acceptable video, okay?"

Smiling, Mary replied, "Okay, Mom."

"I really love you, Mary. I'm so glad God gave you to us as our daughter!"

"Really? Even when I act bad?"

With a big smile, Betty replied, "Yes, really! Could we do the dishes now?"

"Well, if I have to… all right."

THE DYSFUNCTIONAL FAMILY

Some families are chronically weak at meeting the needs of their members. We call these *dysfunctional* families. Sadly, the very factors that hinder the meeting of needs also block the resolution of negative emotions that result. These negative emotions build up in the lives of members of dysfunctional families with devastating effect.

Where do dysfunctional families come from? No one deliberately sets out to create one, so how do they happen? John Bradshaw offers this explanation: "The husband and wife are the architects of the family. Dysfunctional families are created by dysfunctional marriages. Dysfunctional marriages are created by dysfunctional individuals who seek out and marry each other."[6]

Bradshaw further says, "Dysfunctional marriages set up dysfunctional families. Dysfunctional families are the soil for abandonment. One is initiated into addiction through dysfunctional parenting styles and the family systems they create. Addiction and obsessive-compulsive disorders are symptoms of being abandoned and shamed in childhood."[7]

Now let's sketch some of the most common traits of the dysfunctional family.

One or both parents are impaired. In a dysfunctional family, one or both adults are not capable of attending to the needs of other family members. This could be due to addictive behavior such as alcoholism, workaholism, an eating disorder, compulsive gambling, spending, sex, or even religious activity.

Psychological dysfunction or mental illness such as schizophrenia, manic depression, narcissistic personality, or paranoia can also seriously impair a parent. Any physical, mental, emotional, or spiritual problem that hinders the ability of one or both adults to meet each other's or their children's needs leads to the dysfunctional family.

Often, if one parent is an addict or otherwise impaired, the other parent can have little to give the children. The non-addicted parent expends tremendous physical, mental, and emotional effort in coping with the impaired spouse's behavior. That spouse also absorbs the considerable emotional pain the dysfunctional spouse inflicts.

Any physical, mental, emotional, or spiritual problem
that hinders the ability of one or both adults
to meet each other's or their children's needs
leads to the dysfunctional family.

The primary goal in a dysfunctional family. The primary goal of each member in the dysfunctional family is *survival* rather than growth. Thus any pattern of behavior (or non-behavior) that helps with survival becomes deeply ingrained in the lives of both children and adults. Children of dysfunctional families will use these survival techniques long after they have physically left home.

Three rules for survival. Dysfunctional families invariably obey three rules which contribute to individual survival. Regrettably, these rules also serve to maintain the dysfunctional system. They stifle mental, emotional, and spiritual freedom and maturity. Following these rules blocks the meeting of God-given needs.

Rule number one: don't talk. Everyone in the dysfunctional family desperately needs to talk about what is happening to them and around them. However, no one talks about what's really going on. And no one listens to any attempt to break the deadly silence. Instead, everyone pretends that all is well.

Remember Mark, the associate pastor we met earlier in this chapter? During his growing-up years, no one in the family ever talked about anything that was really important to them —for fear that Mark's alcoholic stepfather would get upset. The unstated goal was, "Peace at any price." They never knew what topics might set off an explosion, so it was safer just to keep everything to themselves.

Rule number two: don't feel. "In a dysfunctional family, children do not have permission to feel, or they are afraid of their feelings," explains Linda Kondracki.[8] Because of rule number one, feelings can't be verbally expressed. Also, any non-verbal expressions of feelings are either ignored or rejected. Thus, children may consciously or even subconsciously decide not to feel anything in order to comply with this rule.

Mark actually remembers making a conscious decision to suppress his feelings of hurt and anger. He was twelve years old at the time, lying awake in bed one night as his parents quarreled in the next room. Finally he said to himself, "I've had it! I'm not going to let that man get to me any more! From now on, no matter what he says, no matter what he does, I'm just not going to feel anything."

Rule number three: don't trust. The behavior of the primary dysfunctional parent is chaotic and unpredictable. As a result, neither parent consistently keeps his or her promises. The children are regularly let down and disappointed, thus compounding their emotional pain. Because no one else intervenes to care for the children, they learn that they cannot depend upon parents (and often other siblings). This inability to trust parents and siblings causes even deeper pain. It also promotes an exaggerated self-dependence beyond what children are capable of.

Two other factors intensify the hurt. First, according to rule number one, no one talks about the pain and insecurity or the lack of trust. So the children bear the burden completely alone. Second, children assume that the untrustworthiness of parents is ultimately their own fault. They believe that if they could somehow be better, these others would come through for them. Thus, their feelings of guilt, shame, self-hate, and unworthiness multiply.

DYSFUNCTIONAL FAMILY ROLES

In addition to following these three rules, members of dysfunctional families also typically take on unhealthy *survival roles*. In effect, they adopt a "false self" for purposes of family interaction. Bradshaw writes, "These roles are ways to survive the intolerable situation in a dysfunctional family. They function like ego defenses."[9]

Pat Springle of RAPHA, a large provider of hospital inpatient psychiatric care and substance abuse treatment, summarizes five roles that members of dysfunctional families commonly assume.[10]

1. The *enabler* tries to make everything okay by keeping the primary dysfunctional person happy. They also try to get everyone else to keep that person happy. In so doing, they "enable" that person to continue in the dysfunctional behavior.
2. The *hero* thinks that by being perfect and looking good to the outside world, the problems will go away.
3. The *scapegoat* rebels against the family problems. In order to take the focus off the dysfunctional parent, they are consistently told that they are the problem. They thus end up believing this is actually the case.
4. The *lost child* pulls into a shell, withdraws and isolates himself from meaningful relationships.

5. The *mascot* tries desperately to make everyone laugh in the midst of the tragedy of the family situation.

Bradshaw suggests several other dysfunctional family roles that children take on, such as Little Parent, Family Counselor, Surrogate Spouse, Caretaker, Peacemaker, Mom's or Dad's Buddy, Confidante, Pretty One, Religious One, or Family Referee.[11] Some of these are variations of the above five, but others are distinct roles different from the above.

The Surrogate Spouse role is particularly destructive to children. Every family requires a marriage. If the partners are not meeting each other's needs, they will often turn to one of the children for nurture, approval, or even sex. The child is deeply hurt in two ways. First, the child is abused by the boundary violation of emotional or physical incest with one parent. Second, the child is abused by the non-offending parent's resentment or abandonment.[12]

---

*If the partners are not meeting each other's needs,
they will often turn to one of the children for nurture,
approval, or even sex.*

Playing a role in a family is not intrinsically wrong. People play roles in functional families as well. The problem with dysfunctional family roles is that they are not freely chosen. Bradshaw explains this difference.

The roles in dysfunctional family systems are different. They are not chosen or flexible. They are necessitated by the covert or overt needs of the family as a system. They function to keep the family system in balance. If Dad is a workaholic and never home, one of the children will be Mom's Emotional Spouse since the system needs a marriage for balance.

In an alcoholic family one child will be a Hero because

the family system needs some dignity. If the family system has no warmth, one child will become the emotional Caretaker and be warm and loving to everyone. If the system is ravaged with unexpressed anger and pain, one child will become the Scapegoat and act out all the anger and pain. In every case the person playing the role gives up his own unique selfhood.

In dysfunctional families, the individual exists to keep the system in balance. This is the fate of every individual in a dysfunctional family. The whole family is dis-eased and each person gives up his true self to play a role in keeping the family together. Every single person becomes a co-dependent. Each person lives in reaction to the distress coming from chemical abuse, incest, violence, work addiction, eating disorders, the parents' rage or sickness, or whatever the compulsivity is.[13]

The problem with dysfunctional family roles is that they are not freely chosen.

The debilitating result of dysfunctional family roles is that family members lose (or simply fail to develop) their true identity. Everyone has adopted a "false self." The roles they play are not their genuine identities. These false selves obscure their true personalities. They often wonder, "Who am *I* really? What do *I* really like? What do *I* want to do?"

Betty: case number two. Betty got up from the dinner table. She was pleased that everyone had enjoyed the meal, especially since she got a late start on the soufflé. Somewhat tired from her part-time job at the local bank, she decided to ask her eleven-year-old daughter Mary to help with the dinner dishes.

"No way! You always ask me! Besides, you didn't let me rent the movie I wanted!" Mary stomped down the hall to her room and slammed the door. Betty rushed down the hall after

Mary. Bursting into Mary's room without knocking, she exclaimed, "Mary, please! Control yourself! You know how it disturbs your father when you blow up like that!"

Smoldering, Mary muttered something under her breath. Her mother continued, "Mary, I'm sorry that you are upset, but you know how your father gets this time of night. Besides, I need your help in the kitchen. We've got to keep things peaceful around here. If we'd all pitch in, he wouldn't drink so much."

"I'm not doing any stupid dishes! Get Billy to help you. He never does anything!" Mary knew her mother never asked her seventeen-year-old brother to help.

"Okay, okay. Just don't upset your father. Maybe you should go to Sally's house to do your homework. I don't think he's in a very good mood."

Betty left the room frustrated that she would get no help, but relieved that Mary would not be home to make her husband angry. Mary, for her part, felt good that she had wormed her way out of doing the dishes. She loved the powerful feeling she got from manipulating her mother so effectively.

Betty: case number three. The odor of burned soufflé lingered in the air. Betty walked carefully down the hall. The three highballs made her a little unsteady. Barging into Mary's room, she yelled, "You better get your @#*! in that kitchen right now or you're grounded for the rest of the month!"

"Why can't you ask Billy to help?" Mary whined. "He never does anything!"

"He's busy with his school work. You know how important it is for him to make his grades. He's in line for a scholarship, you know. Besides, you're the girl. You should do the dishes!"

"Ashley's mother doesn't make her help with the dishes! Why should I?"

Mary had pushed Betty's hot button. "You ungrateful little brat! You do nothing but cause trouble! The sooner you grow up and get out of here, the better!" Her mother slapped Mary across the face. "Don't you dare compare me to your friends' mothers! And don't you argue with me again!" she raged. "You better do those dishes or you are going to get worse than a little slap in the face!"

As Betty stormed out of the room, Mary began to sob, wishing she could somehow run away. She knew her mother would not remember hitting her. She went into the kitchen and began washing dishes. No one came to comfort her.

WHERE DO WE GO FROM HERE?

The impact of dysfunctional parents on their children is tragic. While dysfunctional families meet far fewer God-given needs, they also seldom resolve the anger or heal the hurt of those unmet needs. We must also keep in mind that the problems of dysfunction will be passed on to subsequent generations. In their book *Kids Who Carry Our Pain*, Dr. Robert Hemfelt and Dr. Paul Warren equate dysfunction and codependency. They write, "The tragic fact about codependency is this: Unless dealt with, the problem transmits itself from generation to generation, causing misery from father to son to son, down the line."[14]

If we won't seek recovery for ourselves, let's pursue it for the sake of our children and grandchildren! In the next chapter, we will propose just such a recovery process.

CHAPTER 11

Entry into Family Recovery: Steps One through Three

T ODAY'S FAMILY IS A battered institution, assailed by pressures from within and without. It strains under the load of each member's pressing individual needs. The proliferation of such recovery groups as Alcoholics Anonymous, Overeaters Anonymous, and Adult Children of Alcoholics speaks forcefully of these pressures. Dysfunctional family interactions only intensify them.

We offer the following steps to family recovery in the hope that readers will be able to use them to overcome the devastating effects of chronic unmet needs. Regardless of the reason for any specific family's dysfunction, working these steps can help bring hope and healing.

Our model is adapted from the Twelve Steps of Alcoholics Anonymous, to which many recovery programs owe a significant debt. Millions of people have overcome debilitating addictions and compulsive behaviors through various adaptations of the Twelve Steps. We are grateful to those who have blazed the trail before us.

In addition to providing hope and healing for our lives now, we believe that recovery also provides an opportunity to explore issues of eternal importance. In fact, if recovery is pursued for this life only, it will be superficial, self-centered, and incomplete. A spiritual core is essential for genuine recovery. We not only need reconciliation with ourselves and other people, we also need reconciliation with God. May those who work these steps for family recovery experience the freedom and joy of a vital relationship with God—the ultimate source of hope and healing!

Regardless of the reason for any specific family's dysfunction, working these steps can bring hope and healing.

The Twelve Steps to Family Recovery*

1. We admitted that we were powerless over our family dysfunction and its effects—that our lives had become unmanageable.
2. Came to believe that a Power greater than ourselves could restore us to sanity.
3. Made a decision to turn our will and our lives over to the care of God.
4. Made a searching and fearless moral inventory of ourselves.
5. Admitted to ourselves, to God, and to another human being the exact nature of our wrongs and of the effects of others' wrongs upon us.
6. Became ready to have God remove these defects of character, and to forgive others for their defects of character.
7. Humbly asked him to remove our defects of character, and forgave those who had offended us.
8. Made a list of all persons we had harmed and became willing to make amends to them all.
9. Made direct amends to such people wherever possible, except when to do so would injure them or others.

10. Continued to take personal inventory; when we were wrong, we promptly admitted it; when we were wronged, we promptly forgave the offender.
11. Sought through prayer and meditation to improve our conscious contact with God, praying only for knowledge of his will and for the power to live lives pleasing to him.
12. Having had a spiritual awakening as a result of these steps, tried to carry this message to others and to practice these principles in all our affairs.

The Twelve Steps have been called "twelve blows at the roots" of our problems. If that is so, then Steps One, Two, and Three must be considered blows at the "roots of the roots." Working these steps gets us started in family recovery. They force us to deal with such fundamental issues as:

- Do I really have a problem?
- Can I deal with it by myself, or do I need outside help?
- If I cannot deal with it myself, who can? And will I be willing to let them help me?

Answering these questions is foundational to any effort at recovery. Let's take a closer look now at the first three steps.

---

* "The Twelve Steps to Family Recovery" has been adapted from "The Twelve Steps of Alcoholics Anonymous":

1. We admitted we were powerless over alcohol—that our lives had become unmanageable. 2. Came to believe that a Power greater than ourselves could restore us to sanity. 3. Made a decision to turn our lives over to the care of God *as we understood Him.* 4. Made a searching and fearless moral inventory of ourselves. 5. Admitted to God, to ourselves, and to another human being the exact nature of our wrongs. 6. Were entirely ready to have God remove all these defects of character. 7. Humbly asked Him to remove our shortcomings. 8. Made a list of all persons we had harmed, and became willing to make amends to them all. 9. Made direct amends to such people whenever possible, except when to do so would injure them or others. 10. Continued to take personal inventory and when we were wrong promptly admitted it. 11. Sought through prayer and meditation to improve our conscious contact with God, *as we understood Him,* praying only for knowledge of His will for us and the power to carry that out. 12. Having had a spiritual awakening as the result of these steps, we tried to carry this message to alcoholics, and to practice these principles in all our affairs.

The Twelve Steps are adapted and reprinted with permission of Alcoholics Anonymous World Services, Inc. Permission to reprint and adapt the Twelve Steps does not mean that A.A. has reviewed or approved the contents of this publication nor that A.A. agrees with the views expressed herein. A.A. is a program of recovery from alcoholism—use of the Twelve Steps in connection with programs and activities which are patterned after A.A., but which address other problems, does not imply otherwise.

OUT OF CONTROL

1. We admitted that we were powerless over our family dysfunction and its effects—that our lives had become unmanageable. If you have read to this point, it is probably because you feel that something in your life is not quite what you would like. You may believe that your family of origin was dysfunctional. You may have begun to see that you have been affected by unmet needs and unhealed hurts in your own life. Perhaps you are seeing unmet needs and unresolved pain in the lives of your spouse and children as well.

You would like your family to be an environment where legitimate needs are consistently met and where imperfection is forgiven. You want family members to have the courage to honestly face problems as they occur instead of ignoring them. You want your family to contribute to the maturity of every member instead of using members in false roles to maintain the appearance of family stability. More than anything, you want your family to be different from what you experienced growing up. But how do you proceed from this point?

The biggest obstacle to recovery is *denial*—the unwillingness to admit our need for recovery. Step One requires us to squarely face our need for help. To whatever extent we are denying our difficulties, our recovery will be hindered.

Are you in denial? There are several common forms of denial. Honestly evaluate how well the following descriptions fit you.[1]

- *Simple Denial:* pretending that something does not exist when it really does (e.g., discounting physical symptoms that may indicate the presence of problems).
- *Minimizing:* being willing to acknowledge a problem, but unwilling to see its severity (e.g., admitting to estrangement in a relationship when in fact there is overt infidelity).

- *Blaming:* blaming someone else for causing the problem; the behavior is not denied, but its cause is someone else's fault (e.g., blaming your parents for your current inappropriate behavior).
- *Excusing:* offering excuses, alibis, justifications, and other explanations for our own or others' behavior (e.g., calling in sick for a partner when the actual cause of the absence is drunkenness).
- *Generalizing:* dealing with problems on a general level, but avoiding personal and emotional awareness of the situation or conditions (e.g., sympathizing with a friend's flu when you know chemical dependency is the underlying cause of the problem).
- *Dodging:* changing the subject to avoid threatening topics (e.g., becoming adept at "small talk").
- *Attacking:* becoming angry and irritable when reference is made to existing conditions, thus avoiding the issue (e.g., being unwilling to share your feelings).

The more we were hurt in the past, the more we will tend to deny present difficulties to avoid further hurt. Unfortunately, this denial prevents us from dealing with our current problems, making it more likely that they will get worse. Thus we will be hurt even more. That's why our recovery begins when we stop denying our problems.

Our recovery begins when we stop denying our problems.

WHAT CONTROLS US?

Once we become willing to admit that our family dysfunction has affected us, we are ready to consider whether we have the power to overcome these effects. Step One suggests that in fact we do not have the ability to overcome the effects of our family of origin on our own.

What does it mean to be *powerless?* To admit that we are powerless is to admit that we are in bondage—that much of what we do, think, or feel is not freely done, thought, or felt. Rather, we have become a slave to specific effects of our family dysfunction.

We may experience being enslaved to dysfunctional family *rules.* It is essential to see the extent to which we still operate by the survival rules of "don't talk, don't feel, don't trust." Our adherence to these rules presents a major barrier to intimate relationships, yet we still feel compelled to obey them. We can't seem to break free.

Remember Mark? He found it very difficult to share his feelings with any depth, especially with his wife. He seemed unable to rescind his conscious choice of the "don't feel" rule toward his stepfather. The past obedience to the rule carried over to the present—to all his feelings and other relationships. Mark was in bondage to the "don't feel" rule.

Or we may experience slavery to dysfunctional family *roles.* Not only do we follow old rules, we may also continue to play the roles we had in our family: Hero, Enabler, Mascot, Lost Child, Scapegoat, or some combination. If we have changed roles, it is likely only because another family member has changed roles, creating an imbalance in the family system that must be rectified.

This slavery to unhealthy roles was illustrated in one family in this way. The middle daughter played the family Scapegoat role for several years through various forms of rebellion. Finally, she decided to stop defying her parents because she felt guilty for causing them so much grief.

Thus the former Scapegoat now became the family Hero. Her change created the need to find someone else to blame for the family's problems. The youngest of the three daughters, who had previously played the Lost Child role, abruptly became the Scapegoat by trying to commit suicide on three separate occasions over a period of eighteen months.

Powerlessness leads to lack of control in some area of our

lives. Negative emotions, addictive behaviors, and faulty thinking can all control us, contributing to unmanageability of our lives.

Negative emotions may control us. Perhaps the accumulation of negative emotions from long-term unmet needs are in control.[2] The following stories may serve as helpful examples:

Anger may be in control. LuAnn's hostility simmered just beneath the surface as she entered Sharon's office. She explained that she had come at the urging of her brother, who was very concerned about her emotional and spiritual health. This intelligent, capable woman admitted that she was livid with her father, that he had done something that she just could not forgive. Her constant criticism of him resulted in other family members avoiding her.

What had he done that was so terrible? LuAnn's father had remarried two years after the death of her mother. She could not let go of this perceived betrayal. She resisted all encouragement not to hold this offense against her dad. Her anger remained in control, poisoning many of her other relationships as well.

Fear may be in control. Martha's mother had emotionally abused her throughout her life. Her mother always found fault with her efforts, no matter how good they were. So Martha came into her marriage fearful that she would never feel loved. She determined that her husband needed to prove that he loved her.

Predictably, Martha's husband fell short of perfection. She increasingly felt unloved. So she began to treat him the way her mother treated her growing up. Martha always found something to criticize with his efforts. She was never pleased, always hoping that her criticism would control him, making him try harder.

One evening in a marital group session, her husband expressed that he wanted her to tell him that she loved him. Martha admitted that she had never said "I love you" to him. Upon further probing, she tearfully admitted that she was afraid to say that to him. Why? "Because I'm afraid that if I tell him that I love him, he'll quit trying to make me feel loved!" Her fear controlled her and led to her efforts to control her husband.

We may believe that we will never be okay,
that we will never "measure up."
Thus we may become depressed and chronically discouraged.

Other negative emotions may control us. If shame, condemnation, or false guilt are in control, we may chronically feel we are no good and thus unworthy of anything good in our own lives. If hopelessness controls us, we may believe that we will never be okay, that we will never "measure up." Thus we may become depressed and chronically discouraged.

If any of these negative emotions are in control, we may also manifest physical symptoms of emotional turmoil—such as sleep or appetite disturbance, loss of energy, inability to concentrate, or intestinal disorders.

Addictive behaviors may control us. As we have seen, dysfunctional families meet few individual needs. When our needs are not met, we seek something to help us cope with the hurt. We may try to escape the pain through work, drugs and alcohol, sex, religious activity, eating, gambling—almost anything that salves the wound or distracts us from it for a few precious moments.

These behaviors do not just reduce or distract from the pain. They also produce pleasurable feelings—stimulation, excitement, tranquility, or release.[3] Unfortunately, if we practice the escapist behavior long enough, we become enslaved to it: "When you offer yourselves to someone to obey him as slaves you are slaves to the one whom you obey" (Rom 6:16).

No one wants to admit that something they are doing is harming or destroying their own lives or the lives of others. Yet if we are in bondage to addictive or compulsive behaviors, Step One requires that we face the truth and admit these behaviors before we can proceed any further in our recovery.

Some of us may think, "My behavior is not good, but I can stop any time I want." Possibly we have stopped—many times! But can we *stay* stopped? If not, at least that part of our life has become something we cannot manage. In Step One we come to the point of admitting this truth.

The core issue with addiction is: *Who or what is in control?* God is the only one who has the right to control us. He also gives us the ability to have self-control. If we often find that neither God nor we are in control, we need to consider addictions as contributing factors to our unmanageable lives.

The apostle Paul described his own struggle in strikingly appropriate terms: "I do not understand what I do. For what I want to do I do not do, but what I hate I do.... For I have the desire to do what is good, but I cannot carry it out" (Rom 7:15,16,18). Do you identify with his experience?

Faulty thinking patterns can control us. Much of how we feel is triggered not by what happens to us, but by what we *think* about what happens to us. Proverbs says, "As a man thinks within himself, so is he." If the ideas and concepts that influence us conform to reality, both our feelings and our behavior will tend to reflect reality as well. However, if our belief system is not consistent with what is true, then our feelings and behavior will not reflect reality.

Dysfunctional families tend to breed false patterns of thinking. The three rules for surviving the dysfunctional family ("don't talk, don't feel, and don't trust") are good examples of a false belief system: "If I obey these three rules, I will be protected from hurt." Unfortunately, the truth is that obedience to these rules will inflict even more pain on ourselves and others by isolating us from all intimate relationships.

Dr. Chris Thurman has defined several other faulty beliefs which can control us.[4] To the extent we believe these ideas, they *do* control us. Some of the most common lies we believe are:

- I must be perfect in order to be acceptable.
- I must have everyone's love and approval.
- I can't be happy unless things go my way.
- I am only as good as what I accomplish.
- Life should be easy.
- Life should be fair.

Belief in such false ideas begins in childhood. When significant adults frequently criticize children, many will incorporate impossibly high standards for performance. Even though consistent perfection is impossible, much effort is expended to try to be perfect.

RESULTS OF UNMANAGEABILITY

We pay a high price for out-of-control, unmanageable living. It costs us physically, emotionally, and spiritually.

Increased risk of health problems. Whether we live in bondage to unhealthy rules and roles, or whether negative emotions, addictive behaviors, or faulty thinking control us, our bodies may be seriously affected. We have greater likelihood of actual health problems. Worse, we are less likely to do anything positive about these health risks.

Loss of self-respect. Enslavement to addictive behaviors produces dishonesty. We have to lie in order to cover up our behavior and its effects. As we live a lie day in and day out, we slowly but surely lose our self-respect. Not only do we not trust anyone, we know we can't be trusted. We have become the very kind of person who so deeply hurt us as children.

Shame. What is shame? How is it different from guilt? Dr. Charles Whitfield defines shame this way:

> Shame is the uncomfortable or painful feeling that we experience when we realize that a part of us is defective, bad, incomplete, rotten, phoney, inadequate, or a failure. In contrast to guilt, where we feel bad from *doing* something wrong, we feel shame from *being* something wrong or bad. Thus, guilt seems to be correctable or forgivable, whereas there seems to be no way out of shame.[5]

As we live out the effects of our dysfunctional families, we confirm what we learned growing up—we really are bad, rotten, and no good. We no longer simply feel ashamed. We now experience shame as an identity.

Alienation from God. As we previously stated, God is the only one who has a right to control us. If dysfunctional rules, roles, emotions, addictions, or faulty thinking are in control of us, we are alienated from him. He will not seem near to us. We will experience a spiritual void and will not know how to overcome it.

STEP ONE: TAKING ACTION

To recover from the effects of our dysfunctional families, we must give up denial and face reality. We must be willing to admit that our own lives are out of our control. Our own family is threatened because of the unmanageability of our lives. Completing Step One requires us to honestly face two insidiously destructive results of a dysfunctional family: bondage to unhealthy rules and roles, and being controlled by negative emotions, addictive behaviors, and faulty thinking.

More importantly, we admit that on our own, we have not been able to do anything about these problems. As painful as it may be to admit all this, as much of a blow to our pride and self-sufficiency as this admission is, we must come to the place of honestly acknowledging this truth. This honesty is the beginning of the "truth setting us free" (Jn 8:32).

Does your situation seem hopeless? How could anyone ever overcome all these problems? That's it! You've got it! In Step One, we admit that on our own, *we can't*. We need help from something or someone outside of, and greater than ourselves. Step Two invites us to address this critical need. Here are some specific questions to help you take action on Step One:

1. Look again at the forms of denial on pages 208-209. Which of these describe you?
2. To what extent did you follow dysfunctional family rules growing up? To what extent do you follow them now? How are these rules affecting your family life?
3. What role(s) did you play in your family growing up? Are you still playing that role? Does it truly fit you? Are you encouraging your spouse and children to be themselves, or are you requiring them to play roles for the "good of the family"?
4. Are you sometimes controlled by particular negative emotions? Are expressions of anger or fear common for you?
5. Are there any destructive behaviors in your life that sometimes seem to "take over"?
6. Do you find yourself believing any of the common lies listed above? How does belief in these lies affect you? Your family?
7. How successful have you been in overcoming the bondage to rules and roles? To what extent have you overcome the control of emotions, addictions, or false thinking? Are there times when you have wanted to do good (or not do bad) but you were not able?

A HIGHER POWER

2. Came to believe that a Power greater than ourselves could restore us to sanity. In Step One, we came face to face with the fact that we have some real problems that we are not overcoming. And we decided to admit that our own resources are insufficient to solve these problems.

In Step Two, we acknowledge our need for resources beyond ourselves to enable us to overcome the effects of family dysfunction. We go beyond the material world of what we can see, touch, taste, smell, and feel to the world of spiritual reality. Specifically, we come to believe in something or Someone greater than ourselves. And we confront our hopelessness by coming to believe that this Being greater than ourselves can enable us to recover from the deficits of our dysfunctional background.

Not how, but *whom*. The first critical issue in this step is not how strongly we believe. Rather, it is in what or whom we believe. Our faith is only as solid as whatever it is that we have faith in. We may have sincerely strong faith, but be putting that faith in the wrong thing. Many of us put our faith in certain people. We are then greatly disappointed when these people fail us. The strength of our faith is not what matters. Rather, the object of our faith is what counts.

The critical issue is not how strongly we believe. Rather, it is what or whom we believe in.

People with all kinds of beliefs about God realize that they are trapped by an addiction or some other problem and cannot manage their lives. Step Two invites people to be willing to believe—to have some sense of openness to a Power greater than themselves.[6] Some come to believe the Higher Power is within themselves; thus, recovery becomes the process of unleashing their own innate ability to self-heal. For others, a twelve step group becomes their Higher Power. In many twelve step programs, "whatever works" is considered acceptable.

The authors of this book wish to invite our readers to believe in God by name.[7] Be willing to believe in God as he is revealed in his Word, the Bible. We have seen God transform many lives, including our own. His love is infinite, for he *is* love. If you are open to God, you will find him, for he will find you. He promises, "Ask and it will be given to you; seek and you will find; knock and the door will be opened to you. For everyone who asks, receives; he who seeks, finds; and to him who knocks, the door will be opened" (Mt 7:7-8).

Restored to sanity. Step Two invites us not just to believe in a Higher Power, but also that our Higher Power can do something very important for us. We are invited to believe that our Higher Power can restore us to sanity. We define sanity as the ability to face reality honestly, yet relatively free from anxiety. Sane people are characterized by essentially sound thinking and sound behavior.

What do we mean by "sound thinking"? Sound thinking is reasoning according to truth instead of lies. Recall our discussion of "Faulty Thinking," particularly some of the common lies people believe (page 213). Sound thinking enables us to manage our feelings appropriately, rather than letting our feelings control us. Sound thinking is also important because it provides the basis for sound behavior, rather than self-defeating behaviors.[8]

STEP TWO: TAKING ACTION

In Step One, we admit that we cannot overcome the effects of our family dysfunction on our own. In Step Two, we come to believe that there is a Higher Power who can overcome these destructive effects in us. We come to believe that he can do something for us that we cannot do for ourselves: restore us to sound thinking and behavior.

The following questions will help you take action with Step Two:

1. Do you believe in a Higher Power who can restore you to sound thinking and behavior? Do you believe he can enable you to honestly face life relatively free from anxiety? If not, what would it take for you to believe in a Higher Power?

2. Sam Shoemaker, the person credited with the spiritual ideas embodied in the Twelve Steps of Alcoholics Anonymous, often challenged people who did not believe in God to a thirty day experiment: "Just pray every day for thirty days that God will meet you at the point of your greatest need, and see what happens to you."[9] We invite you to do the same. Pray something like this: "God, my greatest need is (name it). If you are really there, please meet me here at this point of my need." Pray this every day for thirty days, and see what happens!

3. Investigate more about who God is. Here are some resources that can help you: *Basic Christianity* by John R.W. Stott; *Mere Christianity* by C.S. Lewis; *Evidence That Demands a Verdict* by Josh McDowell; and *More Than a Carpenter* by Josh McDowell.

SELF-SURRENDER

3. Made a decision to turn our will and our lives over to the care of God. As we complete Step Two, we have hope that someone greater than ourselves can overcome the destructive effects of our dysfunction. However, we may not have decided to allow him to get involved with our recovery. We may not fully understand what such a recovery relationship will involve or how to even have such a relationship.

We may also encounter other obstacles. For example, we may have distorted images of God from our upbringing that make it difficult for us to trust God. We may be confused concerning exactly how to have a relationship with him. Or, we may not understand the implications of new life with God, especially our new identity. Let's examine each of these obstacles.

Obstacle one: distorted images of God. A major obstacle to turning our will and our life over to God may be that we developed a negative understanding of God during our childhood years. According to Dale and Juanita Ryan in their extremely helpful study guide, *Recovery from Distorted Images of God*, "Often our images of God influence us more powerfully than do our ideas or doctrinal statements about God because these images are rooted in powerful emotional experiences."[10]

As long as we hold negative views of God, we will have little desire to entrust ourselves to him. The Ryans go on to identify six common negative images of God and to show how each is rooted in unmet needs in dysfunctional families. These images of God are frequently derived from our view of our parents, particularly our fathers.[11]

These are the six common negative images of God as identified by the Ryans:

1. *The God of Impossible Expectations:* derived from parents who did not meet our needs for unconditional acceptance and approval.
2. *The Emotionally Distant God:* derived from parents who did not meet our need for emotional nurture and comfort.
3. *The Disinterested God:* derived from parents who did not meet our need for attention, understanding, communication, and guidance.
4. *The Abusive God:* derived from parents who verbally, physically, or sexually abused us instead of meeting our needs for affection, discipline, and protection.
5. *The Unreliable God:* derived from parents who fail to consistently keep promises, thus not meeting our need for structure.
6. *The God Who Abandons:* derived when one or both parents are unavailable to us and thus cannot meet most of our needs.

We cannot state too strongly that each of these six images of God are false and distorted. They are all directly refuted by biblical truth. If we replace these false images with true images, we will desire to do exactly what Step Three invites us to do. So what is God really like? Here are six true images of God as revealed in the Bible:

1. *Accepting:* "The Lord is compassionate and gracious, slow to anger, abounding in love" (Ps 103:8); "Therefore, there is now no condemnation for those who are in Christ Jesus" (Rom 8:1).

2. *Emotionally close:* Speaking of Jesus, Paul writes to the Hebrews, "For since he has now been through suffering and temptation, he knows what it is like when we suffer and are tempted, and he is wonderfully able to help us" (Heb 2:18, LB); "This High Priest of ours understands our weaknesses, since he had the same temptations we do" (Heb 4:15, LB).

3. *Intensely interested:* As the psalmist writes,
"O Lord, you have searched me and you know me.
You know when I sit and when I rise;
you perceive my thoughts from afar.
You discern my going out and my lying down;
you are familiar with all my ways.
Before a word is on my tongue
you know it completely, O Lord." (Ps 139:1-4)

4. *Caring and giving:* "If God is for us, who can be against us? He who did not spare his own Son, but gave him up for us all—how will he not also, along with him, graciously give us all things?" (Rom 8:31-32).

5. *Reliable:* "The Lord is faithful to all his promises and loving toward all he has made" (Ps 145:13); "Because of the Lord's great love we are not consumed, for his compassions never fail. They are new every morning; great is your faithfulness" (Lam 3:22-23); "But the Lord is faithful, and he will strengthen and protect you from the evil one" (2 Thes 3:3).

6. *Constantly with us:* God promises his people, "Never will I leave you; never will I forsake you" (Heb 13:5); Jesus said, "Surely I will be with you always, to the very end of the age" (Mt 28:20); "No one can snatch them out of my hand" (Jn 10:28).

As these true images of God replace the old distorted images, we begin to desire to "turn our will and lives over to the care of God."

Obstacle two: uncertainty regarding our relationship with God. Paschal once said, "There is a God-shaped vacuum in every man, waiting to be filled." Augustine said it this way: "Thou hast made us for thyself, O God, and the heart of man is restless until it finds its rest in thee."

Before we proceed any further, how certain are you of your relationship with God and your life with him after physical death? On a scale of zero to one hundred percent, how sure are you that you will spend eternity with God after you die? If you have anything less than absolute certainty, please turn now to Appendix B, "How to Be Certain of Your Eternal Relationship with God."

If you did say you were one hundred percent sure, on what basis do you have this certainty? Check any that apply:

__ Church membership or attendance
__ Parents were Christians
__ My good deeds outweigh my bad deeds
__ I was baptized as an infant
__ Something else that I do or provide

Did you check any of the above? If so, your certainty of eternal life depends on something *you* do. The problem with our eternal life depending on us is this: how can we know for sure that we have done everything well enough? We could be deceived into thinking we have eternal life when in fact we don't!

Rather than our relationship with God depending on anything we do, the Scriptures say that God is the one who took the initiative to provide for us what we could not provide: "But when the kindness and love of God our Savior appeared, he saved us, not because of righteous things we had done, but because of his mercy" (Ti 3:4-5). Also, "For it is by grace you have been saved, through faith—and this not from yourselves, it is the gift of God—not by works, so that no one can boast" (Eph 2:8-9). God is the one who provides what we need through Jesus Christ.

Obstacle three: a distorted view of ourselves. One of the debilitating effects of a dysfunctional family is the assault on each member's personal identity. Because dysfunctional parents are seldom pleased with anyone's behavior, children try to perform to get their God-given needs for affirmation, approval, and acceptance met.

Who we are inevitably becomes linked with what we are able to do—a performance-based system of establishing value and worth. Inevitably, when we don't measure up to standards, we internalize a sense of shame about ourselves. (See our previous discussion of shame, page 215).

Our identity is not based upon anything that we have or have not accomplished. Instead, it is determined by what God has done on our behalf.

But our identity is *not* based upon anything that we have or have not accomplished. Instead, it is determined by what God has done on our behalf. What does God say about our true identity? Each of us is not the great "I Am" (Ex 3:14; Jn 8:24, 28, 58), "But by the grace of God I am what I am" (1 Cor 15:10).

Dr. Neil T. Anderson has compiled a list of statements God makes about his children—those who have received his gift of salvation through believing in Jesus.[12] Read through this list right now to discover who you really are!

- I am the salt of the earth (Mt 5:13).
- I am a son or daughter of God because he is my spiritual father (Rom 8:14-15; Gal 3:26, 4:6.)
- I am a temple of God. His Spirit dwells in me (1 Cor 3:16, 6:19).
- I am a new creation or a new person (2 Cor 5:17).
- Since I am his child, I am an heir of God (Gal 4:6-7).
- I am God's workmanship, born anew in Christ to do his work that he planned beforehand that I should do (Eph 2:10).
- I am righteous and holy (Eph 4:24).
- I am chosen and dearly loved by God (1 Thes 1:4).
- I am a child of light and not of darkness (1 Thes 5:5).
- I am a holy brother or sister, partaker of a heavenly calling (Heb 3:1).
- I am an alien and stranger to this world where I temporarily live (1 Pt 2:11).
- I am born of God and the evil one cannot touch me (1 Jn 5:18).

Once we see our true identity, we have the ability to truly feel loved and accepted by God. Combined with our accurate image of him and our certainty of a relationship with him, we can find ourselves highly motivated to completely surrender to him, entrusting our recovery and necessary changes in our lives to him.

Brennan Manning beautifully expresses this concept:

The only lasting freedom from self-consciousness comes from a profound awareness that God loves me as I am and not as I should be, that he loves me beyond worthiness and unworthiness, beyond fidelity and infidelity; that he loves me in the morning sun and the evening rain without caution, regret, boundary, limit, or breaking point; that no mat-

ter what I do, he can't stop loving me. When I am in conscious communion with the reality of the wild, passionate,
relentless, stubborn, pursuing, tender love of God in Jesus
Christ for *me*, then it's not that I have to or I got to or I must
or I should or I ought; suddenly, I *want* to change because I
know how deeply I'm loved.[13]

KEYS TO RECOVERY

Freedom from fear of rejection. Rejection by fellow human
beings is a fact of life. We are simply not going to be accepted
by some people. However, any of us who grew up in a dysfunctional family frequently experienced the hurt of rejection
from the most significant people in our lives: our parents. We
thus become afraid of rejection and will do almost anything to
avoid that particular hurt, trying our best to please others and
make them happy.

Our complete, unconditional acceptance by God—as indicated by his work in giving us our new identity—speaks directly
to this fear of rejection. We are reassured that God will never
reject us, no matter what we do! He loves us infinitely and perfectly, simply because we belong to him, because we are his
children. There is nothing we can do to cause him to love us
any more than he already does, and there is nothing we can do
to cause him to love us any less than he already does.

Certainly, human rejection still hurts and disappoints us,
but it no longer has to crush or control us. We are free to say
with the apostle Paul, "If God is for us, who can be against us?"
(Rom 8:31). Our awareness of God's perfect love truly "drives
out" our fear (1 Jn 4:18). If we believe what God tells us about
who we really are, we will have little or no doubt that he really
loves us!

Freedom to give up dysfunctional rules of relating. Remember those rules, "Don't talk! Don't feel! Don't trust!"
When we are secure in who we are, we are free to share our-

selves with other people, to be vulnerable about our needs, struggles, and joys. We are free to enter into intimate relationships without being so worried about rejection. We are no longer so concerned about impressing others and have little need to put up facades. We are free to say what we mean.

Since we are secure in our true identity, we are also free to acknowledge our feelings. Recognizing that emotions are God-given, we can allow ourselves to *feel* as part of letting ourselves be human. Beginning to talk and feel provides the foundation for the beginning of trust in our human relationships.

We are not trusting that people will never hurt us or let us down. Instead, we trust that we can be close with others, knowing that when they do let us down, we will not be devastated. We are secure in who we are, rather than finding our security in other people's treatment of us. We also begin to accept our own imperfection, not worrying about how others will respond to our weaknesses.

Freedom from dysfunctional roles. We previously pointed out the various roles that members of dysfunctional families play for survival. Knowing who we really are because of our relationship with God releases us from those false identities. We are truly free to be ourselves. We no longer need to play roles to please others or protect ourselves. We strive to please God, and we are free to let God become our primary protector.

STEP THREE: TAKING ACTION

A concise way to understand the first three steps in sequence is:

- Step One: We admit, "We can't."
- Step Two: We come to believe, "God can."
- Step Three: We decide, "We'll let God do it."[14]

The step of entrusting ourselves to God through Jesus Christ is the spiritual breakthrough of recovery. It requires each person to honestly confront a powerful component of dysfunctionality: the belief that we cannot trust anyone. We directly confront our fear of trusting by deciding to trust God. We also confront and dismantle our shame by deciding to embrace God's view of ourselves in relationship to him. We see that as his beloved children, we truly are "shame-less" before him.

By deciding to entrust ourselves to God, we lay the foundation for the next steps, where we take an honest, thorough look at ourselves. We have become willing to honestly examine ourselves, because we have the internalized personal security that we never had in our dysfunctional families. We are now able to truly believe that we are completely unconditionally loved and accepted. The following questions will help you take action with Step Three:

1. Do you hold any of the six distorted images of God? If you have identified any of the six, we urge you to obtain and work through the study guide, *Recovery from Distorted Images of God,* by Dale and Juanita Ryan, as part of your third step work. If you can do this as part of a group, you will profit even more.
2. Find out more about Jesus in an individual or group Bible study. Go to your local Christian bookstore and get a study guide for this purpose. Two good ones are *One To One* and *Meeting Jesus,* both from InterVarsity Press.
3. Attend church this Sunday. You will probably encounter various styles of worship and music. Keep visiting until you find one that fits your preferences.

CHAPTER 12

Action Steps for Family Recovery: Steps Four through Nine

Effectively working the first three steps brings us to the point of admitting that we need recovery and of entrusting ourselves and our recovery to God. Now we are ready to take a long, hard look at ourselves—our character, our behavior, and our pain.

The next six steps invite us to tackle some tough issues:

- What is the truth about myself? What am I really like?
- How do I deal with my own pain? How do I deal with pain I've caused in others?
- How can I become the person I want to be?

EXAMINING OURSELVES

4. Made a searching and fearless moral inventory of ourselves. Because we are becoming secure in God's love and in our relationship with him, we are free to take an honest look at ourselves. This inventory is *searching*—we intend to thoroughly explore every dimension of our lives, especially our relationships with other people and God. To do this, we will confront a common tendency to ignore or minimize difficult or painful realities. Our recovery depends on our willingness to be honest.

This inventory is also *fearless*—we are willing to look at some painful and uncomfortable areas of our lives without fear, or at least with our fear under appropriate control. What might we be afraid of? We may fear that our shame will be reawakened, that we might begin to believe again that we are fundamentally bad. We may fear feeling guilty as we look at what we've done wrong. We may fear the discomfort of dealing with people we have hurt or failed.

Our recovery depends on our willingness to be honest.

Here, we must remember to complete each step before moving on to subsequent steps. Dealing with those we have offended is a difficult step, but it is not *this* step. It is a future step. "One step at a time!" should be our watchword.

We may also have fears related to considering what others have done to us. We may especially fear the possibility of tapping into our own hurt. We may fear experiencing in the present the hurt that we experienced in the past. No one wants to feel again the deep hurt we experienced in our dysfunctional families. But we must remember that our wounds will not be healed until they are honestly faced. The poison trapped inside must be released.

Taking stock. As the founders of A.A. point out, "A business which takes no regular inventory usually goes broke. Taking a commercial inventory is a fact-facing process. It is an effort to discover the truth about the stock-in-trade."[1] We seek to do the same with our very lives.

In making this inventory, we will specifically seek to identify how we have hurt or offended others, including other people and God. We will also seek to identify how we ourselves have been hurt or offended. How do we go about this? We suggest that you begin with *whom,* and then consider *how.*

Identifying whom we have wronged and who has wronged us. First, in writing, list all your significant relationships. Put the person's name down and leave a few lines of space between each name. Your list might include your father, mother, siblings, spouse, each of your children, specific friends, neighbors, work associates, authority figures—even God. This list identifies those we could have wronged and those who could have wronged us.

Identifying how we have wronged others. Then, pray this prayer from Psalm 139:23-24: "Search me, O God, and know my heart; test me and know my anxious thoughts. See if there is any offensive way in me, and lead me in the way everlasting." Ask God to specifically reveal to you any way that you have wronged any of the people on this list.

Seven deadly sins. Consider this list of the "Seven Deadly Sins" and how you may have committed them in your key relationships.[2]

- *Pride:* inordinate conceit; disdainful behavior or treatment of others; thinking yourself better than others; trying to impress others; pre-occupation with self; self-absorption; independence from God and others; thinking you are smarter, better looking, more talented than others.
- *Greed:* selfishness; materialism; excessive acquisitiveness; valuing things more than people; discontentment.
- *Lust:* indulgence in inappropriate sexual activity; seeking to be sexually stimulated; using others to meet your own sexual needs.
- *Dishonesty:* lying, defrauding, deceiving; justifying behaviors by lying.
- *Gluttony:* covetousness; eating or drinking beyond our genuine needs; overindulgence in anything.
- *Envy:* jealousy; painful or resentful longing for an advantage or benefit enjoyed by another; desire to bring someone else down to your level; inability to "rejoice with those who rejoice."

- *Laziness:* disinclined to activity or exertion; purposeful avoidance or neglect of responsibilities; unwillingness to attend to important matters or put forth necessary effort; low productivity; procrastination.

Dysfunctional tendencies. In addition to these major areas of possible character defects, consider the following common tendencies of people from dysfunctional families which tend to produce hurt in the lives of others, especially close family members.[3]

- *Isolation:* emotional withdrawal; shutting others out; not letting anyone know you; never being vulnerable; not expressing your own needs.
- *Approval-seeking:* people-pleasing; over-sensitivity to criticism; not performing because it is right or appropriate, but in order to look good to others.
- *Care-taking:* making ourselves indispensable: rescuing people; losing our identity; over-responsibility in some relationships to the neglect of others.
- *Controlling:* being overbearing or domineering; being manipulative, judgmental, or rigid; being unwilling to trust anyone else; always having to be "right"; expressing needs or desires in a demanding way.
- *Problems with authority figures:* rebellion against authority; difficulty working within structure; unwillingness to cooperate with others; being intimidated by authorities.
- *Overdeveloped sense of responsibility:* taking life too seriously; having difficulty relaxing or having fun; taking over for others; being rigid; doing too much; being overcommitted.
- *Inappropriate expression of anger:* raging; using verbal abuse, physical abuse, or both; using harsh tone of voice or facial expressions, intending to intimidate others; harsh, vengeful punishment of children instead of loving discipline.
- *Wrong priorities:* neglecting family in favor of other people or activities, such as work, recreation, friends, other family members.

Following dysfunctional family rules. Recall how dysfunctional families follow certain rules, especially "don't talk, don't feel, and don't trust." To what extent have you encouraged your family members to follow these rules?

- *Honest communication:* Are you willing to talk about significant personal issues? Do you encourage your spouse and children to talk honestly as well?
- *Emotional openness:* Are you vulnerable with your feelings? Do you encourage honest expressions of emotions by your spouse and children?
- *Trust:* Are you dependable? Do you consistently keep your promises to your spouse and children?

Encouraging dysfunctional family roles. Recall that dysfunctional families force members into roles which may not fit who they really are. To what extent have you encouraged your family members toward these false roles? For example, have you allowed or subtly encouraged one of your children to become your "surrogate spouse"? (See page 200 to review the concept of dysfunctional family roles.)

Addictive or compulsive behaviors. Evaluate your tendencies toward addictive or compulsive behaviors as described on page 212. Are there any which you are practicing? Look at each of your significant relationships. If so, how have they affected these loved ones?

Faulty thinking. Evaluate your tendencies toward believing lies as described on page 214. Which lies do you tend to believe? How has your belief in these lies affected your significant relationships? Be specific. Write down beside each person's name how you have demonstrated these qualities or committed these sins in your relationship with each one. Now, go back and consider any of these issues which may not be tied to any specific relationship.

By the time you've done all this, you may be feeling pretty bad about yourself. But don't. Remember who you really are.

Remember that the one who is showing you these things about yourself is also the one who absolutely and completely loves and accepts you, even with all your flaws. God is also committed to giving you what you need to rise above them.

You may be experiencing a sense of remorse and regret about what you have done, along with a sincere desire to make it right with others. You are probably feeling a sense of "godly sorrow" which produces "repentance," or appropriate change of mind and heart.

However, you may be experiencing a sense of remorse and regret about what you have done, along with a sincere desire to make it right with others. You are probably feeling a sense of "godly sorrow" which produces "repentance," or appropriate change of mind and heart (see 2 Cor 7:9-11). This repentance is a necessary prerequisite to lasting change of behavior.

STEP FOUR: TAKING ACTION

Once we have admitted our need for recovery (Step One) and have begun to establish a relationship with God as he really is, we can then entrust our recovery and our whole lives to his care (Steps Two and Three). We are then ready to identify just what it is that God would enable us to recover from. Step Four is the beginning of this identification process.

We agree with the traditional twelve step approach of looking at how we have hurt or offended others, paying specific attention to both sinful actions as well as to omissions and character defects which God is bringing to light. But we also believe that it is very important to consider how we have been hurt or offended by others. How others have hurt us is a critical dimension of our personal reality. Thus we include a process which invites us to do just that.

Having considered what God is showing you about yourself, you are now ready to ask God to help you to see what you may have missed and how you may have been hurt. To get in touch with how others have hurt you, whether from your family of origin, current family, or from other sources, complete the following two exercises. (You may be wondering what we will do with these lists. We will use them in Steps Five through Nine. So please be as honest and as thorough as you can now.)

1. Get another sheet of paper and title it, "Hurts from Childhood." Divide it into two columns. At the top of the left column, write: "What I missed growing up." At the top of the right column write, "Feelings I have or had about what I missed." Prayerfully complete both columns in terms of the basic needs we have listed earlier.
2. Another way to approach this issue is to seek to identify toward whom you are harboring resentment. To do this, pray the following prayer: "Lord, please reveal to my mind anyone toward whom I am harboring anger, resentment, or bitterness. Show me whom I need to forgive." As God brings names of people to your mind, write them down.

Completing these exercises is one good way to take action on this step. Completing a fourth step inventory can be a very significant undertaking. For those who wish more detailed help, a number of useful guidebooks are available at your local Christian bookstore.

INTO THE LIGHT

5. Admitted to ourselves, to God, and to another human being the exact nature of our wrongs and of the effects of others' wrongs upon us. In Step Five, we "go public" with the results of our Step Four "searching and fearless moral inventory." As one twelve step writer comments: "Here is a unique opportunity, perhaps for the first time in our lives, to become honest."[4]

Why is this step necessary? Why isn't it enough to just write it all down in our fourth step inventory? Why must we involve God? Why must we involve another person? John Bradshaw helps us at this point: "The admission to self, others, and God in Step Five is a way to come out of hiding. Shame loves secrecy and darkness. To come out into the light is a way to overcome it."[5]

Bradshaw's darkness and light metaphor reflects what God says: "But if we walk in the light as [God] is in the light, we have fellowship with one another, and the blood of Jesus, his Son, purifies us from all sin" (1 Jn 1:7). "Walking in the light" does not imply behavioral perfection. It is simply the willingness to honestly acknowledge how we are behaving. We must also acknowledge the character qualities which produce our behaviors. Finally, we must acknowledge our feelings about others' behavior toward us.

Common fears. Most of us find it hard enough to look at so much unpleasantness in ourselves during Step Four. In this next step, we are now being asked to express all this aloud to someone else. This may also be the first time we have ever thoroughly expressed to anyone what is within us. We may therefore feel afraid to do this step. Moving into uncharted territory does tend to promote fear. What exactly might we feel afraid of?

Rejection. We might fear rejection, especially from the person with whom we share our inventory. We may be afraid that he or she could add to our already heavy burden of shame. No doubt this person should be selected with great care. Consider only someone you know to be fairly "unshockable." Select someone who personally knows God's unconditional love and acceptance, someone who is free from tendencies to pass judgment.

Required response. We may be afraid of what we'll have to do in response to this step. Remember, we are not really doing anything about what is contained in this inventory. We are simply admitting what is there. If there is something we need to do in response to how we have hurt others or how we have been hurt, a subsequent step will deal with it. Remember, "one step at a time."

Confirmation of shame. We may even fear that our deepest beliefs about our own awfulness—about how bad we really are—will be confirmed through this step. If we have this fear, then we need to review Step Three again.

Facing the truth. Step Five calls on us to admit the truth to three people: to ourselves, to God, and to another human being. To some extent, of course, we have already begun to admit our wrongs and our hurts to ourselves as we complete a fourth step inventory. Now we go beyond this previous work to admit these things fully to ourselves.

Begin with the following exercise, adapted from one found in *The Twelve Steps—A Spiritual Journey.*[6] Sit in a chair opposite another chair. Imagine that you are sitting in the other chair. Or, sit facing yourself in a mirror. Now, talk out loud through your inventory with yourself as if you are someone else.

Verbalizing your inventory is very important to this process. For some, a thought unspoken is an indirect denial of current reality. When you are finished, write down any additional insights or new feelings you experienced while doing this exercise.

We are no longer denying or minimizing what we've done, what we are like, or how we've been hurt.

What about admitting our faults to God? Doesn't God already know all about us? Why do we need to admit anything to him? It is not a matter of informing him of what he already knows. Rather, it means we begin to see these matters the way God sees them. It means we are no longer denying or minimizing what we've done, what we are like, or how we've been hurt. It means we express our agreement with him about what he has revealed to us.

How do we make this admission to God? We suggest the following prayer as a way to get started:[7]

> Lord, I understand that you already know me completely. I am now ready to openly and humbly reveal myself to you—my hurtful behaviors, self-centeredness, and character traits. I am grateful to you for the gifts and abilities that have brought me to this point in my life. Take away my fear of being known and rejected. I place myself and my life in your care and keeping.

Next, tell God that you agree with him concerning what he has shown you in your inventory. Express the entire inventory aloud to God in sentences beginning with "Lord, I agree with you that I... (what you did, your character flaw, or how you are hurting from someone else's wrongdoing)." If you are admitting wrongdoing, say so: "Lord, this was wrong."

When we truly see our sin and shortcomings as God does, he then produces in us godly sorrow which leads to genuine repentance: "Godly sorrow brings repentance that leads to salvation and leaves no regret, but worldly sorrow brings death" (2 Cor 7:10). This repentance, or "change of mind" regarding our negative traits and actions, provides the necessary foundation for Step Six. By acknowledging the terrible reality of our personal inventory, we become ready for God to remove these character defects and sinful tendencies from our lives. Real change is now possible, perhaps for the first time.

In addition, we come to see more clearly what God has had to endure because of the sins committed against us. We recognize that he earned the right to judge those who hurt us by dying for them. We see that we are not qualified to be their judge. This perspective provides the necessary foundation for the other aspect of the sixth step, becoming ready to forgive others for their shortcomings.

Finally, when we truly see how bad our sin is by seeing what God the Son had to endure—and yet he forgave us—we are filled with gratitude for what he has done for us. This gratitude helps us become willing to be responsive to God when he asks us to do difficult things, such as forgiving someone who has abused us. We become ready to "forgive each other, just as in Christ, God forgave you" (Eph 4:32).

Admitting to another person. Why do we need to involve someone else? Isn't it enough to just go before God? For many of us, the thought of revealing our personal problems to another person is unthinkable, especially those unpleasant dark secrets many of us have hidden.

For many of us, the thought of revealing personal problems to another person is unthinkable, especially those unpleasant dark secrets many of us have hidden.

A helpful little book, *The Twelve Steps for Everyone*, offers a very important insight: "The further we go into this program, the more humility it requires of us, or rather we require of ourselves. It has taken a great deal of humility to become ready for Step Five. But Step Five is the test of our humility. Are we truly humble, or do we just *think* we are? How can we be sure? Step Five offers us a way to put our humility to the test."[8]

Exposing our true selves—our failings and feelings—tests the limits of our humility. The act of confessing to another human being the "exact nature of our wrongs" casts out the demon of "image management." We have consistently put up a false front to others; that false front will be torn down in this step. This need to "doctor" our image, to manage what others think of us, to "look good" to others, stems from our fear of personal rejection. Yet this same need leads to isolation and loneliness. We are often afraid to just be ourselves.

The root of this fear is pride that says "I must be better than others, I must be liked by others. Therefore I can't expose my true self to others." Pride says, "I don't really need others enough to risk becoming truly intimate with them. I can make it on my own." Doing the fifth step with another person begins to tear down the wall of isolation that pride has built.

Perhaps our need for honest humility was present in God's mind when he said through James: "Therefore confess your sins to each other and pray for each other so that you may be healed" (Jas 5:16).

STEP FIVE: TAKING ACTION

As we have already stated, the person we share with in this step must be selected very carefully. Do it only with someone you believe can keep your inventory confidential. Once selected, set aside a block of time to be together: four to five hours would be best so that no one is distracted by time concerns. Also, eliminate possible distractions of telephone calls, visitors, children, or extraneous noise.

Go through your Step Four inventory, avoiding explanations of how the wrongs came to be or what you plan to do about them. You are not seeking counsel or advice. *The Twelve Steps—A Spiritual Journey* workbook suggests what to do after we have completed this step:

> After completing your fifth step, take time for prayer and meditation to reflect on what you have done. Thank God for the tool you have been given to improve your relationship with him. Spend time rereading the first five steps and note anything you have omitted. Acknowledge that you are laying a new foundation for your life. The cornerstone is your relationship with God and your commitment to honesty and humility.
>
> Congratulate yourself for having the courage to risk self-disclosure, and thank God for the peace of mind you have achieved.[9]

READY FOR RECOVERY

6. Became ready to have God remove these defects of charac-
ter, and to forgive others for their defects of character. "Do
you want to get well?" Jesus asked this seemingly absurd question of a man who had been lame for thirty-eight years (Jn
5:6). Who would not want to overcome such a debilitation?

Apparently, Jesus could see into the man's soul and dis-
cerned that this cripple had adjusted to his malady well—perhaps too well. Perhaps this physical problem had excused the
man from taking responsibility for his own life. Perhaps he had
even come to depend on his handicap for survival. Jesus was
asking this unfortunate man if he was truly ready to recover
from his illness.

Do *you* want to get well? At first glance, this seems to be a ridiculous question. But is it really? We believe that this is an
important question for any of us who are struggling with the
environmental and genetic effects of our dysfunctional families. We were affected by the family we grew up in. We now seek
to overcome whatever harmful effects we have carried into our
present family.

Step Six is a step of readiness to recover. We must ask ourselves whether we really want to get well. Do we want to recover
from the unmet needs and unhealed hurts of our childhood?
Do we really want to stop encouraging dysfunctional rules and
dysfunctional roles in our present family? Do we want to stop
harboring resentment and bitterness toward those who have
offended us? Do we want to give up the enjoyment or escape of
our compulsive eating, drinking, sex, or work? Are we ready for
real change?

Step Six is a process—"becoming" ready. Readiness to recover is not automatic. Some of us may need time to consider
what we may give up in recovery. Like the man Jesus spoke to,
we have necessarily adjusted to our dysfunction—its rules and
roles. Our idealization of our parents has protected us from
the reality of their imperfection. We have learned to depend

on dysfunctional patterns of relating in our families for survival. Our addictions and compulsions give us pleasure or anesthesia from life's pain and tedium. We may not be ready to give up these coping behaviors.

Change is often uncomfortable, even threatening. Change may lead to growth, but it always involves loss. Though we gain freedom to become who we really are, we lose the familiar, the comfortable. Do we really want to get well?

Readiness to recover is not automatic. Some of us may need time to consider what we may give up in recovery.

The agent of our recovery. Our dysfunctional family taught us to take care of ourselves, so we naturally assume that our own effort is required for these proposed changes and improvements. We may even assume that our recovery ultimately depends solely on our own ability to accomplish it. Recovery is "self-help," right?

Wrong. In Step Six we become ready to specifically surrender our change process to God. We become ready for God to do something in our lives which we cannot do for ourselves: remove our character defects and replace them with the character strength of Jesus Christ.

We laid the foundation for our willingness to have God change us in Step Five, especially as we sought to allow God to produce in us a "godly sorrow leading to repentance." When we see that Jesus had to suffer and die for the things that we desperately want to hang on to, then we genuinely desire for God to remove these defects.

Recovery won't happen any other way. God never commands us to reform ourselves. Rather he urges us to present ourselves to him "as those who have been brought from death to life" (Rom 6:13). Brennan Manning says it this way: "I can't free myself. I have to be set free—the role of the Holy Spirit is to form Christ in us. I give him my presence and let him make the changes in me that I can't make myself."[10]

Why don't our own efforts to change succeed? Again Manning is helpful: "I would say that every attempt to change myself is motivated either by self-hatred or guilt in some form."[11] If our motivation for change springs forth as a response to our shame, it is just one more effort to perform to gain approval. Anything less than perfection brings more shame and condemnation. Our self-hatred and guilt thus act as barriers to lasting change.

When God changes us, he makes no appeal to our shame. Instead, he tells us in advance, *before* we have changed, an incredible truth—that he has removed the basis for our shame: "There is now no condemnation for those who are in Christ Jesus" (Rom 8:1). When God changes us, he makes no appeal to our guilt. Rather, he tells us how he will remove it. He tells that if we will simply agree with him about what we have done wrong, he will forgive us, thus removing our guilt completely.

The whole thrust of our true identity as God's beloved children is to directly counteract and remove our self-hatred. All he asks of us is that we simply become ready to let him change us.

When God changes us, he makes no appeal to our shame or to our guilt.

Can God really change us? Becoming ready for God to change us means believing that he can do it. How can we be sure of this? First, believe that God is in the business of removing our character defects. In fact, he has planned to do this all along! According to the Living Bible translation of Romans 8:29, "From the very beginning, God decided that those who came to him—and all along he knew who would—should become like his Son."

Second, believe that he really *wants* to do this work in our lives. This is what he is already doing, as we cooperate with him: "And we... are being transformed into his likeness" (2 Cor 3:18). When we become discouraged, thinking we can't change, let's remember: "What is impossible with men is possible with God" (Lk 18:27).

THREE KEYS THAT UNLOCK OUR READINESS TO FORGIVE

Part of our fourth step inventory involves identifying how others had hurt us. We ask God to show us the particular hurts of unmet needs and our feelings associated with what we missed. We also ask God to show us toward whom we had resentment and bitterness. As we do this, we may become aware of unresolved anger, resentment, and bitterness toward those who had offended us.

In Step Five, we honestly acknowledge to ourselves, God, and another person the extent of our unresolved hurt and anger. Our recovery from these hurts begins with this step, because we began to have our feelings of sadness, fear, and anger accepted and validated by another person.

In Step Six, we become ready to release any resentment and bitterness which continue to hold us in bondage to painful events and people of our past. We become ready to forgive others for their character defects and the ways those defects have hurt us. Here are three keys that unlock our readiness to forgive:

1. Who is the judge? The first key has to do with who really has the right to pass judgment. When we made our searching and fearless moral inventory, we asked God to show us what he wanted us to see about ourselves. In doing this, we acknowledge that he really is the only one who has the right to judge us.

Other people can often discern what is wrong in us—what needs to change. We ought to listen to what they have to say for our own well-being and for the good of others we affect.

God may be speaking to us through them. However, God does not grant any human being the right to pass judgment on another human being. In fact, he commands us not to judge (Mt 7:1-5). God as our perfect Creator and Redeemer is the only one who can properly pass judgment on our character and behavior. And we are rightfully bothered when we sense that others are judging us.

Just as God is the only one who has the right to pass judgment on us, he is also the only one who has the right to pass judgment on those who have hurt us. When we harbor resentment and bitterness, we are passing judgment. We are saying, "These people are bad. I deserved better. I have a right to evaluate them, find them lacking, and then hold their shortcomings against them."

We become ready to forgive those who have sinned against us only when we see that we *don't* have the right to hold anything against anyone, no matter what they did to us. Only God has the right to sit in the judge's chair. So forgiveness means deciding not to judge any longer. We are letting the offenders "off our hook." This may be difficult because we don't think they *deserve* to be off the hook. Actually, even though we let them off our hook, offenders are still on God's hook. They must answer to him for what they have done.

We are the ones who suffer from our resentment,
and we are the ones who benefit when we let it go.

---

2. Who benefits from forgiveness? Many of us resist forgiving our offenders because we think forgiveness is intended to benefit the offender. Most of the time, however, offenders are unaware or unwilling to admit that they have even done anything wrong. It is difficult to provide a benefit to someone who sees no need for it!

The fact is, *we* ourselves are the ones who suffer from our resentment, and we are the ones who benefit when we let it go. As we have seen, unresolved anger allows the devil to have a foothold or place of influence in our lives. When we forgive our offenders, we derive the significant benefit of closing off a major inroad of the devil in our lives. We become ready to forgive when we see that we are the ones who stand to benefit, not those who hurt us.

3. Forgive as we have been forgiven. When we see how bad our own sin really is and see also that God has forgiven us totally, we can then see how unreasonable it would be for us not to forgive someone else.[12] If we are having trouble seeing how much God has forgiven us, we need to review Step Five. If we believe we have been forgiven only a little, we will forgive only a little. If we believe that we have been forgiven much, we will be readier to forgive much.

STEP SIX: TAKING ACTION

We have become ready for God to bring about our recovery when we:

- Give up the idea that we can accomplish our own recovery.
- Decide that we will be better off when we are free from all the aspects of our dysfunctional background and present reality.

We have become ready to forgive others when we:

- Decide that we have no right to take God's place as judge.
- See that we will benefit greatly when we forgive.
- Appreciate how forgiven we are.

Step Six is not so much an action as it is a state of being. It is similar to the second step, where we come to believe that Someone greater than ourselves could intervene to restore us. In this step, we make sure that we are really ready for this Someone to do the work of restoration by changing our character. This sixth step requires us to trust God with our recovery. It also requires us to trust him with dispensing justice to others who have offended us.

The following questions and prayers will help you take action on Step Six:

1. Are you ready for God to change your character? If so, then express your readiness to him: "Lord, I realize that I strive to hang on to my weaknesses and flaws, particularly those which give me momentary pleasure. I confess that I have tried to change myself in my own strength, but it will never work. You are the only One who can truly change me for the good. I am ready for you to do your good work in me. Amen."

2. Are you ready to forgive those who have hurt you? If so, express your readiness to God through a prayer like this one: "Lord, I confess that I have harbored resentment and bitterness toward those who have hurt me. I recognize that you are the only one who has the right to judge them. I also see that I will benefit greatly by forgiving. I also affirm that my forgiveness of others is entirely appropriate in light of all that you have forgiven me. I am ready to forgive. Amen."

GETTING FREE

7. Humbly asked him to remove our defects of character, and forgave those who had offended us. In Step Six, we became ready for God to remove our character defects. We also became ready to forgive those who have offended us. In this step, we will actually go before God to ask him to do his work of character transformation. And we will let go of the resentment toward those who have hurt us. Step Seven is the action step for which the previous step prepared us.

In this age of glorification of power and strength, Rambo and the Terminator provide significant role models for many.

Value and worth is measured by performance and accomplishment. Acceptance must be earned. Forgiveness is for weaklings. In stark contrast, the twelve steps require us to admit that we really are not doing very well. We admit that left to ourselves, we are powerless.

This admission in Step One is our first step toward the godly quality of humility. A recurring theme throughout the twelve steps, humility is the central idea of Step Seven.[13]

Pride is essentially self-confidence. Humility is also confidence, but it is confidence properly placed.

What is humility? We can understand humility best when we see it contrasted to pride. Pride is essentially *self*-confidence. Pride says, "I can do it on my own. I don't need anyone's help." We idolize our own abilities, accomplishments, and strength. Pride says, "What I want is most important. I reserve the right to determine what is best for me."

On the other hand, humility is also confidence, but it is confidence properly placed.[14] The humble person says, "I can't do it on my own. I must have God's help. I have confidence that God can do what he has promised to do." Humility focuses on God, rather than self—what God wants for me, rather than what I want for myself.

In Step Four, we ask God to show us what needs to change in us. Now, we confidently ask him to do in our lives what he has already said we need. With assurance, we ask him to accomplish the transformation of our character.

Because our focus is on God, we grant him the right to take whatever time he wishes to build the character of Jesus in us. We determine to be patient, resisting the temptation to put God on our timetable. Since our needed character work may require a major overhaul, we recognize that God's slowness to change us may be designed to give us and others time to adjust to the necessary losses change always brings.

Humility is required for genuine forgiveness as well. If we are humble, we appreciate that we did not deserve the forgiveness we have received. We did nothing to merit the free gift that God extended to us. We can thus extend forgiveness to others, not taking pride in the fact that we have done this good thing for God. Instead we recognize that it is only reasonable in light of all the forgiveness we have received.

STEP SEVEN: TAKING ACTION

Are you willing for God to use suffering to remove character flaws and to build the character of Jesus in you? Are you willing for God to cultivate in you new patterns of perseverance instead of bailing out when the going gets rough? If so, ask him to remove your character defects, humbly giving him the freedom to accomplish this work according to his plan: "Lord Jesus, I am now willing that you should have all of me, good and bad. I ask that you remove from me every defect of character that stands in the way of my usefulness to you and others. Give me the strength I need to persevere when suffering comes. Please do whatever it takes to produce in me the character of Jesus Christ, for your honor and glory and for my good. Amen."

Express to God your forgiveness of those who have offended you. To forgive means letting go of resentment and bitterness. We decide to no longer pass judgment—to not hold the offense against the offender. We do this for our own benefit, for the emotional and spiritual freedom we gain. With your list of "Whom I Need to Forgive" from Step Four in hand, pray the following prayer: "Lord, I forgive (name of person) for (specifically identify whatever you hold against that person)."

Go down your list, person by person. Don't leave one until you are finished. Do not rush through it. Let yourself feel your feelings! Honestly acknowledge your hurt, anger, sadness, shame, and even hate. Your forgiveness will be more complete if you first recognize your hurt and resentment. This is "forgive your brother from your heart" (Mt 18:35).

If you find that you can't do this on your own, seek help from a trusted friend or counselor. Your Step Five person might be a good candidate.

MAKING AMENDS

8. Made a list of all persons we had harmed and became willing to make amends to them all. Steps Eight and Nine are action steps. We will act to bring healing and reparation to others. We will also gain a clear conscience for ourselves. In the eighth step, we will develop a plan to make amends to those we have harmed. In the ninth step, we will actually carry out the plan.

A crucial part of Step Eight is becoming willing to make these amends. Remember, in this step we are not actually making the amends. Rather, we are honestly confronting our resistance to this idea and becoming *willing* to do it. Only after becoming willing do we actually contact the appropriate people and tangibly make amends to them in the next step.

A dictionary definition of making amends is "to attempt to compensate for offensive conduct; to make reparation for loss, damage, or injury."[15] Thus, we begin to make amends by expressing our regret, and then making restitution for damage we caused.

One author explains that making amends means "fully and completely acknowledging our part of every dispute in which harm came to someone as a result of our action or inaction, regardless of cause, no matter how justified we may have felt."[16] Focusing on just *our* part prevents us from slipping into the trap of "justifiable sin." Sometimes we admit we did wrong, but we justify or excuse our wrong by blaming the other party: "I wouldn't have done what I did if he had not hurt me first." We must be willing to take responsibility for our wrong, regardless of what others may have done.

We should also keep in mind that apologies are a good start, but they are not enough. We must become ready to make physical, mental, emotional, and even financial restitution for each harm we caused.

We must be willing to take responsibility for our wrong, regardless of what others have done.

Why making amends is necessary. To God, making amends when we've done wrong takes priority even over worship: "Therefore, if you are offering your gift at the altar and there remember that your brother has something against you, leave your gift there in front of the altar. First go and be reconciled to your brother; then come and offer your gift" (Mt 5:23-24). Why might this be?

For others' healing. God can use our amends to help our victims recover. While making amends does not undo what we've done, it can soften the blows and heal the hurt. Wouldn't we feel better if someone who had offended us came to us, admitted what they had done, and sought to make amends?

Making amends develops humility. Making amends to those we have harmed also deepens God's work of producing humility in us. Humility grows in us as we gradually give up our false confidence in self and increase our confidence in God and his care for our lives. In Step Eight, we need to become willing to face our victims—people we have wounded, let down, and hurt. We must first deepen our dependency upon God and his care in our lives, or we will probably not become willing to take this difficult step.

This is tough! If you feel stuck here, it might be beneficial to review Step Three. Have you entrusted your life and will to God, or is your fear a symptom of clinging to self-protection? Are you clear about your identity as a child of God? Our confidence and security in God's love are the basis of our ability to risk being rejected by those we have harmed.

To gain a clear conscience. Making amends is necessary in order to clear our own conscience. The goal is to be able to face anyone, anytime—that there would be no one we want to avoid because of how we had harmed them.

Once we are willing to make amends, we are ready to identify those we may have harmed. We began to do this in our fourth step inventory. As before, we are only interested in God's direction concerning to whom we should go. Friends or family members may offer advice or suggestions concerning whom we have harmed. We should listen and consider what they say. However, we are depending on God's guidance to direct us to the people he has prepared for us.

STEP EIGHT: TAKING ACTION

In this step, we define what it means to make amends to those we had harmed and determine why making amends is so important to our recovery process. This understanding helps prepare us for the very difficult work of Step Nine— actually facing our victims. We observed the possible need to go back to Step Three if we are having difficulty with this step. We also ask God to guide us in making our list of those to whom we need to make amends. Then we complete this step by seeking God's direction concerning how we could make amends to these people.

1. Make a list of all persons you have harmed. Look again at your Step Four list of significant relationships. Pray this prayer (or a similar one), then write down whomever God brings to your mind: "Lord, I know that I have harmed many of the people on this list. I am willing to make amends to them all as you enable me. Help me to identify whom I have harmed and how I could make amends

to them. If there is anyone else who is not on this list, bring them to my mind now."

2. For each person on your list, identify what you need to do to make amends for the harm you have done. Since we have entrusted our lives to God's care, again we seek his guidance concerning how he would want us to make amends. Pray this (or a similar) prayer: "Lord, you know the harm I have done to these people. You know the hurt they have lived with. You also know what I am capable of doing for them through your enabling, and how they would be helped by my amends. As I consider each person on my list, please guide me to identify what you want me to do now to make amends for what I have done."

3. Ask yourself: Are you truly willing to do what God has directed you to do? This may be one of the most difficult aspects of the recovery process. Don't forget why making amends is so important. Imagine the impact on those we have harmed when we humbly go to them, admitting what we did wrong and seeking to make up for it in a tangible way. Especially consider what it will mean to our closest loved ones—our spouse and children.

GOING INTO ACTION

9. Made direct amends to such people wherever possible, except when to do so would injure them or others. This is the second step of the action plan for "social housecleaning." In Step Eight, we made a list of those we had harmed and became ready to make amends to them all. In Step Nine, we implement our plan by actually going to those persons on our list, seeking to make restitution wherever possible.

Completing this step requires at least two character qualities: humility and courage. If humility was required to "become willing" to make amends, how much more humility is needed to actually face those we have harmed! But imagine for a moment what it would be like to be able to go anywhere without fear of running into someone you have harmed. This peace and freedom from anxiety is available for all who complete this step. Ask God to produce in you a depth of humility—confidence in him and his empowering—beyond what you have ever known. Trust that he will answer this prayer.

When we made our lists of people we had harmed, someone likely emerged whom we would rather not face. Perhaps we still feel guilty about how we harmed that person. Perhaps we are afraid that this individual will not receive us well. We may fear rejection or condemnation. Maybe we fear the awkwardness of the encounter. Perhaps we sense our lack of control of the situation, because of our subordinate position in this contact. Perhaps we are not quite sure what we fear.

What is genuine courage? It is being "strong in the Lord and in his mighty power" (Eph 6:10). Spiritual courage recognizes that if we are doing what God wants us to do in his way, he will supply what we need to accomplish the task.

Spiritual courage recognizes that if we are doing
what God wants us to do in his way,
he will supply what we need to accomplish the task.

Are we sure you have heard from God concerning those to whom you should make amends? If not, return to Step Eight. If so, depend on his strength to overcome these fears.

Let us share a true example of courage and humility with you. Joey had become aware that God was asking him to make amends to many people he had harmed. Single, about thirty years of age, he had grown up in the "fast lane." His father was a professional gambler who had taught his son all the ways to win big—both honestly and dishonestly.

Four years earlier, on the verge of suicide, Joey had received Jesus Christ as his Savior. In subsequent months, God drew him away from his compulsive and dishonest gambling lifestyle.

Gambling had been lucrative, however, and he was still living off the investment income generated by years of winnings.

Joey's Step Eight list included several people he had cheated out of thousands of dollars. Some went back several years. Some of his Christian friends even suggested that God was blessing him by allowing him to keep the money. Joey, however, did not have peace about keeping the money. He knew that God was directing him to go to every person he could find whom he had cheated. He knew that he needed to admit his dishonesty. And he knew that God wanted him to give them back whatever he had gotten from them—with interest.

Over the next few months, with humility and courage, Joey did just that. He gave back more than sixty thousand dollars to several utterly flabbergasted former gambling associates. Step Nine cost him a lot of money. It required great courage to execute his plan. But Joey gained two priceless qualities: spiritual freedom and spiritual peace. He also became much more humble and courageous! His example should help motivate us toward Step Nine courage when we need to go to people we have harmed.

Like Joey, we may need an extra measure of humility and courage to face all the people we have harmed. Believe that God will provide what we need. And believe that these qualities will increase in us as we allow God to work in our lives.

Making amends for emotional isolation. Many of us respond to family hurt by emotionally isolating ourselves. This isolation may take the form of surface communication, keeping everything on the factual level. Or it may take the form of physical absence—certain family members trying to be gone as much as possible.

The simplest, yet possibly most harmful, form of isolation is the failure to be vulnerable to share any of our own needs. When we do not express our needs, we harm our families by making it impossible for anyone to meet our needs, because no one knows what they are. We may be ensuring dysfunctionality by hindering the ability of the family to meet our own needs.

Husbands and wives sometimes withhold expressing needs to each other. Any chance for intimacy dies with this decision to withdraw emotionally. These same adults tend to model non-expression of needs to their children. They subtly teach their children that honest expression of needs is not appropriate. The children may even conclude that they really don't have any legitimate needs, since Mom and Dad never discuss the subject. Even worse, children may know they have needs, but feel bad about themselves because of it, as if something were wrong with them for having needs.

Out of hiding. Why do we hide our needs? We may fail to share our needs out of fear—fear that our needs will again not be met. We stop sharing our needs to avoid being hurt. We may fail to share needs because of resentment. Our withdrawal is designed to punish significant family members for how they have failed us. Perhaps we fail to share our needs because we are not aware that we have them. We learned in our families to hide or deny our needs, believing that we were strong if we had no needs.

One of the best ways to make amends to our families is to commit ourselves to sharing our needs in an undemanding way. As we begin to express our own needs, we send a clear message to other family members that they too have legitimate needs that can and should be shared. As needs are shared, family members have new opportunities to meet needs because they are now aware of them. Family members, especially parents, begin to ask others what their needs are, inviting more possibilities for healthy meeting of needs. The whole family takes a major step toward functionality.

How do we overcome our fear of being hurt or our resentment from past hurts? Our work in previous steps has laid the foundation for overcoming these hindrances. In Step Three, we turned our will and our lives over to the care of God. The answer to fear is not to naively trust people; rather, we put our trust in God. We give others the opportunity to meet our needs, trusting God to take care of us should these people hurt us.

Then in Step Seven, we asked God to remove our defects of character, recognizing that he often uses pain and suffering in this process. The hurt we feel when someone close to us chooses not to meet our needs may be something God is using to develop within us the character of Jesus.

The hurt we feel when someone close to us chooses not to meet our needs may be something God is using to develop within us the character of Jesus.

This previous work provides the basis for managing our fear of being hurt, preventing it from being in control of us. We are free to say to our spouse, "Honey, right now I think I need some attention from you. Do you think that we could sit and talk sometime soon?" If we find that our fear of being hurt still controls us—hindering our ability to lovingly express our own needs—we ought to thoroughly review Steps Three and Seven.

What about overcoming the barrier of resentment? In Step Six, we became ready to forgive those who had hurt us. In Step Seven we expressed our forgiveness. Clearly, if we are withholding expression of our needs and not inviting others to share their needs because of resentment, our forgiveness has been incomplete. Our personal recovery as well as that of our families is seriously blocked at this very point. We must go back and thoroughly review Steps Six and Seven.

Let's dismantle our family dysfunction by giving up emotional isolation. Let's make amends to our families by committing to express our needs. Let's give our loved ones the opportunity to meet our needs. Let's also invite other family members to do the same. We will experience the joy of knowing that we are lovingly meeting their needs for understanding and nurture when we encourage them to share their needs as well.

The danger of injuring others. Step Nine recognizes the possibility that directly making amends could actually cause additional injury to that person or to others. We need to exercise caution in this step. As one person suggested, "We cannot rush about brashly reopening old wounds or exposing dirty linen which might hurt the person to whom we are making the amends or to a third party."

For example, someone may have been involved in an extramarital relationship. We believe that the offender should not seek to make amends by telling his or her own spouse, going to the spouse of the other person, or by contacting the former partner in the affair. Rather, such people should make amends *indirectly* by rededicating themselves to being the mate that God wants them to be, seeking to unselfishly understand and meet the needs of their partner. The offenders should also make indirect amends by cooperating with God's program of spiritual recovery as outlined in these steps. They are then increasingly capable of loving their spouse as God intends.

---

*We should also be very cautious if honest confession
and making amends might lead
to serious consequences for our family.*

We should also be very cautious if honest confession and amends might lead to serious consequences for our family. Loss of employment, imprisonment, or other major financial or social impact on our families should be weighed very carefully. We should discuss these issues with a trusted advisor if we have any doubts.

Sometimes emotional wounds may appear to be healed but are really not. A husband may not want to reopen an old marital wound because of the pain it causes his wife. But such a decision may be a necessary part of his Step Nine work. That husband does not necessarily need to rehash in great detail all of his past offenses. But, if God so directs, he should admit to his wife (and children, if applicable) his sins of emotional isolation, selfishness, undependability, insensitivity, or wrong priorities—with specific examples of these flaws. He should then try to make amends to whatever extent possible. He should do this, even if he knows that opening the old wounds will stir up feelings of hurt and anger in his wife. Reopening the wound is a prerequisite for complete healing.

How can we know with confidence whether the Step Nine "Exception Rule" applies in our case? How can we tell whether to proceed when we are unsure? *The Twelve Steps for Everyone* comments:

> The important thing to bear in mind is that we should not be deterred from making amends by fear for ourselves, but only by the real possibility of injury to others. We will only have to suffer later for any "excuses" we make for ourselves at this point. Our lack of candor or courage or willingness at this or any other point in the program will delay our growth or prevent us from growing further.

If you're still unsure about your particular case, consult with a trusted counselor, pastor, or friend for guidance.

STEP NINE: TAKING ACTION

Anyone pursuing recovery from the effects of a troubled family needs to adopt *new rules*. Making amends to family members is a direct assault on dysfunctional rules and roles! We have determined in previous steps that it is okay to feel our feelings. But here in Step Nine, we are following a new "It's okay to talk" rule. We are practicing God's rules for a functional family:

- "Talk!" (Eph 4:15, 25, 29)
- "Feel!" (Eph 4:26-27)

- "Trust God!" (Prv 3:5-6)
- "Love People!" (1 Cor 13)

1. Develop a specific plan for making direct amends to each person on your list.

   - When will you contact this person?
   - How will you contact them (letter, phone call)?
   - What exactly will you do to make amends to this person?

2. If you need to make amends to family members, carefully consider the "Healing Family Hurts" plan in Appendix Three.
3. Have you harmed your family through emotional isolation? Consider making a new commitment to share your own needs as a significant way to make amends to your family members. Commit also to inviting family members to share their needs with you as well.
4. Ask God to give you the humility and courage you need to carry out your plan for making amends.

CHAPTER 13

Growing in Recovery: Steps Ten through Twelve

T O THE EXTENT THAT we have thoroughly and honestly worked the first nine steps, we have completed our initial "personal housecleaning." These steps were likely the most rigorous and searching look at our lives that we have ever undertaken.

We have thus made a significant commitment to personal and family recovery. Our loved ones—family, friends, even work associates—begin to benefit as we become more capable of giving and receiving unselfish love. And our own souls are more at peace when we have an emotional and relational "clean slate."

We now come to Steps Ten through Twelve, which enable us to maintain the recovery process we have begun. These steps also help us to continue to grow in our recovery, especially on the spiritual plane. These last three steps engage us in the following issues:

- Is my work over? If not, what more should I do?
- How can I grow in my relationship with God?
- Can I help others toward recovery? If so, how?

STAYING ON COURSE

10. Continued to take personal inventory; when we were wrong, we promptly admitted it; when we were wronged, we promptly forgave the offender. We are now ready for the "continuation step," Step Ten. John Blattner comments: "It indicates that the repentance process of Steps Four through Nine is not to be a one-time experience, but is to be built into one's whole approach to life."[1] Like physical, mental, and emotional growth, spiritual growth is a continuing process. Thus we need to continue to take personal inventory.

How? The same way we do in our fourth step inventory. We regularly come before God with the words and attitude of the psalmist:

> Search me, O God, and know my heart;
>   Test me and know my anxious thoughts.
> See if there is any offensive way in me,
>   and lead me in the way everlasting. **Ps 139:23-24**

Then we respond appropriately to what we find. If we have done wrong, we promptly admit our offense. When we are wronged, we promptly forgive the offender.

Conquering guilt. *Guilt* is one of the most significant blocks to spiritual development. We exposed and removed our pervading sense of guiltiness or shame in Step Three. But all of us continue to do wrong and thus rightfully feel true guilt again. We must regularly deal with these guilty feelings and remain free of them to continue our recovery.

How? Not by ignoring our guilt or denying that we have done anything wrong. Not by somehow being perfect—an impossible task! Instead, we continue to identify both what we have done wrong and the underlying sin. Then we promptly admit these wrongs and sins to God and to the person we have offended. If possible, we "make amends" to whomever we have wronged.

Reaffirming reliance on God. In Step Three, we made a decision to turn over every area of our lives to God's management and care. The predominant challenge of our continuing recovery and spiritual development is to deepen our dependency upon him for everything.

Klass reminds us that inventory is not history; it changes from day to day.[2] Regular moral inventory will surface subtle intrusions of old patterns of self-will and self-management. We should regularly ask ourselves: Has greed crept back in? Dishonesty? Lust? Have we drifted back into following old "don't talk" or "don't feel" rules?

Are we subconsciously measuring our worth in the old currency of performance, achievement, or appearance? Are we unimpressed by the sacrifice of our Savior on the cross for us? Have former patterns of pride, resentment, self-pity, shame, or self-condemnation taken root? Are we playing, or encouraging others to play, outmoded dysfunctional family roles?

Do we thoroughly accept God's management of our lives?
Or are we trying to take over again?

Do we thoroughly accept God's management of our lives? Or does our egotism, greed, dishonesty, self-pity, resentment, envy, jealousy, worry, depression, hatred, or fear indicate that we are not accepting his dealings with us? Do they reveal that we are trying to take over again?[3]

Whenever we see that we are not accepting God's management of our lives, we promptly admit this wrong to him and receive the wonderful gift of his forgiveness (1 Jn 1:9).

Rooting out resentment. Resentment hinders recovery and stunts spiritual growth. In Step Seven we explained how resentment or unresolved anger gives the devil significant influence in our lives. Therefore, we continue to survey our personal inventory to see if we are holding anything against anyone who has hurt us.

People are imperfect. They will inevitably fail us. We will sometimes be hurt and we will feel angry about what was done to us. We must not ignore these feelings as was once our practice. Instead, we honestly acknowledge our feelings of hurt and anger. We honestly admit our feelings—not to blame the offender, but so we can respond appropriately to these emotions. In so doing, we consistently implement our new "It's okay to feel" rule.

We then must consistently decide to not hold perceived wrongs against those who offend us. Instead, we entrust them to God's dealing. As he directs, we also follow our new "It's okay to talk" rule. We sit down with the person who hurt us and resolve the conflicts, free from the baggage of accumulated resentment.

STEP TEN: TAKING ACTION

1. Try a "seven day inventory" experiment. Pray Psalm 139:23-24 each day for one week. Write down whatever God shows you. Is there a previous step that needs to be addressed again? If so, go back to that step. Consider continuing to take five minutes at the end of each day for this kind of inventory.

2. Did the seven day experiment reveal any new area of your life which needs attention? Apply Steps One to Nine to this problem. For example, your initial fourth step inventory may not have surfaced a current problem of worry. Or, you now may be struggling with a rebellious teenager. Apply Steps One to Nine to this particular problem.[4]

3. Ask someone close to you (spouse, parent, sibling, roommate, friend) for feedback concerning what character quality God may desire to develop in your life now. Then ask this person to pray for you that God would accomplish this work in your life.

KNOWING GOD'S WILL

11. Sought through prayer and meditation to improve our conscious contact with God, praying only for knowledge of his will and for the power to live lives pleasing to him. We are committed to the concept that everyone has physical, emotional, and spiritual needs. Each person's own unique environmental and genetic circumstances determine the extent to which these needs are met. When these needs consistently go unmet, a variety of dysfunctions develop, many of which need formal treatment. We believe that most treatment efforts are directed at physical and emotional dimensions of dysfunction.

We are convinced, however, that recovery which excludes or dilutes the spiritual dimension is incomplete. Thus, our Twelve Step Program of Family Recovery has required us to explore this dimension of our being.

In Step Two we acknowledge that we need help from a "Higher Power" to do for us what we could not do. Step Three requires us to turn our lives and will over to God. As part of this step, we are challenged to renounce distorted images of God. We are also invited to enter into a personal relationship with God's Son, Jesus Christ, and to discover our new identity in relationship to him.

Our relationship with God continues to be a central aspect of our recovery in Steps Four through Nine. In Step Four, we ask God to direct our moral inventory. In Step Five, we confess the results of that inventory to him. In Step Seven, we ask God to remove these defects of character. In Step Nine, we entrust ourselves to God as we pursue making amends to those we have wronged. In Step Ten, we regularly ask God to guide our moral inventory and appropriate ways to respond.

Clearly these steps embody a spiritual recovery process that affects every dimension and relationship of our lives. Our next-to-last step invites us to deepen and strengthen our relationship with God through the practices of prayer and meditation. These spiritual disciplines provide the vital link between

God and ourselves—relationship-builders that put us in touch with the one who loves us most.

---

*Prayer is two friends taking time
to enter each other's worlds.*

Talking with God. Prayer is two-way communication—dialogue, not monologue. It is two friends taking time to enter each other's worlds. When we pray, we are asking God to act. But we are also expressing *our reality* in order to more fully enter *his reality*. We not only ask God to do things, we also ask questions and seek insight. For this reason, we stop and listen to what he has to say in response.

The cardinal rule for all prayer was articulated by Martin Luther several hundred years ago: "Don't lie to God in prayer!" Be honest! If you hate someone, even yourself, tell God about it. If you are angry at God, tell him. If you think life is miserable, tell him. If you think church stinks, tell him. If you think the twelve steps are worthless, tell him. If you are not sure you believe he is really there, tell him that, too.

Let's not forget that God already knows these things anyway. Our honesty may threaten some people, but not God. Having once walked this earth among us, he thoroughly understands our present reality and our pain. And he is big enough to receive us as we pour out our most negative emotions to him.

Soaking up the truth. Biblical meditation is not the emptying of our minds of all conscious thought in order to see what comes in. It is not focusing on some nonsense syllable in order to enter an altered state of consciousness. Instead, biblical meditation is focusing our thoughts on truth, and then allowing this truth to soak into our consciousness as it applies to us.

God urges us to consistently fill our minds with spiritual truth: "Set your minds on things above, not on earthly things" (Col 3:2). "Finally brothers, whatever is true... think about such things" (Phil 4:8). Jesus pointed to truth as the means of spiritual freedom: "You will know the truth, and the truth will set you free" (Jn 8:32). He also prayed for his followers: "Sanctify them by the truth; your word is truth" (Jn 17:17).

Clearly, knowing and believing the truth of God's Word is crucial to our recovery process. We meditate when we quietly focus on a particular truth, seeking to picture and be impressed with its relevance to us. *The Twelve Steps for Christians* offers this helpful description of meditation:

> In the act of meditating, we recall, ponder, and apply our knowledge of God's ways, purposes, and promises. It is an activity of holy thought, consciously performed in the presence of God, under the eye of God and by the help of God, as two-way communion with him. Its purpose is to clear our mental and spiritual vision and let his truth make its full and proper impact on our minds and hearts. Meditation humbles us as we contemplate God's greatness and glory and allow his Spirit to encourage, reassure, and comfort us.[5]

Prayer and meditation improve our conscious contact with God. As this happens, we'll find it increasingly natural to trust our heavenly Father with everything.

What do we pray for? The apostle Paul's prayer recorded in Colossians 1:9 best captures our Step Eleven prayer: "Asking God to fill you with the knowledge of his will through all spiritual wisdom and understanding."

"Knowledge of his will." Most prayer is self-centered. Often we ask God to give us what we have already selfishly determined we want and deserve. Paul's prayer is quite different. He prays that believers would simply know God's will in a way that would make a difference in their lives. We might assume that

knowing God's will means knowing what he wants us to do. This prayer probes much deeper. It is a request to know what *God* is doing in and around us, and what he wants to accomplish in our circumstances.

What might God be doing? He might be building the character of Christ in us or in someone else. He might be seeking to show someone their desperate need for him. He might be deepening our perception of his character or unconditional love. He might be seeking to get someone's attention through painful circumstances. Gaining a sense about God's activity and intention provides the basis for us to discern more clearly what he wants us to do.

We seek to know what God is doing in and around us, and what he wants to accomplish in our circumstances.

"Spiritual wisdom and understanding." Spiritual wisdom is insight into the nature of reality. This wisdom recognizes that reality includes not just the material world but also the unseen, spiritual world. In the broader view that spiritual wisdom offers, God is active and all powerful. But he is also being opposed by evil beings: "For our struggle is not against flesh and blood, but against the rulers, against the authorities, against the powers of this dark world and against the spiritual forces of evil in the heavenly realms" (Eph 6:12).

Spiritual understanding is the ability to put the insight of spiritual wisdom into practice. Spiritual wisdom discerns what God and the opposition are doing. Spiritual understanding determines what we need to do in light of what is really happening around us.

STEP ELEVEN: TAKING ACTION

A modern paraphrase of the prayer in Colossians 1:9 might be: "God, show us what you are doing so we can get in line with it!" Our Step Eleven prayer seeks discernment of God's activity and purposes so that we can mentally, emotionally, and behaviorally align ourselves with him. We can also follow Paul's example and pray this prayer for others.

Our objective is not to please self *or* others. Instead, we strive to please God. As we comprehend what he is doing and how he wishes us to participate in fulfilling his plan, we will often be led to help others. Sometimes we will sense that God wants us to attend to our own needs and thus say no to others. But always we seek his direction concerning what to do in every situation. Why? Because our new aim is to please God rather than to please others or ourselves.

Let your mind imagine for a moment what happens in a family when even one member improves his conscious contact with God—praying to know God's agenda and for the power and will to please him!

1. Pray each day, asking God to make you aware of and sensitive to what he is doing in your life. Ask him to show you how to get "in sync" with him. Ask him to empower you to live pleasing to him every day.

2. Identify a current need or struggle in your life. What Scripture speaks to this need? Meditate on that passage, seeking its relevance for you. Ask God to make this truth real to your mind and heart.

3. Consider joining a Bible study group in order to help you meditate more on God's truth. Check your church's opportunities, as well as other studies such as Bible Study Fellowship, Community Bible Study, and Precept upon Precept. These studies are offered in most major cities and in many rural areas as well. Check your phone book for listings or call local churches for information.

SHARING THE MESSAGE

12. Having had a spiritual awakening as a result of these steps, tried to carry this message to others and to practice these prin-

ciples in all our affairs. The increasing awareness of our spiritual nature and the reality of God comprises our spiritual awakening. We "wake up" spiritually when we realize how much God loves us and how much we need him.

The twelve steps require us to honestly admit exactly what we need to change. They also invite us to recognize that our needed change will not happen unless God produces it. Thus, our proper response is to entrust our recovery to him, cooperating with God as he builds our character into the likeness of Jesus Christ. Genuine recovery is spiritual at its core. And spiritual recovery requires spiritual awakening.

Millions of people grow up in dysfunctional families. Millions struggle with addictions, compulsions, unresolved emotional issues, and alienation from God. Having worked our way through eleven of the steps, we are ready for Step Twelve. We are positioned to help others with similar needs.

In good time. Someone has said, "We cannot impart what we do not possess." We have credibility to the extent that we ourselves have experienced change and growth as guided by these steps. "We must have already had a spiritual awakening in order to tell others how they, too, may achieve one. We must be in God's hands in order to extend the hand of God."[6]

This means not just reading the steps, simply being familiar with them. It means having thoroughly and honestly worked the steps to the best of our ability, applying the spiritual and behavioral principles to our lives.

Arrival at Step Twelve certainly does not mean we are finished recovering or that we have somehow achieved perfection. It means that we have tangible evidence of recovery— improved dimensions of our behavior and character along with a gradual resolution of emotional and spiritual conflicts. We will be experiencing recovery and growth in our family relationships as well.

Milestones in recovery. What does "tangible evidence of recovery" look like? How would we know we are making progress in our recovery? *The Twelve Steps—A Spiritual Journey* offers an encouraging list of "Milestones in Recovery" which we have lightly edited:[7]

- We have a clear sense of who we are in Christ as God's much-loved children.
- We feel comfortable with people, including authority figures.
- We generally accept others apart from their behavior.
- We accept and use personal criticism in a positive way.
- We accept responsibility for our own thoughts and actions.
- We feel comfortable standing up for ourselves when it is appropriate.
- We are enjoying peace and serenity, trusting that God is guiding our recovery.
- We love people who love and take care of themselves.
- We are free to feel and express our feelings even when they cause us pain.
- We have a healthy sense of self-esteem based on our identity in Christ.
- We are developing new skills that allow us to initiate and complete ideas and projects.
- We take prudent action by first considering alternative behaviors and possible consequences.
- We rely more and more on God as our higher power.

Genuine progress in recovery naturally leads
to the desire to help others.

The power of testimony. Genuine progress in recovery naturally leads to the desire to help others. Carrying the message of spiritual recovery to others is also a necessary dimension of our own continuing recovery.

Our experience of recovery can help others. Painful experiences hurt even worse when we see no benefit coming from them. Twelfth step work involves us not only in sharing our struggles and painful experiences, but also sharing how God has enabled us to overcome them. Some people may decide to keep going, gaining hope through our testimony. Others may be comforted through our understanding compassion. Our suffering holds more meaning when we see how it enables us to help others.

Sharing our recovery reinforces the practice of these principles. Working with others in their recovery requires that we continue to live according to the principles. Any drift or slip away will be exposed sooner or later to us or to those whom we are helping. This is especially true if we are involved with a twelve step group.

Beware of trying to fix people. As we encourage others with their recovery and practice of these steps, we seek to avoid a common caregiving pitfall: trying to "fix" other people. Our job is to "testify." Once we have shared our recovery story, we leave the rest up to God. "If we try to fix others, we may make matters worse for them."[8] We are the care-givers; God is the cure-giver.[9]

Some people will want us to fix them. They will subtly try to get us to take responsibility for their recovery. The founder of Alcoholics Anonymous, Bill Wilson, suggests: "Burn the idea into the consciousness of every man that he can get well.... The only condition is that he trust God and clean house."[10]

STEP TWELVE: TAKING ACTION

By taking these twelve steps, we have begun to deal with many core issues of our lives. We have faced the effects of unmet needs and unhealed hurts from our families of origin. We have begun to take responsibility for our own lives, for now we are "playing the hand we were dealt." We have entrusted our lives to God and begun to depend upon him more and more. We are in the process of dealing with current difficulties, and we have become better equipped to face other issues in the future.

We are care-givers; God is the cure-giver.

Practicing these principles in every aspect of our lives and in every relationship is important for our own sake. But no one will believe a message that is not truly working in our own lives. Our message is effective because it is true. But others doubt its validity unless they see the evidence.

1. Ask God to direct you to people who could benefit from your journey of recovery. Ask him to give you what to say and what to ask.
2. Help start a twelve step group. Many helpful resources provide guidance and structure in a helpful workbook format. We especially recommend *The Twelve Steps—A Spiritual Journey* and *God Help Me Stop*. Rapha's *Twelve Steps for Overcoming Codependency* workbook and the *Serenity Bible* have also helped many in their recovery.

AFTERWORD

THE SCIENCE OF CHEMISTRY studies the effects of combining various elements together. Depending on many factors, these mixtures cause different chemical reactions—some beneficial, some destructive. In much the same way, our families also produce various chemical reactions as each individual reacts to other family members according to his or her unique genetic inheritance and special circumstances.

Chemists learn to control reactions by understanding the specific characteristics of each element involved. We can also benefit from a greater understanding of not only ourselves but also the other members of our families. As we seek to comprehend the genetic predispositions and special characteristics each person brings to the family unit, preventive action may be taken for improved health.

Unlike a scientist who performs controlled experiments in a sterile laboratory, families must live in a very imperfect and often unpredictable world. Having to face the many unexpected stresses in our lives gives us all the more reason to be as fully prepared as possible—not only for today but also for the trials tomorrow may bring. Understanding the family as a single unit bound by physical, emotional, and spiritual ties, allows us to see it as a source of strength when facing such trials.

Acquiring this knowledge demands a response on our part. We can either incorporate the elements of change which we perceive as beneficial, or we can reject these concepts of family interaction as unimportant or lacking relevance for our own personal situations. Such an act of decision serves to focus our attention on our own needs and those of our families, at least for the moment. Careful consideration of the issues raised in this book will also highlight the necessity of periodically reassessing our physical, emotional, and spiritual needs. We can expect change and continue to look for new approaches as specific difficulties arise.

Viewing the family as a unit with multi-faceted strengths and weaknesses allows us to see the complex nature of our family structure. Focusing our attention too specifically on just one area which seems to be crying out for help may be short-sighted. We may end up only putting a bandaid on a deeper wound. Our human nature is to avoid more painful remedies as long as possible. Yet because physical illness frequently carries broader consequences, we may be forced to deal with emotional issues when physical pain becomes unbearable.

Failing to recognize the inherent spiritual nature of human beings and families inevitably leads to frustration and anxiety. We must consider the need for health not only in our physical and emotional beings, but in our souls as well. Greater awareness of the emotional needs of our families may improve communication and lessen the possibility of dysfunctional behavior. Opening ourselves up to the spiritual needs of each family member may further expand the depth of our relationships.

A common example of these interactions is that of the impaired family with one or more members involved in some addictive behavior. It could range from an addiction to a substance—such as alcohol, drugs, or food—or even to sexual abuse or the abuse of power within a relationship. Typically, we see the family in our clinic as a result of the physical problems of one family member who is least equipped to handle the current stress.

A variety of symptoms may bring someone to our doorstep, such as headaches, abdominal pain, or insomnia. It is tempting for both the patient and the health care provider to simply treat the current complaint. But when underlying issues are involved, superficial treatment seldom resolves the person's problem.

Suppose the patient has a bona fide medical condition which is poorly controlled, such as diabetes. Unmet emotional problems may be contributing to an inappropriate diet or improper monitoring of blood glucose levels. Failing to address these needs will hinder the best medical efforts.

Two of the most prevalent emotional disorders we see today are depression and anxiety. Treating emotional problems without considering the physical effects on the body is an incomplete assessment. Failure to consider a person's spiritual condition in the face of extreme emotional turmoil provides just as incomplete a picture.

If the family chemistry concept teaches us anything, it is to consider the individual and the family as a product of their combined environmental and genetic factors, current medical problems, and spiritual status. Until we routinely address the patient as a complete person, help for many of today's problems will be inadequate, falling far short of total healing.

The family is a group of individuals who, by their proximity and heritage, deeply affect the other members. This is not a particularly new concept, yet one easily forgotten in our highly mobile and increasingly impersonal society. Many voices today are urging a holistic view of people as individuals, rather than just a collection of isolated body parts. Likewise, we have seen an increasing awareness of the innate spiritual nature of humankind, and thus a desire on the part of many to clearly delineate what comprises this spirituality.

Before we prescribe medication or treatment, we must first diagnose the problem. Taking an inventory of our physical, emotional, and spiritual status is a crucial step in improving not only our own well being, but that of our families as well. Healing within the family begins with the individual member who is willing to be honest and face their current situation with determination. We invite you to be that person, beginning with a sincere effort to better understand your own family chemistry.

APPENDIX

How to Be Certain of Your Eternal Relationship with God

How does finite humanity gain a a relationship with the infinite God? By simply putting our trust in his Son Jesus as our savior. We are then open to the fullness of God's healing power to enable us to recover.

You may be thinking, "Isn't it arrogant to think that I can be one hundred percent sure of my relationship with God?" Indeed, it would be arrogant if we were trusting in our own abilities, actions, or good deeds to earn our salvation. However, if we are trusting in something or someone else besides ourselves, then one hundred percent certainty is a response of humility and thankfulness, not arrogance.[1]

In what sense do we decide to trust in him? We essentially come to believe in four specific truths.[2] *First, we come to believe that we have lived our lives in a less than perfect manner—that we have all fallen short in some way.* We admit that we have done some things we shouldn't have done. We also admit that we have not done some things we should have done. We recognize that no one is perfect: "For all have sinned and fallen short of the glory of God" (Rom 3:23).

Second, we come to believe that our less-than-perfect manner of living has caused a separation between us and God—a spiritual separation which the Bible calls spiritual death. We have earned this spiritual separation from God because of our sin: "For the wages of sin is death" (Rom 6:23).

Third, we come to believe that God the Father overcame this spiritual death penalty by providing his own Son Jesus to take this penalty in our place: "But God demonstrates his own love for us in this: While we were still sinners, Christ died for us" (Rom 5:8). We begin to realize that Jesus is someone who can really identify with us, since he experienced so much of the same harsh realities of life on an imperfect planet populated by imperfect people: "He was despised and rejected by men, a man of sorrows, and familiar with suffering" (Is 53:3); "He himself suffered when he was tempted" (Heb 2:18).

Yet Jesus was perfect and thus did not deserve to die: "For we do not have a high priest who is unable to sympathize with our weaknesses, but we have one who has been tempted in every way, just as we are—yet was without sin" (Heb 4:15).

Fourth, we come to believe that since God has provided the gift of a relationship with himself, all we need to do is receive this gift: "The gift of God is eternal life in Christ Jesus our Lord" *(Rom 6:23).* We receive him by simply deciding to trust in Jesus' payment for our sins on the cross: "Yet to all who received him, to those who believed in his name, he gave the right to become children of God" (Jn 1:12). "For God so loved the world that he gave his one and only Son, that whoever believes [trusts] in him shall not perish but have eternal life" (Jn 3:16).

Jesus said, "For my Father's will is that everyone who looks to the Son and believes in him shall have eternal life, and I will raise him up at the last day" (Jn 6:40). Have you received God's gift of eternal life through Jesus Christ? Would you like to accept this gift right now? You might use this prayer to express your desire:[3] "Lord Jesus, I need you. I want you to be my Savior and my Lord. I accept your death on the cross as payment for my sins. I now entrust my life to your care. Thank you for forgiving me and giving me spiritual life. Thank you for giving me the opportunity for abundant life now. Please help me to grow in my understanding of your love and power so that my life will bring glory and honor to you. Amen."

If you have previously received Jesus Christ as your savior, you may want to reaffirm your faith in him through the following prayer: "Lord Jesus, I need you. Thank you that I am yours. I confess that I have sinned against you. Thank you for continuing to forgive me of all my sins. I renew my commitment to serve you. Thank you for loving me completely and unconditionally. I entrust my life to your love and care. Please give me your strength and wisdom to continue growing in you, so that my life can bring glory and honor to you. Amen."

If either one of these prayers expresses the desires of your heart, you have taken a major step in your recovery. However, trusting in Christ does not release us from our problems. Though we will continue to have difficulties, we can be encouraged that God forgives us of all our wrongdoing; that we are restored to a relationship with God that will last through eternity; that we will receive his unconditional love, acceptance, strength, and wisdom as we continue to grow in recovery.[4]

N O T E S

TWO
Diseases that "Run in the Family"

1. Hanson, J.W., and Barclay, A.M., *Textbook of Family Practice*, R.E. Rakel, ed. (Toronto: W.B. Saunders Company, 1991), 1552.
2. Nora, J.J., and Fraser, F.C., *Medical Genetics* (Philadelphia: Lea & Febiger, 1989).
3. Albano, W., and Lynch, H., et al., *Cancer*, 47, 1981, 2113.
4. Longenecker, M.P., et al., *Journal of the American Medical Association*, 260, 1988, 652.
5. National Research Council, *Diet and Health* (Washington, D.C., National Academy Press, 1989).
6. Kelly, P.T., *Current Problems in Cancer*, VII (12), 1983, 15.
7. Kelly, *Current Problems in Cancer*, 15.
8. National Research Council, *Diet and Health*.
9. National Research Council, *Diet and Health*.
10. Garn, S.M., *Current Problems in Pediatrics*, 15, 1985, 1-47.
11. Wilber, J., *Journal of the American Medical Association*, 266, 1991, 257.
12. Minirth, F., Meier, P., Hemfelt, R., and Sneed, S., *Love Hunger: Recovery from Food Addiction* (Nashville: Thomas Nelson Publishers, 1990).

THREE
Addiction: All in the Family

1. Food addiction inventory from Minirth, Meier, Hemfelt, and Sneed, *Love Hunger*.
2. Minirth, Meier, Hemfelt, and Sneed, *Love Hunger*.
3. Pihl, R.O., and Perterson, J., *Journal of Abnormal Psychology*, 99, 1990, 291.
4. Institute of Medicine, *Causes and Consequences of Alcohol Problems*, (Washington D.C.: National Academy Press, 1987).
5. Shapiro, S., et al., *Archives of General Psychiatry*, 41, 1984, 971.
6. Warner, R.H. and Rossett, H.L., *Journal of Studies on Alcohol*, 36, 1975, 1395.
7. Bleuler, M., *Etiology of Chronic Alcoholism* (Springfield, Connecticut: Thomas O. Diethelm, ed., 1955), 110-16.
8. Kaij, L., *Alcoholism in Twins* (Stockholm: Almqvist and Wiksell, 1960).
9. Hrubec, Z., and Omenn, G.S., *Alcoholisms: Clinical and Experimental Research*, 5, 1981, 207-15.
10. Gurling, H., Murray, R., and Clifford, C., *Twin Research 3: Epidemiologic Clinical Studies* (New York: Liss, 1981), 77-87.
11. Pickens, R., and Svikis, D., *The Twin Method in the Study of Vulnerability to Drug Abuse* (Washington D.C.: NIDA Research Monograph, National Institute of Drug Abuse, U.S. Government Printing Office, 1989).

12. Pickens and Svikis, *The Twin Method in the Study of Vulnerability to Drug Abuse.*
13. Pickens and Svikis, *The Twin Method in the Study of Vulnerability to Drug Abuse.*
14. Boyd, J., Seissman, M., Thompson, W., and Myers, J., *American Journal of Psychiatry*, 140, 1983, 1309-13.
15. Pickens and Svikis, *The Twin Method in the Study of Vulnerability to Drug Abuse.*
16. Hayashida, M., et al., *New England Journal of Medicine*, 320, 1989, 358-65.
17. Rakel, R.E., and Blum, A., *Textbook of Family Practice* (Toronto: W.B. Saunders Company, 1991), 1552.
18. Pickens and Svikis, *The Twin Method in the Study of Vulnerability to Drug Abuse.*
19. Snadler, D., Everson, R., and Wilcox, A., et al., *American Journal of Public Health*, 75, 1985, 487-92.
20. Abelson, H., and Miller, J.D., *National Institute of Drug Abuse Research Monogram Series*, 61, 1985, 35-49.
21. Robins, L.N., *Psychological Medicine*, 8, 1978, 611-22.
22. Madden, J.S., *A Guide to Alcohol and Drug Dependence* (Bristol, UK: John Wright and Sons, 1979).

FOUR

The Power of Family Emotions

1. Examples of stress-induced coping failure adapted from Rakel, R.E., *Textbook of Family Practice*, Fourth Edition (Philadelphia, PA: W.B. Saunders Company, 1990), 1586.
2. *Topics in Psychiatry*, LP Communications, Inc., Vol. 1, No. 5, Summer 1990.
3. McGuffin, P., and Katz, R., *British Journal of Psychiatry*, 155, 1989, 294-304.
4. Rakel, *Textbook of Family Practice*, 1587.
5. Thomas, A., and Chess, S., *Temperament and Development* (New York: Bruner/Mazel, 1977).
6. Pederson, N., Plomin, R., McClearn, G., and Friberg, L., *Journal of Personality and Social Psychology*, Vol. 55, 1988, 950-57.
7. Pederson, et al., "Genetic and Environmental Influences of Type 'A'-like Measures and Related Traits," *Psychosomatic Medicine*, Vol. 51, 1989, 428-40.

FIVE

Especially for Women

1. Sneed, S.M., and McIlhaney, J., *PMS: What It Is and What You Can Do About It* (Grand Rapids: Baker Book House, 1988).
2. Sneed and McIlhaney, *PMS.*
3. Sneed and McIlhaney, *PMS.*
4. Kantero, R.L., and Widholm, C., *Acta Obstetrica Gynecologia Scandinavia* 14, 1971, 17-18.
5. Kantero and Widholm, *Acta Obstetrica Gynecologia Scandinavia*, 17-18.
6. Kantero and Widholm, *Acta Obstetrica Gynecologia Scandinavia*, 17-18.
7. Sneed and McIlhaney, *PMS.*

SIX

Stages of Family Life

1. Liese, B.S., and Price, J.G., *Textbook of Family Practice.*
2. Erikson, E.H., *Childhood and Society*, Second Edition (New York: W.W. Norton, 1963).

3. Sheehy, G., *Passages: Predictable Crises of Adult Life* (New York: Dutton and Co., 1976).
4. Liese and Price, *Textbook of Family Practice.*
5. Sheehy, *Passages.*
6. From *Women in Mid-Life Crisis* by Jim and Sally Conway (Wheaton, Illinois: Tyndale House, 1985). The list applies equally well to men and women.
7. Carter, E., and McGoldrick, M., *The Family Life Cycle: A Framework for Family Therapy,* (New York: Gardner Press, 1980).
8. Liese and Price, *Textbook of Family Practice.*
9. Liese and Price, *Textbook of Family Practice.*
10. Liese and Price, *Textbook of Family Practice.*
11. Liese and Price, *Textbook of Family Practice.*
12. Frank, E., Anderson, C., and Rubenstein, D., "Frequency of Sexual Dysfunction in 'Normal' Couples," *New England Journal of Medicine,* 299(3), 1978, 111-15.

SEVEN
Fussing and Fighting: the Family in Turmoil

1. Christoffel, K., and Liu, K., *Child Abuse and Neglect,* 7, 1983, 339.
2. Wyatt, G., and Peters, S., *Child Abuse and Neglect,* 10, 1986, 241-51.
3. Russell, D., *Child Abuse and Neglect,* 7, 1983, 133.
4. Rakel, *Textbook of Family Practice,* 127.
5. Gelles, R., and Straus, M., *Contemporary Theories About the Family,* Vol. 1, 1979.
6. Gelles, R., *The Dark Side of Families: Current Family Violence Research* (Newbury Park, California: Sage, 1983).
7. Taler, G., and Ansello, E., *American Family Physician,* 32(2), 1985, 107-14.
8. Hetherington, E., and Arasteh, J., *The Impact of Divorce, Single-Parenting, and Stepparenting on Children* (LEA Publishers, 1988).
9. Glick, P., *Journal of Family Issues,* 5, 1984, 7-26.
10. Rakel, *Textbook of Family Practice,* 137.
11. Somers, A., *Journal of the American Medical Association,* 241, 1979, 1818-22.
12. Hetherington, E., *Remarriage and Stepparenting Today* (New York: Guildford Press, 1987).
13. Hetherington and Arasteh, *The Impact of Divorce, Single-Parenting, and Stepparenting on Children.*
14. Kelly, J.B., "Long-term Adjustment in Children of Divorce." *Journal of Family Psychology,* 2, 1988, 119-40.
15. Kelly, "Long-term Adjustment in Children of Divorce."

EIGHT
Charting a New Course

1. Rogers, J., Durkin, M., and Kelly, K., *New Jersey Medicine,* 82, 1985, 887.
2. Rakel, *Textbook of Family Practice.*
3. Smilkstein, G., *Journal of Family Practice,* Vol. 6, 1978, 1231-39.

NINE
First Steps Toward Change

1. Hofling, C.K., and Lewis, J.M., *Family Evaluation and Treatment* (New York: Brunner/Mazel Pub., 1979).

2. Rollins, B.C., and Cannon, K.L., *Journal of Marriage and Family*, 36, 1974, 271.

TEN
Hope and Healing, Today and Forever

1. This list of needs has been influenced by Dennis Guernsey in *The Family Covenant* (Elgin, IL: David C. Cook Publishing Company, 1984), 6-18, 65-66. See also Bradshaw, *On: The Family* by John Bradshaw (Deerfield Beach, FL: Health Communications, Inc., 1988), 42-44. We are also greatly indebted to an outstanding marriage and family therapist, David Ferguson, for his insights on fundamental God-given human needs. See especially *Marriage and Family Intimacy* Newsletter, Vol. 1, No. 12.
2. Heitritter, Lynn, and Vought, Jeanette, *Helping Victims of Sexual Abuse* (Minneapolis: Bethany House Publishers, 1989), 54, citing Dr. David Seamands, "Healing Distorted Concepts of God" (Minneapolis, Minnesota: National Counseling Conferences, Crystal Free Evangelical Church, May 14-16, 1986.)
3. See Dennis Guernsey, *The Family Covenant*, 6-9, for a clear, inviting elaboration of unconditional love.
4. For further elaboration of what the functional family is like, see Bradshaw, *On: The Family*, Chapter Three entitled, "Profile of a Functional Family System."
5. Bradshaw, *On: The Family*, 54-55.
6. Bradshaw, *On: The Family*, 61.
7. Bradshaw, *On: The Family*, 70.
8. Interview with Linda Kondracki, *Steps* Newsletter, Vol. 2, No. 2, 7.
9. Bradshaw, *On: The Family*, 78.
10. With some elaboration, this list comes from Pat Springle, *Rapha's Twelve Step Program for Overcoming Chemical Dependency* (Houston: Rapha Publishing/Word, Inc., 1990), xii.
11. Bradshaw, *On: The Family*, 83.
12. See *Marriage and Family Intimacy* Newsletter, Vol. 2, No. 10, for more detail about this problem.
13. Bradshaw, *On: The Family*, 77-78.
14. Hemfelt, Robert, and Warren, Paul, *Kids Who Carry Our Pain* (Nashville: Thomas Nelson Publishers, 1990), 16.

ELEVEN
Entry Into Family Recovery: Steps One through Three

1. *The Twelve Steps—A Spiritual Journey* (San Diego: Recovery Publications, 1988), 33-34.
2. *The Twelve Steps—A Spiritual Journey*, 35.
3. Ferguson, David, "Emotional Capacity," *Marriage and Family Intimacy*, I (November, 1989), 3.
4. Thurman, Chris, *The Lies We Believe* (Nashville: Thomas Nelson Publishers, 1989).
5. Whitfield, Charles L., M.D., *Healing the Child Within* (Deerfield Beach, FL: Health Communications, Inc., 1987), 44.
6. Miller, J. Keith, *A Hunger for Healing* (San Francisco: Harper Collins, 1991), 32.

7. If we pursue our investigation of truth in the Bible, we discover nothing less than a genuine encounter with the God of the Bible, through his Son Jesus Christ. It is beyond the scope of this book to argue for the existence of God or prove the uniqueness of Jesus. However, we invite you to study the New Testament and discover Jesus who claimed to be God (Jn 10:30) and claimed to reveal God fully (Jn 14:9). He claimed to be the embodiment of truth and the way to God (Jn 14:6). Jesus promised those who believed in him both eternal life (Jn 3:16) and the abundant life (Jn 10:10). He did not leave us the option of considering him as merely a good man or a great teacher. Either Jesus Christ is truly Lord, or he was a liar or a lunatic.

8. For an excellent discussion of the importance of sound thinking as the basis for healthy behavior, see Neil T. Anderson, *Victory Over the Darkness* (Ventura, CA: Regal Books, 1990), especially Chapter Seven: "You Can't Live Beyond What You Believe."

9. Miller, *A Hunger for Healing,* 36.

10. Ryan, Dale and Juanita, *Recovery From Distorted Images of God* (Downers Grove, IL: Intervarsity Press, 1990), 12.

11. See Seamands, David, *Healing for Damaged Emotions* (Wheaton, IL: Victor Books, 1981), 92-94. See also Springle, Pat, *Your Parents and You* (Houston: Rapha Publications, 1990).

12. Reprinted by permission from Anderson,, *Victory Over the Darkness* , 45-47.

13. Brennan Manning interview, *Wittenburg Door,* No. 63 (October-November 1986), 15.

14. Davis, Patty. Lecture notes on the Twelve Steps for Westlake Bible Church, June 5, 1991.

TWELVE

Action Steps for Family Recovery: Steps Four through Nine

1. *Alcoholics Anonymous,* Third Edition (New York: Alcoholics Anonymous World Services, Inc., 1976), 64.

2. A helpful exercise form for this list is contained in *The Twelve Steps—A Spiritual Journey,* 85. Our definitions are adapted from those in this handbook.

3. This list is adapted from *The Twelve Steps—A Spiritual Journey,* 46-68.

4. Klass, Joe, *The Twelve Steps to Happiness* (New York: Ballantine Books, 1990), 85.

5. Bradshaw, *On: The Family,* 202.

6. *The Twelve Steps—A Spiritual Journey,* 77.

7. *The Twelve Steps—A Spiritual Journey,* 76.

8. *The Twelve Steps for Everyone* (Minneapolis: CompCare Publishers, 1975), 37-38.

9. *The Twelve Steps—A Spiritual Journey,* 77.

10. Manning interview, 14-15.

11. Manning interview, 15.

12. See the "parable of the unforgiving servant" (Mt 18:21-35) for a penetrating portrayal of this truth.

13. *The Twelve Steps—A Spiritual Journey,* 89.

14. *The Twelve Steps for Everyone,* 62-63.

15. *The Twelve Steps for Everyone,* 70.

16. *The Twelve Steps for Everyone,* 71.

THIRTEEN
Growing in Recovery: Steps Ten through Twelve

1. Blattner, John, "The Twelve Steps: Where They Work; How They Work," *Pastoral Renewal*, Volume 13, Number 6 (May/June 1989), 10.
2. Klass, *The Twelve Steps to Happiness*, 130.
3. Joe Klass provides an insightful explanation for the connection between these negative qualities and the "violation of our Step Three contract" with God. *The Twelve Steps to Happiness*, 129-33.
4. *The Twelve Steps—A Spiritual Journey*, 146-47, has an excellent worksheet to help with this kind of exercise. This workbook may be ordered from Tools for Recovery, 1201 Knoxville St., San Diego, CA 92110 (619-275-1350).
5. Friends in Recovery, *The Twelve Steps for Christians From Addictive and Other Dysfunctional Families* (San Diego: Recovery Publications, Inc., 1988), 106.
6. Klass, *The Twelve Steps to Happiness*, 147.
7. *The Twelve Steps—A Spiritual Journey*, 153.
8. Claire, W., *God Help Me Stop* (San Diego: Books West, 1982), 77.
9. Haugk, Kenneth, *Christian Caregiving—A Way of Life* (Minneapolis: Augsburg Publishing House, 1984), 19-24.
10. *Alcoholics Anonymous*, 98.

APPENDIX
How to Be Certain of Your Eternal Relationship with God

1. Springle, Pat. *Rapha's Twelve Step Program for Codependency*, 56.
2. All Scripture references are from the New International Version, unless otherwise noted.
3. These two prayers are lightly edited from material in Springle, *Rapha's Twelve Step Program for Codependency*, 57.
4. Springle, *Rapha's Twelve Step Program for Codependency*, 57.

Other Books of Interest
from Servant Publications

Forgiving Our Parents, Forgiving Ourselves
From the Minirth-Meier Clinic
Dr. David Stoop and Dr. James Masteller

Many of us desperately want to change but can't stop behaving in
ways that hurt ourselves and those we love. What's keeping us so
stuck? Can we ever hope to get unstuck?

Forgiving Our Parents, Forgiving Ourselves begins by exploring
the family patterns that perpetuate dysfunction. Step-by-step, readers
will learn to construct a psychological family tree that will help them
uncover family secrets and family habits that have profoundly
shaped their adult identity.

As they develop greater understanding of their family of origin
and its effect for good or ill, they will be able to take the essential
step of forgiveness. When that happens, they will find themselves
moving into a place of profound spiritual healing which will change
their lives forever. **$10.99**

Healing Adult Children of Divorce
Taking Care of Unfinished Business
So You Can Be Whole Again
Dr. Archibald D. Hart

When parents divorce, the children usually grow up with unfinished
business to resolve. Chances are they were left with emotional
wounds, the scars of which remain with them even as adults. *Healing
Adult Children of Divorce* examines the long-term effects of this traumatic event, the damaging consequences that follow children of
divorce, and ways to resolve past hurts that have shaped their lives.
$16.99